Introducing Second Language Assessment

Many books have been written on the topic of second language assessment, but few are easily accessible for both students and practicing language teachers. This textbook provides an up-to-date and engaging introduction to this topic, using anecdotal and real-world examples to illustrate key concepts and principles. It seamlessly connects qualitative and quantitative approaches and the use of technologies, including generative AI, to language assessment development and analysis for readers with little background in these areas. Hands-on activities, exercises, and discussion questions provide opportunities for application and reflection, and the inclusion of additional resources and detailed appendices cements understanding. Ancillary resources are available, including data sets and videos for students, PowerPoint teaching slides, and a teacher's guide for instructors. Packed with pedagogy, this is an invaluable resource for both first and second language speakers of English, students on applied linguistics or teacher education courses, and practicing teachers of any language.

Gary J. Ockey is Professor of Applied Linguistics and Technology at Iowa State University, USA. Professor Ockey currently teaches language assessment courses to graduate students and has previously taught English as a second or foreign language in elementary school, high school, university, and adult language schools in Asia and the US and worked at the Educational Testing Service. Professor Ockey has co-authored/edited several books, has been published in various journals, and served as the editor of *TOEFL Research Report Series* and *Language Assessment Quarterly*.

"This textbook addresses a real need in the field: a language assessment book that makes theory interpretable and comprehensible, while providing practical examples and applications that will help students become better language testers. The end-of-chapter discussion questions are an invaluable resource for instructors."

Elvis Wagner, Temple University

"This is a genuinely easy-to-read, comprehensive introduction to the complexities of language assessment. Many personal anecdotes, reflection questions, non-technical hands-on exercises, examples from real language classrooms, and supplementary online materials make this an engaging, state-of-the-art resource, valuable for language teachers, language teacher educators, students of applied linguistics, and everyone who wants to better understand the basics of language assessment."

Benjamin Kremmel, University of Innsbruck

"This book is an invaluable resource for educators, students, and researchers alike. It offers accessible insights into language assessment, focusing on practical implications. With clear guidelines for integrating cutting-edge technology such as Chatbots and virtual environments, it provides hands-on training and fosters critical discussions on language testing techniques. It is a must-read for anyone passionate about second language assessment."

Nasser Jabbari, University of Essex

"An indispensable resource, this textbook deftly bridges the theoretical and practical realms of second language assessment. Enhanced by cutting-edge technologies like generative AI, it offers both novices and experienced practitioners a profound and accessible exploration of the field."

Jessica Wu, Language Training and Testing Center, Taiwan

"Ockey bridges the worlds of language testing and educational assessment to give a comprehensive grounding in the principles of effective practice. The historical context is especially valuable in supporting more critical evaluation of current testing practices. I will be using this book with master's and doctoral students in TESOL because it shows how educators can use assessment to drive learning, building on key concepts such as assessment use arguments and needs analyses."

Mark Carver, University of St. Andrews

"*Introducing Second Language Assessment* provides an engaging overview of assessment practices by blending theory, practice, and personal experience. Ockey's adept and accessible exploration illuminates the importance of effective assessment design and is sure to resonate with undergraduate students who are just beginning their teaching journey."

Suzanne Johnston, University of Central Arkansas

"This is a timely addition to the shelves of applied linguists, students, and practicing teachers. In a clear and accessible way, Ockey presents a comprehensive overview of the key issues related to second language assessment, with a focus on developing practical understanding of research findings in this area and their relevance to language education. Of particular value are the numerous hands-on activities, discussion points, and additional teaching resources interspersed throughout the chapters, as they will undoubtedly assist the use of this book as both a textbook and a springboard to reflect on the role of assessment in the language learning and teaching process."

Pawel Szudarski, University of Nottingham

"In *Introducing Second Language Assessment*, Gary Ockey draws on decades of experience as an assessment developer, teacher, and world-class researcher to provide an overview of language assessment fit for the modern age. The book is written in an accessible style, suitable for those exploring the field of language assessment for the first time, with particularly clear explanations of statistical analyses. Each chapter includes case studies, reflection questions, exercises, and recommendations for further study, making for an engaging read. There is also a welcome focus on the role of new technologies in language assessment. This book will be of great use to anyone who seeks to develop their language assessment literacy."

Luke Harding, Lancaster University

Introducing Second Language Assessment

GARY J. OCKEY
Iowa State University

Shaftesbury Road, Cambridge CB2 8EA, United Kingdom

One Liberty Plaza, 20th Floor, New York, NY 10006, USA

477 Williamstown Road, Port Melbourne, VIC 3207, Australia

314–321, 3rd Floor, Plot 3, Splendor Forum, Jasola District Centre, New Delhi – 110025, India

103 Penang Road, #05–06/07, Visioncrest Commercial, Singapore 238467

Cambridge University Press is part of Cambridge University Press & Assessment, a department of the University of Cambridge.

We share the University's mission to contribute to society through the pursuit of education, learning and research at the highest international levels of excellence.

www.cambridge.org
Information on this title: www.cambridge.org/highereducation/isbn/9781316512487

DOI: 10.1017/9781009067461

© Gary J. Ockey 2025

This publication is in copyright. Subject to statutory exception and to the provisions of relevant collective licensing agreements, no reproduction of any part may take place without the written permission of Cambridge University Press & Assessment.

When citing this work, please include a reference to the DOI 10.1017/9781009067461

First published 2025

A catalogue record for this publication is available from the British Library

A Cataloging-in-Publication data record for this book is available from the Library of Congress

ISBN 978-1-316-51248-7 Hardback
ISBN 978-1-009-06605-1 Paperback

Additional resources for this publication at www.cambridge.org/ockey

Cambridge University Press & Assessment has no responsibility for the persistence or accuracy of URLs for external or third-party internet websites referred to in this publication and does not guarantee that any content on such websites is, or will remain, accurate or appropriate.

To my daughter, Shelly, who has taught me that intelligence can take you a long way in life, but persistence will take you further.

Contents

List of Figures page xv
List of Tables xvii
List of Guidelines xviii
List of Examples xix
Preface xxi
Acknowledgments xxiii

PART I Engaging with Language Assessments 1

1 Language Assessments and Tests: What We Need to Know and Why We Should Care 2
   Introduction 3
   What We Mean by Language "Assessment" and "Test" 3
   Misuses of Language Assessments 4
      Intentional Misuses 4
         The Shibboleth Test 4
         The Australian Dictation Test 5
         The Louisiana Literacy Test 5
      Unintentional Misuses 6
         A Private Conversation School's Test of Oral Communication 6
         A Poor-Quality Writing Test 7
   Effective Uses of Language Assessments 7
      How a Language Test Positively Affected the Life of Sonca Vo 7
      Language Assessments vs. Other Selection Options 9
   Language Assessment Literacy 10
   Conclusion 12
   Questions for Discussion 13
   Exercises 14
   Additional Resources 15

2 Making Sense of the Many Approaches to Language Assessment 16
   Introduction 17
   Characterizing and Distinguishing among Language Assessments 17
      Stakes 18
      Objectiveness 18
      Frame of Reference 19
         Criterion-Referenced Tests 19
         Norm-Referenced Tests 20
   General Purposes of Language Assessments 22
      Dynamic Assessment 22
      Learning-Oriented Assessment 23

Self-Assessment	24
Formative Assessment	24
Portfolio Assessment	25
Diagnostic Tests	25
Placement Tests	25
Proficiency Tests	26
Summative Tests	26
Standardized Tests	26
Conclusion	27
Questions for Discussion	28
Exercises	28
Additional Resources	30

PART II Gaining Knowledge of Language Assessment Principles — 33

3 Context, Purpose, and Impact: The Situation Matters — 34

Introduction	35
Social Influences	35
Sociopolitical Factors	35
Cultural Factors	37
High- vs. Low-Context Cultures	37
Effects of Culture on Language Assessments in Local Contexts	38
Educational Factors	39
Assessment Design	39
Equipment	40
Managing Social Influences	40
Purposes and Impacts	41
Impact on Stakeholders	41
Test Takers and Their Families	42
People Who Have a Close Relationship with Test Takers	43
People Who Do Not Have a Close Relationship with Test Takers	43
Impact on Language Learning Practices	43
Availability of Resources	44
Human Resources	46
Space	46
Material Resources	46
Balancing Assessment Goals and Available Resources	46
Conclusion	46
Questions for Discussion	47
Exercises	47
Additional Resources	48

4 What and Who Are We Measuring? Validity and Alignment — 49

Introduction	50
Validity	50
Defining Constructs	51
Language Theory	52

Language Needs Analysis	54
Corpora	56
Curriculum Objectives	57
Alignment	57
Test Content	58
Response Processes	59
Other Sources of Validity Evidence	60
Other Approaches to Validity	61
The Socio-cognitive Framework	61
Argument-Based Validation	61
Conclusion	62
Questions for Discussion	63
Exercises	63
Additional Resources	64

5 Language Assessment Consistency: Uniformity and Reliability — 65

Introduction	66
Uniformity	67
Setting	68
Physical Environment	68
Equipment	68
Administrative Procedures	69
Content	69
Instructions	69
Item Type	69
Language Input	69
Non-language Input	71
Scoring	71
Types of Scoring	71
Error Avoidance	71
Reports and Storage	71
Uses of Technology to Increase Uniformity	72
Reliability	73
Test-Retest Reliability	73
Parallel Forms Reliability	74
Internal Reliability	75
Important Points about Reliability	75
Conclusion	76
Questions for Discussion	76
Exercises	76
Additional Resources	77

PART III Right or Wrong — 79

6 Assessing Comprehension and Knowledge with Dichotomously Scored Item Types — 80

Introduction	81

Dichotomously Scored Item Types	81
Selected Response Items	81
Multiple-Choice Items	82
True–False Items	83
Short-Answer Items	84
Variations of Item Types	85
Assessing Receptive Language Understanding and Knowledge	85
Instructions	86
Item Type	86
Language Input	87
Genre	87
Topic Accessibility	87
Delivery	87
Speaker Selection	90
Length	91
Grammatical Complexity and Vocabulary Difficulty	91
Non-language Input	91
Conclusion	92
Questions for Discussion	92
Exercises	93
Additional Resources	93

7 Analyzing Dichotomously Scored Items for Selecting the Most Proficient Test Takers   95

Introduction	96
Using Content Analysis to Evaluate Language Assessment Validity	96
Content Analysis of Language Input	97
Genre Provides Potential to Assess Targeted Construct	97
Topic Is Accessible to Test Takers	98
Delivery Is Appropriately Authentic	98
Length Is Sufficient to Assess Targeted Construct	98
Grammatical Complexity and Vocabulary Difficulty Are Appropriate	98
Non-language Input Is Appropriate	99
Content Analysis of Selected Response Items	99
Items Should Assess Only the Targeted Construct	99
Information in One Item Should Not Influence Responses to Another	100
Items Should Be Straightforward	100
Options Should Be Syntactically Parallel, Similar in Length, and Concise	100
Options Should Follow a Systematic Order	101
Items Should Have Only One Best Answer with All Other Options Reasonable	101
Comprehension Items Should Require Test Takers to Understand the Input	101
Using Descriptive Statistics to Evaluate a Test	102
Summary Statistics	104
Minimum and Maximum	104
Range	104
Mean	104

Variance and Standard Deviation	106
Score Distributions	107
Skewness	107
Kurtosis	108
Histogram of the Grammar Tense Test Scores	110
Conclusion	111
Questions for Discussion	111
Exercises	112
Additional Resources	114
Appendix 7A Using ChatGPT to Create Reading Passages	114
Appendix 7B Using ChatGPT to Create MC Reading Items	115
Appendix 7C Guidelines for Scoring MC Items with Excel	116
Appendix 7D Calculating Descriptive Statistics in Excel	117

8 Judging the Effectiveness of Dichotomously Scored Items — 119

Introduction	120
Item Analysis	120
Item Facility	120
Point-Biserials	121
Correlation: The Principle Underlying PBs	121
Uses of PBs	124
Content Analysis, PBs, and IFs to Judge the Effectiveness of Test Items	126
Evaluating IFs for the Grammar Tense Test	127
Evaluating PBs for the Grammar Tense Test	128
Analyzing Item 3 of the Grammar Tense Test	128
Analyzing Item 7 of the Grammar Tense Test	129
Analyzing Other Items of the Grammar Tense Test	129
Reliability	129
Cronbach's Alpha	129
Interpreting Cronbach's Alpha and Other Reliability Estimates	131
Cronbach's Alpha for the Grammar Tense Test	131
What to Consider When Using Cronbach's Alpha	131
Ways to Increase the Reliability of Test Scores	132
Conclusion	132
Questions for Discussion	132
Exercises	133
Additional Resources	133
Appendix 8A Calculating IFs and PBs in Excel	134
Appendix 8B Calculating Cronbach's Alpha in Excel	135

9 Identifying the Masters: Evaluating Criterion-Referenced Assessments — 137

Introduction	138
Vocabulary Test 1	138

Content Analysis for CRTs	139
Judging the Test Format, Overall Construct Representation, and Relationship among Items	140
Evaluating Item Content	141
Selecting Content Judges	142
Standard Setting	143
The Angoff Method	143
The Contrasting Groups Method	144
Multiple Cut Scores	146
Descriptive Statistics	146
The Median	146
Mastery Rate	146
Statistical Item Analysis	147
Item Facility	148
The B-Index	148
Using Content Analysis and Statistical Analysis to Judge Item Quality	148
Dependability	150
Conclusion	151
Questions for Discussion	152
Exercises	152
Additional Resources	153
Appendix 9A Calculating the Median and Mastery Rate in Excel	153
Appendix 9B Calculating the B-Index in Excel	154

PART IV Judging Test Taker Performances — 157

10 Being Creative: Types and Delivery of Performance Assessments — 158

Introduction	159
Independent, Integrated, and Interactive Tasks	159
Independent Tasks	159
Integrated Tasks	160
Interactive Tasks	160
Independent Test Tasks for Assessing Speaking and Writing	160
Prepared Oral Presentation Tasks	161
Picture Tasks	161
Knowledge-Based Tasks	163
Tasks for Assessing Integrated Language Skills	163
Retell and Summary Tasks	163
Synthesis Tasks	164
Roleplay Tasks	164
Interview Tasks	166
Paired and Group Oral Discussion Tasks	168
Elicited Imitation and Indirect Tasks for Assessing Speaking and Writing	169
Delivery of Performance Assessment Tasks	170
Face-to-Face Delivery	170
Virtual Delivery	171
Video-Mediated Communication	171

Virtual Environments	171
Computerized Delivery	172
Spoken Dialog Systems	172
Complex Language-Processing Models	173
Conclusion	173
Questions for Discussion	174
Exercises	174
Additional Resources	175
Appendix 10 Using ChatGPT to Create a Prompt for a Synthesis Task	175

11 Scoring Performance Assessments: Rating, Rating Scales, and Raters — 177

Introduction	178
A Listening and Writing Assessment for Young Saudi Learners of English	178
Context and Purpose	178
Constructs and Alignment	179
Task	179
Scoring Performance Assessments	180
Holistic Rating Scales	181
Analytic Rating Scales	182
Comparison between Holistic and Analytic Rating Scales	182
Considerations for Creating, Selecting, and Using Rating Scales	185
Strong and Weak Sense of Language Performance Assessment	185
Test Takers' Characteristics	186
Specificity	186
Physical Layout	186
Weighting of Analytic Rating Scale Scores	186
Approaches to Creating Rating Scales for Performance Assessments	187
Adapting Existing Scales	187
A Standards-Based Approach	187
A Theory-Based Approach	188
A Performance-Driven Approach	188
Preparing for Scoring Performance Assessments	191
Human Scoring	191
Rater Training	191
Rater Norming	192
Computer Scoring	192
Hybrid Scoring	193
Conclusion	193
Questions for Discussion	193
Exercises	194
Additional Resources	195
Appendix 11 Using ChatGPT to Help Create Rating Scales	196

12 Judging the Effectiveness of Performance Assessments: Validity, Reliability, and Dependability — 197

Introduction	198
The Assessment of Academic Oral Communication	198

Assessment Context and Purpose	198
Assessment Constructs and Alignment	198
Assessment Task	199
Test Administration and Scoring	200
Validity of Performance Assessment Scores and Their Interpretations	200
Tasks Elicit Language Appropriate for Measuring Targeted Ability	200
Tasks Elicit Sufficient Language	204
Instructions Are Clear for Test Takers and Administrators	204
Scoring Criteria Are Appropriate for Measuring the Targeted Construct	205
Scoring Criteria Are Clear	205
Rating Scale Proficiency Levels Are Appropriate for Making Judgments about Targeted Language Abilities	205
Reliability and Dependability of Performance Assessments	205
Dependability	209
Reliability	210
Conclusion	212
Questions for Discussion	212
Exercises	212
Additional Resources	213
Appendix 12 Using Excel to Calculate Average Covariance and Average Variance for Performance Assessment Scores	213

PART V   Reflecting and Self-Assessment   215

13 Evaluating Our Language Assessment Literacy   216

Introduction	216
Judging Our Language Assessment Literacy	217
The Language Assessment Literacy Test	219
Evaluating a Multiple-Choice Reading Assessment	219
Reading Test 1: Visiting the Zoo with My Family	219
Reading Test 2: Seemi's Math and Art Classes	220
Evaluating an Oral Communication Performance Assessment	222
Evaluating Our Own Performance on the Language Assessment Literacy Test	224
Conclusion	225
Glossary	226
References	236
Index	240

Figures

1.1	A person writing Chinese characters on a blackboard	*page* 2
1.2	The unfairness of the Shibboleth Test, the Australian Dictation Test, and the Louisiana Literacy Test	6
1.3	Sonca Vo, whose life was positively affected by good language testing practice	8
1.4	Kremmel and Harding's (2020) aspects of LAL and the level of expertise required of researchers, test developers, and teachers	11
2.1	Use of the wrong type of assessment can have serious negative consequences	16
2.2	The stakes of an assessment range from low, like a classroom quiz, to high, like a test for employment	18
2.3	Assessments can range from subjective, like individuals' judgments of their own abilities, to objective, like a true-or-false question	19
2.4	Scores on a CRT. A line separates students who pass from those who fail	20
2.5	Normally distributed scores for an NRT. Most scores are near the average	21
2.6	Seven dimensions of LOA	23
2.7	Traditional standardized test with bubble mark sheet	26
3.1	Cultural, sociopolitical, and educational backgrounds are important contextual variables for language assessments	34
3.2	Comparison of communication styles in high- and low-context cultures	38
3.3	Relationship between contextual factors, test purposes, and test impacts	42
3.4	Potential stakeholders for our English-speaking Thai nurses example	44
3.5	Relationship between contextual factors, purposes, and impacts in the English-speaking Thai nurses example	45
4.1	Real-world language use on the playground	49
4.2	Using language theory to create language constructs that we can assess	52
4.3	Steps in a language needs analysis for creating language constructs	54
4.4	COCA corpus example of *strong argument*	56
4.5	A language construct and the test content that the test measures	59
4.6	A test can measure some parts of a construct and not others	59
4.7	Bachman and Dambock's (2017) argument-based validation model for classroom teachers	62
5.1	Effective clocks are reliable. They keep time consistently	65
5.2	Design for assessing test-retest reliability	74
6.1	Selecting an answer	80
6.2	A scripted listening input. Actors memorize exactly what to say	88
6.3	An authentic listening input which comes from a real-world listening context	88
6.4	An authenticated listening input. Actors follow a general outline but create the exact language while they speak	89
7.1	A group listening to a person using statistics to explain an information pattern	95
7.2	Positively and negatively skewed score distributions	108

7.3	Score distributions with positive and negative kurtosis	109
7.4	Histogram of the Grammar Tense Test. The scores are quite normally distributed	110
8.1	A person using statistics and figures to help understand test results	119
8.2	Scatter plot of reading and listening quiz scores	122
8.3	Scatter plot of reading and grammar error quiz scores	123
9.1	A panel of teachers setting standards for an assessment	137
10.1	University students having a discussion in the target language use situation	158
10.2	Students taking the role of a prince and a princess in a classroom roleplay test task	165
10.3	Three test takers completing a group oral discussion task	168
10.4	A face-to-face oral interview task	170
10.5	Virtual delivery model: An interviewer is giving an oral interview to a test taker	171
10.6	Virtual environment of a roleplay with an interviewer and a businessperson	172
11.1	A 10-point rating scale	177
11.2a	Effective-level writing sample for Saudi Young Learner English Assessment (Naila)	189
11.2b	Approaching-Effective-level writing sample for Saudi Young Learner English Assessment (Akeem)	189
11.2c	Emerging-level writing sample for Saudi Young Learner English Assessment (Farah)	190
11.3	Writing sample for Saudi Young Learner English Assessment for Discussion Question 11.1	194
11.4	Saudi Young Learner English Assessment for Exercise 11.1	195
12.1	Judges providing different ratings for the same performance	197
13.1	Reflecting on what we have learned	216

Tables

1.1	Recording language assessment literacy responses	page 14
2.1	Some ways to characterize and distinguish among language assessments	18
4.1	Using theory to define a construct: ELF principles, description of principles, and constructs based on the principles	53
4.2	Using language needs analysis to guide construct development	55
5.1	Aspects important to the uniformity of language assessments	67
7.1	First ten students' selected options on the Grammar Tense Test	103
7.2	Scored responses for first ten students on first administration of the Grammar Tense Test	105
7.3	Calculation of the variance and SD of the first ten students' scores on the Grammar Tense Test	107
7.4	Scores of test takers 11–20 on first administration of the Grammar Tense Test	113
7D.1	Excel commands for max, min, mean, variance, standard deviation, skewness, and kurtosis	118
8.1	Assumed reading and listening quiz scores for ten students	122
8.2	Reading and grammar error quiz scores for ten students	123
8.3	Items, answer key, IFs, and PBs for the Grammar Tense Test	126
8.4	Correlations among items of the Grammar Tense Test	130
9.1	A teacher's judgment of the percentage chance that a minimally competent student would have of answering an item correctly	145
9.2	Scores of the thirteen most proficient test takers on Vocabulary Test 1	147
9.3	Item numbers, answer key, IFs for masters and non-masters, and B-Index for Vocabulary Test 1	149
9.4	Contingency table for mastery and test administration of Vocabulary Test 1	151
11.1	Holistic rating scale for the Saudi Young Learner English Assessment	181
11.2	Analytic rating scale for the Saudi Young Learner English Assessment	183
12.1	Analytic rating scale for the Assessment of Academic Oral Communication	201
12.2	Scores from two raters for each of the four rating categories on the Assessment of Academic Oral Communication	207
12.3	Contingency table for mastery and non-mastery of the Assessment of Academic Oral Communication	209
12.4	Calculation of Cronbach's Alpha for the Assessment of Academic Oral Communication	211
13.1	Scale for self-assessment of LAL	217
13.2	Levels of LAL before and after reading this book	218

Guidelines

1.1	Kremmel and Harding's (2020) nine aspects of LAL	*page* 12
7.1	Content guidelines for reading and listening input	96
7.2	Systematically evaluating selected response items	99
7.3	Steps for calculating SD	106
8.1	Judging IF for NRTs	121
8.2	Judging items based on PBs	125
9.1	Rating scale for judging a CRT with selected response items	140
9.2	Rating scale for judging MC item content on CRTs	141
12.1	Creating or evaluating performance assessment tasks	204

Examples

1.1	Ways to identify potential students with sufficient English proficiency	*page* 9
2.1	A formative self-assessment with can-do statements	29
2.2	A true-false formative assessment	30
2.3	A short-answer formative assessment	30
3.1	A culturally biased analogy question	39
6.1	Parts of MC items, including terms for describing them	82
6.2	A true-false item	83
6.3	A short-answer vocabulary item	84
6.4	A reading comprehension short-answer item that requires a few words for an effective response	84
7.1	Two MC items that a teacher brought to assess reading comprehension of Passage 2	100
7.2	Revised item based on a content analysis	101
7.3	MC university-level Grammar Tense Test	102
8.1	Items 3, 7, and 22 of the Grammar Tense Test	128
9.1	Items 1, 2, 24, and 25 of Vocabulary Test 1	139
10.1	A prepared oral presentation task	161
10.2	A picture task	162
10.3	An independent writing task for a university placement exam	163
10.4	An oral retell task for a university placement context	164
10.5	A synthesis read-write task for a university placement context	165
10.6	A roleplay task for a university placement context	166
10.7	An oral interview task for beginning-level young learners	167
10.8	A paired oral task for a university placement context	168
11.1	The Saudi Young Learner English Assessment	179
12.1	The Assessment of Academic Oral Communication	199
13.1	Reading Test 1: Visiting the Zoo with My Family	220
13.2	Reading Test 2: Seemi's Math and Art Classes	221
13.3	Roleplay task for assessing hotel receptionists' abilities to interact with hotel guests	223

Preface

Introducing Second Language Assessment takes readers on an engaging journey into the world of second language assessment. It introduces them to key concepts and principles that they will need in order to select, create, and effectively use second language assessments for various purposes and in diverse contexts. The book's primary audiences are graduate and advanced undergraduate students in language teacher training courses, students in TESOL/TEFL certificate programs, and practicing second language teachers. I take the approach that most assessment principles apply in various language assessment contexts. However, to engage the primary target audience, most of the examples are based on classroom contexts. I have written the book with the assumption that readers have very limited or no background knowledge about second language assessment. However, experience of teaching and/or learning a second language and giving and/or taking second language assessments will help readers better relate to the book's content.

I became interested in language assessment while teaching and assessing English as a second or foreign language in various contexts, including a medical school in Thailand, an adult conversation school in Taiwan, a middle school and high school in Taiwan, a language university in Japan, an English-medium graduate university in Japan, and multiple universities and community colleges in the United States. In these contexts, I saw the power of assessments and how good ones can help with making appropriate decisions about individuals. For example, they can help an employer determine whether or not a job applicant has sufficient language ability to be successful, or help teachers decide which students they should place into a particular writing or reading group in their classes. I also saw how effective language assessments could lead to successful language learning practices. These positive (along with some negative) experiences, coupled with my formal training, have helped me gain an understanding about assessing a second language that I believe will benefit readers of this book.

The approach I take in the book is based on what I have discovered about learning and teaching during my more than sixty years of learning and forty years of teaching. In my experience, students learn best from examples, anecdotes, connecting new concepts to their own experiences, and hands-on activities. I therefore use these learning approaches throughout the book. With the aim of making language assessment principles and concepts as accessible as possible, I include the following learning aids:

- At the beginning of each chapter, a language assessment anecdote from my own experience that prepares readers for the concepts that they will learn
- "Time to Think" activities, throughout the chapters, that encourage readers to connect the concepts they are learning to their own language assessment contexts and experiences and monitor their understanding of the information in the chapter
- Sets of guidelines that are helpful for remembering key content
- Examples that help readers digest important language assessment principles and concepts
- End-of-chapter questions for discussion that provide learners with opportunities to further increase their understanding of the concepts by discussing them with others

- End-of-chapter exercises that give learners a chance to further engage with the materials through hands-on and thought-provoking activities
- A section on additional resources that points readers to readings, videos, or assessments that they can use to further increase their understanding of each chapter's contents
- Appendices with explanations and examples for how to complete data analyses in Excel and use artificial intelligence (AI) technologies such as ChatGPT to help create language assessment inputs, questions, and rating scales
- Online videos that provide step-by-step examples of how to complete additional data analysis activities and how to use AI to help create language assessment inputs and questions
- Additional online data sets that teachers can use to provide further opportunities for students to practice using content and statistical assessment evaluation techniques
- Online PowerPoint slides that teachers can use to help them present the materials in the book
- A teacher's guide that provides teaching ideas for each chapter, example responses to "Time to Think" activities, and answers to exercises.

The book is unique in various ways. First, it emphasizes the importance of assessing language in the same ways that students use and learn it in the real world and the language classroom. It moves assessment beyond language as simply the four skills of listening, reading, speaking, and writing, to language as communication for particular purposes. Second, it recognizes that language teachers and other language professionals need to be familiar with various types of technology that people use to design, create, and score language assessments. It discusses these technologies and provides examples of how we can appropriately use them in simple, accessible ways. Technology is an integral part of the book, rather than a standalone chapter. Third, the book emphasizes how we can use both content and statistical analyses to help evaluate the effectiveness of language assessments. It introduces statistical analysis through examples and simple explanations and demonstrates how we can use it to support content analysis. Finally, it emphasizes the importance of context, including sociopolitical, cultural, and educational context, when assessing a second language.

The book has five sections. In Part I, Engaging with Language Assessments, which includes Chapters 1 and 2, readers engage with the topic of language assessment, gain an appreciation for the value of language assessment literacy, and explore some of the types of assessments they will discover and use. In Part II, Gaining Knowledge of Language Assessment Principles, which contains Chapters 3 through 5, readers learn about the basic principles for selecting, creating, and analyzing language assessments. In Part III, Right or Wrong, which includes Chapters 6 through 9, readers go through the processes of selecting, designing, creating, and interpreting scores from dichotomously scored items. In Part IV, Judging Test Taker Performances, which contains Chapters 10 through 12, readers learn about selecting, designing, creating, scoring, and interpreting performance assessments. The final part of the book, Reflecting and Self-Assessment, which consists of Chapter 13, takes readers through the process of self-evaluation of their level of language assessment literacy and setting goals for how they will further learn and apply their knowledge. The chapters build on each other and it may be best to use them in chronological order. I hope that this book is effective in helping readers discover the exciting and important field of second language assessment.

Acknowledgments

I wish to thank the many people who helped me write this book. First, I would like to thank Lyle Bachman and Adrian (Buzz) Palmer, my PhD (University of California, Los Angeles) and MA (University of Utah) major professors, who taught me much of what I know about language assessment and inspired me to be the best language assessment teacher and researcher that I could be. I am also indebted to Professor Noreen Webb, who taught me about assessment, quantitative research methods, and how to make complex concepts transparent.

I am highly indebted to two of my graduate students, Fatimah Aseeri and Ananda Muhammad. Both spent many hours helping with the supplementary materials and providing feedback on the book chapters. Fatimah also spearheaded the effort to create and administer the Saudi Young Learner English Assessment. I also appreciate the efforts of the unnamed young Saudi learners and their parents who allowed me to use their test responses in the book. Sonca Vo, another of my graduate students, agreed to tell her story about the positive impact of a language test and helped inspire me to write a book that includes many stories and anecdotes. I also benefited from the efforts of Jayme Wilkin, who helped create the supplementary materials. Many of my graduate students read some or all of the book, completed activities, and provided feedback, including Reza, Febriana, Widya, Hardi, Ma-aruf, Danilo, Seemi, Ali, Ben, Droste, Shangyu, Gi Jung, In Young, Duong, Maksim, Qi, Hannah, Burak, Shuhui, Abdulrahman, and Liberato. I also benefited from the anonymous feedback of more than twenty-five language assessment teachers, to whom I owe my gratitude.

I am also indebted to the editors and support staff at Cambridge, including Rowan Groat, Rachel Norridge, Helen Shannon, Rebecca Taylor, Simone Chiara van der Merwe, and Emily Watton.

I am indebted to my children, John, Matt, and Shelly, who sacrificed time with their dad so that I could write the book. Last, but certainly not least, I am grateful to my wife, Emiko, who helped me with the artwork and provided continued support and encouragement throughout the project.

PART I
Engaging with Language Assessments

CHAPTER 1

Language Assessments and Tests: What We Need to Know and Why We Should Care

FIGURE 1.1 A person writing Chinese characters on a blackboard.
Source: Leren Lu/Stone/Getty Images.

Just like every other class for the entire semester, I could feel my hands beginning to sweat. In a minute or two, the teacher would walk through the door and maybe ask everyone to take out a piece of paper – except the unlucky student. And, just like every day, I was afraid that student might be me. I was in a university second-language Chinese class, and the teacher would sometimes begin class by requiring us to write the short story that we read in the previous class. These tests had strict time limits, and it was challenging to finish writing the story on a piece of paper in the time the teacher gave us for the test. It was bad enough to have to write these stories so quickly on paper, but sometimes it was even worse. As a way of providing immediate feedback to the class, the teacher would ask one student to go to the back of the classroom and write the story on the chalkboard. Because it was much harder to write quickly on the chalkboard, and I got embarrassed in front of others easily, I knew that if I ever had to write my story on the chalkboard, I would have no chance of a passing grade.

My heart sank when the teacher walked into the classroom and pointed at me to go to the back of the room. I was very nervous as I tried to remember and then write what I had practiced. When the timer rang, I stared at my work. Despite the fact that I had practiced writing my story many times, what I had written on the chalkboard was hardly readable. Even though I was in my early twenties, I had to fight back the tears when the teacher wrote on the board that I had failed the test and then criticized almost every word that I had written while the other students listened. I wished at that moment that no one should have to take a language test ever again.

> **Time to Think 1.1**
> What are some strengths and weaknesses of the **assessment** described in the story you have just read?
> What could the teacher do to limit the weaknesses?

Introduction

The effects of language assessments are widespread. Language assessments may impact test takers' circumstances, including passing a class or immigrating to another country. They may also affect teaching practices, an instructor's pay, and family members' livelihoods. Because of these powerful effects, like I did when I had to write a story on the classroom chalkboard, many language teachers, test takers, and others have learned to distrust and even hate language assessments. This, of course, is not the way it should be. Language assessments should help learners in their language acquisition journeys and should help us identify learners who have the necessary language skills to be successful in a particular language use situation. For instance, assessments can help identify a learner's language abilities, with the aim of placing them into courses most appropriate for their needs. They can also provide feedback on what learners do and do not know, give an indication of the extent to which learners have the necessary language skills to successfully study in a particular situation, and encourage effective language learning practices.

In this first chapter, we will begin by discussing what we mean when we talk about language assessments. Next, we will discuss some of the ways people have used language assessments unfairly. The aim of this section is to give readers an opportunity to explore their own concerns about language assessments. After describing some of the potential problems related to language assessment, we will discuss some of their potential advantages, including providing individuals with opportunities to demonstrate their abilities. Finally, we will discuss what we need to know about language assessment to be effective in our work.

What We Mean by Language "Assessment" and "Test"

It is important to begin by indicating what we mean when we talk about language assessment. People use "assessment" to mean any way of collecting evidence about a test taker or group of test takers for the purpose of estimating their knowledge of and ability to use a language. The term "assessment" seems to have become more popular than the term "test" for many writers and researchers. In fact, some view all measurement instruments that we refer to as tests negatively and all those we refer to as assessments more positively. Because people sometimes use these terms differently, and at other times synonymously, it is important to discuss how various writers and researchers use them.

Writers and researchers who use "test" and "assessment" differently generally view language tests as formal tools for identifying how much a test taker knows about a particular language. They may view tests as inflexible instruments that can unfairly label test takers. An example of a test to these individuals would be a vocabulary translation test, where test takers see a word in the language they are learning and write the word in their first language. On the other hand, these writers and researchers usually view assessments as less formal or less threatening ways of collecting evidence for understanding what test takers know about or can do with a language. These individuals might view self-evaluations in the form of written reflections as assessments rather than tests. Throughout the book, we will use the term **test** for formal measurements and assessment more broadly to include both formal and informal measurements (Earl, 2013).

Misuses of Language Assessments

Intentional Misuses

For many centuries, people have used language assessments for unethical purposes. Language has been, and continues to be, a source of identity and sometimes a way of grouping people. Deceptive people have used language tests in unfair ways, and this is a major reason why some people dislike them. Unfortunately, people can create language tests with the aim of disadvantaging certain groups or individuals, and people can use even the best-made tests in inappropriate ways. It is extremely important that language teachers, researchers, administrators, and others are careful to create and use ethical assessments. In the next sections, we will discuss examples of three unfair tests that people commonly discuss in the language assessment field. As you read through these examples, think about a language test that you have taken or know about that may be intentionally unfair.

The Shibboleth Test

The Book of Judges in the Bible tells of a misuse of a language assessment. According to this account, the Gileadites used a one-word language assessment to identify and then kill their Ephraimite enemies, who spoke a very similar dialect of the same language. The Gileadites controlled a passage across the Jordan River. When an Ephraimite or a person they thought might be one wanted to use this passage, they would engage the individual in a conversation about the flooding problems related to the river. The Gileadites' aim was to get the person to use the word "Shibboleth," which meant "flood water." The Gileadites would then assess whether the person pronounced the word as "S̲h̲ibboleth," as most Gileadites would, or "S̲ibboleth," as most Ephraimites would. If the individual pronounced the word as "S̲ibboleth," as judged by the Gileadites, they would immediately kill the person. The Gileadites killed more than forty thousand individuals that they judged to be Ephraimites based on their pronunciation of the word "Shibboleth" (McNamara, 2005).

There are many ethical problems with the Shibboleth test. First, the Gileadites did not use the test to determine whether or not a test taker had the language ability to be successful in a particular language context. They used it as a way to discriminate between two groups of people. Second, the individuals taking the test did not know the aim of the test. They were not aware of what the objective of the test was and what an appropriate response would be. Finally, with only one test question (sh vs. s in one word), the results may not have accurately distinguished between an Ephraimite and a Gileadite.

The Australian Dictation Test

Australian officials claimed to use the Australian Dictation Test (1901–1957) as one way of determining if a person had the language skills needed to immigrate to Australia. Test administrators read a passage of roughly fifty words out loud, and test takers wrote down the passage. While the passages contained unusual sentence structures and low-frequency vocabulary, this was not the major concern about the fairness of the test. Immigration officials, who were also the test administrators, talked with test takers and learned what European languages they could speak. Then, the test administrators gave a test in a language that the test taker could *not* speak. They followed this procedure because the test's aim was to fail anyone who took it, and immigration officials had already identified individuals who took the test as ones the government did not want in the country. In its early years of administration, a few test takers actually passed, but as the test administrators became aware that the aim of the test was to stop everyone who took it from immigrating to Australia, the pass numbers dropped. After 1910, no one passed the test, until the officials finally stopped administering it in 1957 (McNamara, 2005).

The Australian Dictation Test was obviously unethical. The immigration officers did not administer the test to determine whether or not a test taker had sufficient language ability to succeed in a particular situation. Instead, they used the test to discriminate against potential immigrants who were "undesirable" in the eyes of the immigration authorities in Australia.

The Louisiana Literacy Test

White people in Tangipahoa Parish, and possibly other parts of the state of Louisiana in the United States, created and used the Louisiana Literacy Test to reduce the African American vote in 1964. Since voting ballots were in English only, the test creators' logic was that it would be necessary to read the ballot to vote. The test creators wrote the test so that essentially no one, even people highly literate in English, could pass it. People who had to take the test to vote had ten minutes to complete thirty questions. If they answered one question wrong, they failed. The questions were more like riddles than an English literacy test. For example, one question required test takers to "Spell backwards, forwards," while another asked test takers to "Write the word 'noise' backwards and place a dot over what would be its second letter should it have been written forward" (Onion, 2013). Neither question had a clear answer, so if examiners wanted to fail a test taker, they could interpret the question differently than the test taker did.

Some people used the Louisiana Literacy Test as a way to capitalize on a society's trust in tests as fair measures of ability. In fact, the Louisiana Literacy Test was not an objective measure of language ability by any standard, since the test administrators could score the tests based on their prejudices and preferences for who they wanted to pass.

Interestingly, the Shibboleth Test, the Australian Dictation Test, and the Louisiana Literacy Test probably did effectively fulfil their designers' aims. However, despite achieving their purpose, they clearly were not fair or appropriate. We can see a summary of some of the reasons for the unfairness of the Shibboleth Test, Australian Dictation Test, and the Louisiana Literacy Test in Figure 1.2.

1 LANGUAGE ASSESSMENTS AND TESTS: WHAT WE NEED TO KNOW

Shibboleth Test	Australian Dictation Test	Louisiana Literacy Test
• Purpose was discrimination • Allowed subjectivity • Aim wasn't clear to test takers • Inadequate # of questions	• Purpose was discrimination • Allowed subjectivity • Pre-determined outcome	• Inappropriate question types • Allowed subjectivity • Standard for passing was too high (100%) • Inadequate time to complete it

FIGURE 1.2 The unfairness of the Shibboleth Test, the Australian Dictation Test, and the Louisiana Literacy Test.

Time to Think 1.2

Have you ever taken a test that you think was biased against certain test takers? If so, how did it influence your view of assessment?

Unintentional Misuses

While the Shibboleth Test, the Australian Dictation Test, and the Louisiana Literacy Test were intentionally unfair, unintended bias in language assessment is a much more common situation. People who select tests for a given situation, or even individuals who create assessments, may not be knowledgeable about best test practice. These people may unknowingly use or create unfair tests.

A Private Conversation School's Test of Oral Communication

Maybe the best way to illustrate this point is to tell you about the experience that got me interested in language assessment more than thirty years ago. My first experience teaching English and working with language tests came when I went to Taiwan to teach English at a private conversation school. The majority of the students at the school were adults who desired to improve their abilities to communicate orally with other English speakers. After I had taught for a year or two, my boss asked me to be a rater for the school's two-part placement test.

In the first part, the test taker completed a grammar and vocabulary test. The scores on this first part determined whether or not a test taker completed an oral interview and, if they did, the types of questions the interviewer would ask them. It was common to have test takers who got all of the grammar and vocabulary questions correct in the first part of the test but who were unable to answer simple questions in the oral interview. However, because these test takers got high scores on the vocabulary and grammar tests, we would place them in an intermediate-level oral communication course that was too difficult for them.

Unfortunately, the two-step assessment process did not allow test takers with low scores on the grammar and vocabulary tests to have an oral interview. They joined a low-level class, based solely on their scores on the vocabulary and grammar test. I met many of these students during class recesses, and after speaking with them I was surprised that they were in a low-level course. Importantly, no one aimed to be unfair to any of the test takers. The problem was with the tests and testing procedures, which did not effectively measure test takers' oral communication ability.

A Poor-Quality Writing Test

One of my doctoral students from Saudi Arabia told me a story about a poor-quality writing test and agreed that I could share it in this book. The student was an English major at university in a program that required courses in listening, reading, speaking, and writing. Unfortunately, based on the student's opinion, the course and the assessments were not appropriate for teaching students to write, nor to assess writing ability. The instruction and the assessments focused on knowledge of grammatical structures. For example, tests included questions such as, "Complete the following sentences with an adverb" or "Write the correct preposition in the blank." The student felt that the instructors chose fill-in-the-blank questions because they were easier to grade than judging the quality of an essay. As a result, the class did not achieve its stated aim of preparing the student for a written graduate-level entrance examination or equipping the student with the writing skills necessary to be successful in a graduate program.

My experience at a conversation school in Taiwan and my student's experience in a university writing class suggest that we cannot assume tests will be fair for everyone simply because the test developers have good intentions. Given its importance, we will continue to discuss test fairness throughout the book, particularly in Chapter 3.

Time to Think 1.3

Have you ever taken a language test that was unfair because of poor design or implementation? If so, how would you redesign the test to make it more fair? If you have not taken a language test that you thought was unfair, describe a fair test that you have taken and discuss why you think it was fair.

Effective Uses of Language Assessments

If they have such a tendency to be either intentionally or unintentionally unfair to test takers, at this point you may be wondering why we would want to use language tests. The simple answer is that we have been discussing unusual situations. Most language assessments do have a positive effect on test takers' lives.

How a Language Test Positively Affected the Life of Sonca Vo

We can see an example of the positive effects tests can have on our lives by considering the case of a former graduate student of mine, Sonca Vo (Figure 1.3).

1 LANGUAGE ASSESSMENTS AND TESTS: WHAT WE NEED TO KNOW

FIGURE 1.3 Sonca Vo, whose life was positively affected by good language testing practice.
Source: Courtesy of Sonca Vo.

I (Sonca Vo) grew up in a small village in Vietnam and was unable to take any English classes until high school, due to the lack of English teachers in my area. When I started taking English classes in high school, I was so amazed by the English language that I began to dream of becoming a university English teacher. Unfortunately, such a dream did not seem possible, because I was from a poor village; in fact, my family was the only household in the village that did not have electricity. Therefore, apart from the textbooks that I used at school, I did not have access to any other resources to practice English. Realizing that I would probably not be able to enter a good university, I considered how I might prove myself worthy of this goal. I did not have friends who could help me get into a good university, nor any of the other potential advantages of the students studying in prestigious high schools, such as private tutors. However, Vietnam uses a national university examination that pays no attention to one's financial status, living conditions, or any other such factor. University selection decisions depend completely on a student's performance in the test.

Thus, I studied hard for the exam. All of my efforts throughout my high school years paid off when I passed the national examination with a very high score. I was so happy to be able to join an English education program at a prestigious university in a big city in my country. The national examination played a very important role in helping a poor student from a small village like me achieve my educational goals. I now hold a PhD and am a university professor. I will forever be thankful for that test. It did not discriminate against me because I was a poor person from the countryside. Instead, it gave me the same opportunity to be successful as everyone else.

Language tests can provide a fair opportunity for individuals to demonstrate their ability, just like the Vietnamese national exam did for Sonca. The major aims of language assessments are to provide an accurate indication of a test taker's language ability or achievement and to promote effective language learning practices. The Vietnamese university entrance exam made it possible for Sonca to show sufficient English language ability to be successful in a prestigious university. In addition, it gave her, and probably others, motivation and direction for how to study English.

Language Assessments vs. Other Selection Options

Let's consider an example to further illustrate the point about the potential value of language assessments in providing opportunities to many individuals. Let's assume we have a hundred English language learners (English is not their first language) who have applied to a biology department at an English-medium university. Based on courses they took in their first language, each has the necessary biology background knowledge to be successful in the program. However, we are not sure if these applicants have the necessary English proficiency to be able to succeed in an English-medium university. We ask a group of English language teachers to identify twenty students (this is their maximum capacity) with the best English skills from this group. The teachers create a list of ways to identify potential students with sufficient English to be successful in an English-medium university; we can see this list in Example 1.1.

Example 1.1 Ways to identify potential students with sufficient English proficiency.

- Prestige of the student's high school
- Educational and/or financial status of the student's parents
- Grades the student achieved in high school English classes
- Recommendation letters from high school English teachers
- Self-evaluation (a can-do list of statements about the student's English abilities)
- A set of English tests (targeted at oral communication and literacy for biology)

Time to Think 1.4

Before you continue reading, think about the strengths and weaknesses of each of the measures in Example 1.1. Which one (assume you could only use one) do you think would be the most appropriate for identifying the twenty students who are most likely to succeed in the course?

The first two approaches (*Prestige of the student's high school* and *Educational and/or financial status of the student's parents*) may unfairly exclude some excellent student applicants. Just like Sonca, who was from a poor family and who studied at a high school with little prestige, students in this situation may come from relatively humble circumstances but be well prepared for studying in the biology program. Moreover, even if such criteria were effective, we could not consider them fair.

The next three approaches (*Grades achieved in high school English classes*, *Recommendation letters from high school English teachers*, and *Self-evaluation*) all depend on a particular student applicant's previous learning context. For example, grades in high school English classes depend on the grading practices of the particular high school that a student attended. Some high schools might have strict grading practices; for example, they might require teachers to give only a limited number of high grades. Other high schools may encourage lenient grading practices as a way to promote student confidence. As a result, the use of English course grades may be unfair to students who attended the first type of high school. Similarly, the teaching contexts and values of teachers may impact the recommendation letters that they write. For instance, teachers in schools with many highly proficient students may write less positive recommendation letters for students with an average level of English proficiency than teachers in schools with students who generally have lower levels of English proficiency.

Context may also affect student applicants' self-evaluations. For instance, if they are studying in schools where the English proficiency of most students is high, they may assume their English proficiency is low. On the other hand, students studying in schools with low English proficiency overall may assume their English abilities are strong. In addition, students' levels of confidence may result in subjective evaluations of their own abilities.

A set of English tests (like Sonca's university entrance exam) may lead to decisions less dependent on the student applicants' individual previous learning contexts and accompanying subjectivity than the other selection approaches. Moreover, students may believe that a set of English tests is a fairer approach to selection. This potential of assessments has led many professionals to select formal tests over other measures of language ability when attempting to identify the most qualified individuals for a particular language use context. It is important to note, however, that formal tests are not always the best option for language assessment situations. Moreover, for tests to be a good choice, we must design, administer, score, and interpret the results correctly.

Time to Think 1.5

Have you ever taken a (language) test that you thought was fair and that had a positive impact on your life? If so, how has it impacted your view of assessment and what can you learn from this test about the value of good assessments?

Language Assessment Literacy

Language assessment literacy (LAL) refers to what language teachers and other language experts need to know about assessment to be effective in their work (Giraldo, 2022). Some language experts have argued that they do not need to know anything about language assessment. For example, some teachers believe that they are language instructors, not assessment experts, and that they should therefore spend their time developing their teaching skills rather than wasting time with assessment issues. However, as we will soon discover, this view is not very widespread. More commonly, teachers and others involved in language education believe that they need to know about assessment.

With the aim of determining what language experts need to know about LAL, two researchers, Benjamin Kremmel and Luke Harding (2020), asked three groups of people – language teachers, language assessment/test developers, and language assessment researchers – the following question: "How knowledgeable do people in your chosen group/ profession need to be about various aspects of language assessment?" Following this were seventy-one phrases, such as "how to prepare learners to take language assessments." The researchers asked more than a thousand people to indicate the level of knowledge they needed for each of the seventy-one aspects of LAL by indicating one of the following: Not knowledgeable at all, slightly knowledgeable, moderately knowledgeable, very knowledgeable, or extremely knowledgeable. Based on these seventy-one survey questions, they found the nine aspects of LAL in Guidelines 1.1 to be important for language professionals.

Kremmel and Harding also learned that the three groups of language professionals believed that different aspects of LAL were more important for some groups than others. We can see these findings in Figure 1.4.

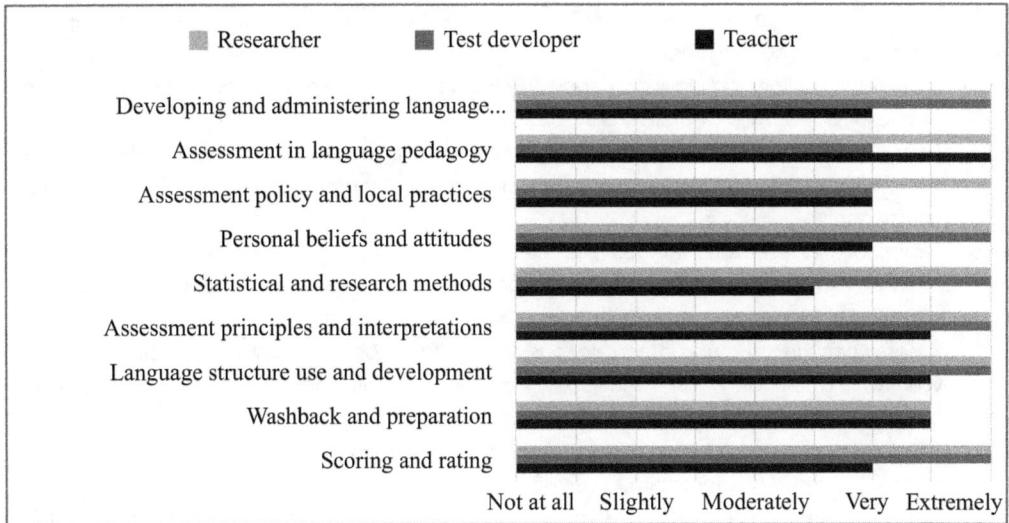

FIGURE 1.4 Kremmel and Harding's (2020) aspects of LAL and the level of expertise required of researchers, test developers, and teachers.

What is clear from the research is that all three groups believed they needed at least moderate amounts of expertise for all nine aspects of LAL. Researchers needed to be very to extremely knowledgeable for all nine areas except washback and preparation, for which they needed to be very knowledgeable. Test developers needed to be extremely knowledgeable for all but assessment in language pedagogy, assessment policy and local practices, and washback and preparation. In these areas they needed to have moderate to very high levels of expertise. Teachers believed that they needed at least moderate levels of expertise in all areas and to be very to extremely knowledgeable about assessment in language pedagogy. This suggests that all of these groups need to have at least moderate knowledge of language assessment in each of the areas that we see in Guidelines 1.1 and higher levels in some of these areas, depending on their role. These nine areas of LAL have helped to shape the contents of this book.

Time to Think 1.6

What do you find interesting about Kremmel and Harding's research findings?

Which aspects of LAL do you think are most important for you to develop?

Are there other aspects of LAL that you would add to the nine we can see in Guidelines 1.1? If so, what?

> **Guidelines 1.1** Kremmel and Harding's (2020) nine aspects of LAL.
>
> 1. *Developing and administering language assessments*: The procedures for creating language tests, providing training for others who need to understand language test development, and the processes of administering a language test.
> 2. *Assessment in language pedagogy*: The utilization of language assessments for teaching and learning a second language.
> 3. *Assessment policy and local practices*: The local practices of assessment and their relationship to local teaching and program policies.
> 4. *Personal beliefs and attitudes*: Individuals' own views about language assessment, how these views might impact assessment practices, and their relationship to others' views of language assessment.
> 5. *Statistical and research methods*: The use of statistical methods and other methods, such as interviewing test takers about the effectiveness of the test questions to understand an assessment's effectiveness.
> 6. *Assessment principles and interpretations*: Knowledge of basic assessment principles, such as validity and reliability, and the ability to appropriately interpret scores resulting from a particular assessment.
> 7. *Language structure use and development*: Knowledge about aspects of the particular language that test developers aim to assess.
> 8. *Washback and preparation*: The knowledge that language experts need to prepare language learners appropriately for a particular assessment and the ways in which assessments can change the ways that programs and/or instructors provide instruction for learners.
> 9. *Scoring and rating*: The ability to effectively grade or rate particular test questions.

You may have noticed that LAL theorists and researchers do not include the test takers themselves as individuals who need a certain level of LAL. This is likely because we do not usually consider test takers as responsible for determining the tests they take. However, test takers should play an active role in the assessment process. We should encourage them to develop and use their LAL to help with language assessment design and procedures. Having learners with LAL would help to make language teachers, developers, researchers, and administrators more responsible in their assessment practices. Even with little understanding of language assessments, test takers may be able to provide insights into what abilities they use when completing an assessment and, with some basic LAL training, they would be able to provide advice to those adapting and developing tests. This does not mean that anyone who takes a language test should have to be language assessment literate, but it implies that discussing some basic assessment principles with test takers and asking for their feedback on how we evaluate their language abilities can lead to better assessment practices.

Conclusion

In this chapter, we have discussed what we mean when talking about tests and assessments. We can view assessments as a way of collecting evidence about a test taker or group of test takers for the purpose of estimating their knowledge of and ability to use a language. We sometimes consider tests as a particular category of assessments that are more formal than other assessments. We also discussed a number of language tests that people have used to favor a particular group or individual over another. Such unfair assessment practices can lead to various problems for test takers, programs, institutions, businesses, and others. Next, we discussed some advantages of assessments and how they can have positive impacts on individuals' lives. The chapter ended with a discussion of what language teachers and others involved in second language education need to know about assessment to be effective in their roles.

We will conclude by returning to my language assessment experience that we discussed at the beginning of the chapter. The teacher in the story probably believed that having students write their responses on the chalkboard to allow for immediate feedback was an effective assessment technique. However, the teacher did not have the language assessment training necessary to avoid discouraging at least one student from learning a second language. I am glad that I did not give up my dream to become competent in a second language based on this experience. A major reason I decided to write this book was to help ensure that language teachers obtain the assessment knowledge they need, so they will not discourage students from learning a second language.

In the journey on which this book takes readers, I hope it will become clear that while we can use language assessments in inappropriate ways, we can also use them to place test takers in appropriate language use contexts and to promote their language learning aims. They can and should help us reach fair decisions about a test taker's language ability or achievement and support the language learning process. Effective language assessments require a basic understanding of language learning and assessment principles, along with the values and forces that shape a language assessment context. Readers of this book will benefit from gaining this knowledge, because it can empower them to play a positive role in making language assessment a more valuable part of language learning. In the next chapter, we will look at some types of assessments and their characteristics. It should become clear that language teachers need to be familiar with many types of language assessments to be effective educators.

Questions for Discussion

1.1 Share an experience you have had with a language test that you thought was intentionally or unintentionally unfair. Then discuss whether you think the tests that you or your classmates described were intentionally or unintentionally unfair.

1.2 Share an experience you have had with a language test that you thought was fair and that had a positive influence on your language learning experience and/or life. Then discuss why you think it was fair and see if your classmates agree with your judgment about the fairness of the test. Should we judge fairness based on whether or not you or a classmate passed the test? Why or why not?

1.3 Think of a formal language assessment that is familiar to everyone in your group. Then look at some of the alternatives to language assessments in Example 1.1. Would you prefer the formal assessment or one of the alternatives? Why?

1.4 Some tests can seriously affect the lives of test takers; their families, friends, and teachers; and others. As a result, test takers (and others) often blame the test when they fail to pass and need an excuse for this failure. How might we design tests so test takers (and others) cannot blame them for their failures?

Exercises

1.1 Explain what an intentionally unfair test is to a few people and then ask them if they have ever taken such a test. Try to find at least one person who has taken one and write a paragraph about the person's experience. Do you agree that this test was intentionally unfair? Why or why not?

1.2 Search the Internet for the Louisiana Literacy Test (you might be able to find the test at http://bit.ly/3SqtybE). Try answering the questions and see how you do. Write about your opinion of the fairness of such a test for determining whether someone should have the right to vote.

1.3 Do a quick search of the Internet for the terms "test" and "assessment." In what ways do people use these terms similarly and differently? Do the results of your internet search agree with your view? Explain how your view is the same or different from what you found on the Internet.

1.4 Judge your own language assessment literacy. Refer to Kremmel and Harding's LAL framework in Figure 1.4 when answering the following questions. Use Table 1.1 to record your responses.

TABLE 1.1

Recording language assessment literacy responses.

	1 0–19%	2 20–39%	3 40–59%	4 60–79%	5 80–100%
1. Developing and administering language assessments	1	2	3	4	5
2. Assessment in language pedagogy	1	2	3	4	5
3. Assessment policy and local practices	1	2	3	4	5
4. Personal beliefs and attitudes	1	2	3	4	5
5. Statistical and research methods	1	2	3	4	5
6. Assessment principles and interpretations	1	2	3	4	5
7. Language structure use and development	1	2	3	4	5
8. Washback and preparation	1	2	3	4	5
9. Scoring and rating	1	2	3	4	5

1.4.1 What is your main purpose for learning about language assessment? (language teacher, language assessment developer, language assessment researcher, or another purpose)

1.4.2   Rate your current level of LAL on the five-point scale for each of the nine aspects of Kremmel and Harding's framework.

1.4.3   Use the same five-point scale in Table 1.1 to indicate how much you think you need to know about each of these nine aspects of LAL.

1.4.4   Add up your ratings across the nine aspects for both what you believe you know and what you think you need to know. You will have between one and five points for each category. For example, if you believe you have 0% to 20% LAL in all aspects, you will have a score of 9 x 1 = 9 for what you believe you know. Calculate your total score for both what you believe you know and what you think you need to know. Your score for each will be between nine and forty-five.

1.4.5   Set goals for how much you want to learn about each of the nine LAL aspects by referring to the rating system that you used in 1.4.2. Keep these goals in a place where you can revisit them often. At the end of the book, we will reflect on how well you think you have met your goals.

Additional Resources

Brown, J. D. (2013). Teaching statistics in language testing courses. *Language Assessment Quarterly, 10*(3), 351–369.

This article discusses the importance of including statistics as part of LAL. The author suggests various ways to engage students with statistics as an important component of LAL. Readers who are nervous about learning statistics may find this easy-to-read article useful.

Giraldo, F. (2022). *Language Assessment Literacy and the Professional Development of Pre-service Foreign Language Teachers*. Editorial Universidad de Caldas.

This book provides a comprehensive look at what language assessment literacy is, its history, and how to create language assessments for teachers, particularly ones in pre-service courses. Readers may find chapters 1 and 2 particularly useful in helping them further understand the concept and practice of language assessment literacy.

Kremmel, B., & Harding, L. (2020). Towards a comprehensive, empirical model of language assessment literacy across stakeholder groups: Developing the language assessment literacy survey. *Language Assessment Quarterly, 17*(1), 100–120.

The article discusses the procedures that Kremmel and Harding used to identify the areas of LAL that teachers and others believe are most important. It describes the context of their study, making it possible for readers to determine how useful the researchers' findings might be for their own language assessment contexts.

McNamara, T. (2005). 21st-century Shibboleth: Language tests, identity and intergroup conflict. *Language Policy, 4*, 351–370.

This very accessible journal article provides a more in-depth discussion of some ways that people use tests in unethical ways. It provides an excellent reminder that we need to do all we can to avoid the unethical use of language tests.

CHAPTER 2

Making Sense of the Many Approaches to Language Assessment

FIGURE 2.1 Use of the wrong type of assessment can have serious negative consequences.
Source: salihkilic/E+/Getty Images.

Many years ago, I joined an English-medium university graduate program in a country where students and faculty used English as a foreign language. One of my job responsibilities was to serve as the coordinator of the English language assessments. Requirements for admission to the university included a certain score on a standardized assessment such as the Test of English as a Foreign Language (TOEFL) or International Language Testing System (IELTS), tests for showing general English proficiency. Students who scored above a certain score on one of these tests but below another could enter the university. However, prior to beginning study of content coursework they had to take intensive English support courses.

When I arrived, the intensive English program was under pressure from administrators who felt that the English preparation program was not effective. The administrators pointed to data which showed that about one-third of students had actually decreased in English proficiency by the end of the two-month intensive English program. To determine the effectiveness of the program, students took one of the standardized tests at the end of the summer program, and teachers compared how they did on the same standardized assessment when they entered the program. The problem with this approach was that these standardized tests serve as general indicators of academic English ability, not as summative assessments, which show mastery of a curriculum. Changing the program's exit tests from standardized to summative resulted in a more appropriate evaluation of the program, and we soon discovered that the program was quite effective in achieving its aims.

Introduction

In this chapter, we will discuss some of the types of language assessments that language professionals use. Language assessments should achieve two major aims: providing an accurate indication of a test taker's language ability or achievement and promoting effective language learning practices. There are numerous types of language assessments, and while we should use all of them with these two general aims in mind, each also has a more specific purpose. Professionals involved in selecting, adapting, evaluating, using, or developing language assessments should know the various types that exist and the accompanying characteristics, strengths, and weaknesses of each of them. We will begin with a discussion of some of the features that we commonly use to describe and distinguish among assessments. Next, we will explore some of the types of language assessments along with their uses. Notably, we will examine most of these types in more detail in later chapters.

Various types of language assessments exist, and we should use them for their intended purposes. In fact, using one for an inappropriate purpose can be meaningless or even harmful. We can compare the use of language assessments to the use of medical equipment. While proper use of medical equipment can be extremely helpful to doctors in diagnosing a patient's health problems, improper use may not have any value and might even have a negative impact on the patient's health. Language assessments can have a similar effect. Using one that is appropriate for its intended purpose can lead to appropriate judgments about a test taker's language ability or achievement and promote effective learning. On the other hand, using an assessment that is not appropriate for its intended purpose can provide an incorrect indication of test takers' language ability or achievement and have negative impacts on learning, which can negatively impact the test taker and others. For example, test takers may need to unnecessarily review course materials, enroll in classes that are not at a proper level, inappropriately fail to gain acceptance into a university, or unfairly lose a job opportunity. The test takers' instructors, family, supervisors, and others might also experience negative impacts from an inappropriate use of a test. For instance, if test takers have to take a language course that requires language above their ability level, instructors may need to adapt materials and pay extra attention to the student. Family members may suffer financial hardship if test takers have to complete unnecessary coursework that requires them to spend money and time on a course when they could be working to provide income for the family.

Time to Think 2.1

Have you ever been affected by the results of a language assessment? If so, how did it affect your life?

Did you think the test was appropriate for its purpose? If not, what changes would you recommend?

Characterizing and Distinguishing among Language Assessments

We commonly characterize and distinguish assessments based on certain criteria. These criteria help us to select or create the type of test that will be most useful for our particular purpose. We often use stakes, objectiveness, and frame of reference to help us characterize and distinguish among language assessments (Table 2.1). We will discuss each of these criteria separately.

2 MAKING SENSE OF APPROACHES TO LANGUAGE ASSESSMENT

TABLE 2.1

Some ways to characterize and distinguish among language assessments.

Stakes	Objectiveness	Frame of reference
Low stakes	Subjective	Criterion-referenced
High stakes	Objective	Norm-referenced

Stakes

We often refer to assessments as high **stakes** or low stakes. Stakes relate to the seriousness of the impact an assessment has on test takers and others, such as teachers, families, and institutions. We can judge the strength of an effect by considering how easy it is to reverse the results of the assessment. Results based on high-stakes assessments have important consequences that we cannot easily reverse, such as whether or not test takers have sufficient language skills for employment. For instance, if a test incorrectly leads to a company hiring test takers that do not have the skills they need to be successful in the job, and if the test fails to identify test takers that do, it may be extremely difficult and costly for the company to replace the unqualified workers with qualified ones. Conversely, results from low-stakes assessments do not generally have serious consequences, and we can easily reverse the decisions that stem from these results. For example, teachers can usually change a decision to move on to the next unit, based on an ineffective classroom quiz, if the teacher later discovers the students are still struggling with the content of the previous unit. Figure 2.2 lists some assessments along a continuum from high to low stakes.

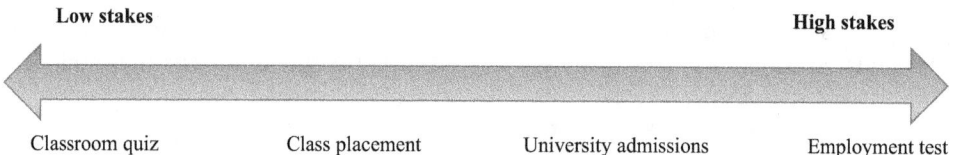

FIGURE 2.2 The stakes of an assessment range from low, like a classroom quiz, to high, like a test for employment.

Objectiveness

We can think of assessments as existing along a spectrum, with objective at one end and subjective at the other. We usually consider **objective assessments** as ones that we score according to a predetermined answer, for example tests which require students to select whether a statement about the content of a reading passage is true or false. We will discuss true–false tests in some detail in Chapter 6. Toward the other end of the spectrum is an assessment that requires responses that we judge subjectively. **Subjective assessments** are measures that rely on human judgments, such as test takers' self-assessment of their own language abilities.

Importantly, however, we should recognize that every assessment has elements of subjectivity. True or false statements might have only one correct answer, but decisions about what to assess and how to write each question are subjective. Computer-automated essay assessments are on the objective end of the spectrum because they use a systematic algorithm for scoring. However, many decisions about what to and not to evaluate mean the assessments are subjective. Figure 2.3 shows some types of assessment and their relative objectiveness.

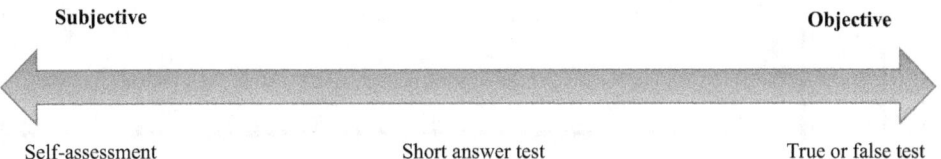

FIGURE 2.3 Assessments can range from subjective, like individuals' judgments of their own abilities, to objective, like a true-or-false question.

Time to Think 2.2

Do you find yourself more comfortable taking a test toward the objective or subjective end of the spectrum? Why?

Which do you think will give you a better learning experience?

Which do you think will give you a more accurate indication of your language ability or achievement?

Frame of Reference

In this section, we will differentiate between language assessments that can identify individuals with the necessary language ability to be successful in a particular language use situation and ones that select the most able individuals from a particular group.

Criterion-Referenced Tests

Criterion-referenced tests (CRTs) compare a person's knowledge or skills against a predetermined standard, learning goal, performance level, or other criterion. When we use CRTs, we compare each test taker's performance directly to a standard, without considering how other students perform on the test. We use CRTs to determine whether or not a test taker has the ability to meet a certain standard, such as basic, proficient, or advanced.

We use CRTs for various purposes. In school settings, for example, we can use them to assess whether students have appropriately mastered the course content. In other instances, we can use them to determine whether a test taker has sufficient ability to undertake a particular course of study. To illustrate how a CRT functions, we will assume that the data in Figure 2.4 represent scores on an end-of-unit 100-point foreign language high school vocabulary assessment. The students appear as people, and their scores on the assessment, ranging from 0 to 100, are on the left side of the figure. As is typical of a classroom test where students study and practice the same vocabulary words that are on the test, many students achieved a high score. In fact, nine of the twenty-five students got a perfect score of 100, six got 90, and three got 80. Only a few students scored between 10 and 70, while three scored 0. The line drawn at 60 represents the score that students need to achieve to pass the test. We consider students with scores at or above this line to have mastered the vocabulary in the unit, while students below this line have not (see Figure 2.4).

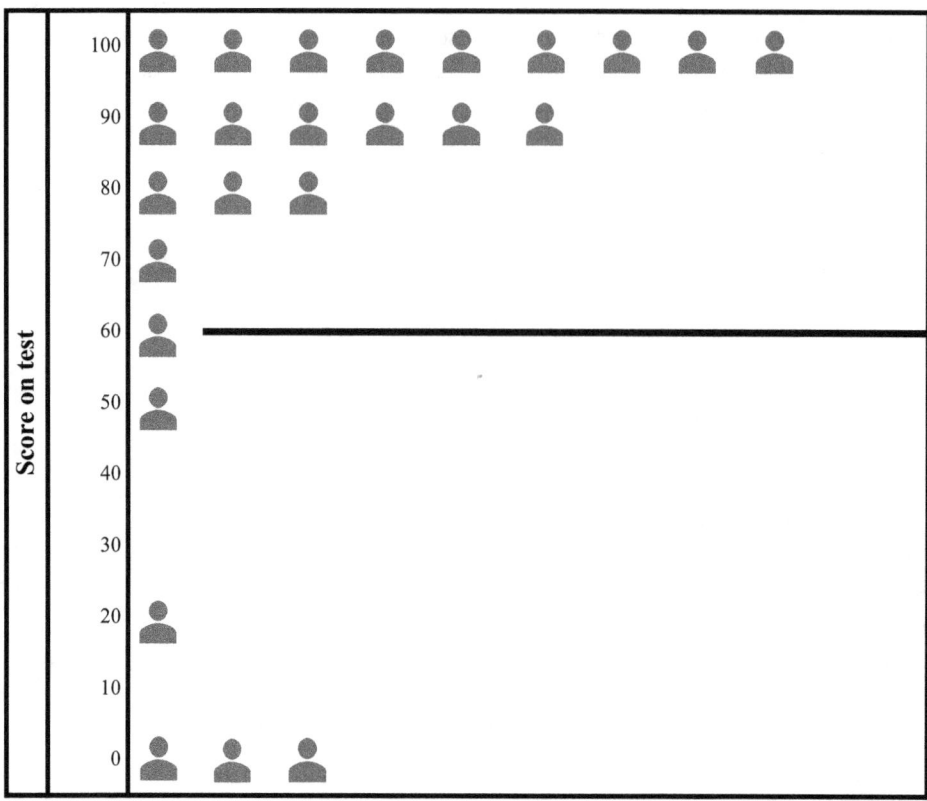

FIGURE 2.4 Scores on a CRT. A line separates students who pass from those who fail.

In a professional setting, CRTs can help a company determine whether or not a job applicant has the skills necessary to be successful in a particular occupation. For instance, they can help determine whether an applicant for a nursing position has sufficient language skills to work in a hospital. We can also use CRTs to determine if pilots have the language skills they need to effectively communicate with a control tower. We will discuss CRTs in more detail and explore their application in classroom settings in Chapters 9 and 12.

> **Time to Think 2.3**
> Describe a CRT that you have taken.

Norm-Referenced Tests

We design **norm-referenced tests (NRTs)** with the aim of ranking test takers from most to least proficient in a language, making it possible to identify the test takers in a certain group who have the highest level of language ability. In NRTs, we compare test takers' scores to other test takers' scores, not to a criterion. When we use NRTs, we assume that test takers' abilities range from high to low, with many test takers getting scores near the average and few test takers getting very high or very low scores. We refer to this spread of scores as a **normal distribution**.

To demonstrate how an NRT functions, we will assume that our high school class of twenty-five students who took the CRT vocabulary test also took a comprehensive language exam with an NRT design. The teacher used the test to help select a few of the students with the strongest language ability to join a study-abroad group. A strict limit on the number of students who could be part of this group required the teacher to select only a few. Let us assume that the students got the scores shown in Figure 2.5. As we can see, the distribution of the scores for the NRT are different from those for the CRT. For the NRT, only a few students got high or low scores. Most of them got scores near the middle. For example, five students achieved a score between 50 and 59, while only one managed a score between 90 and 99 and only one received a score between 10 and 19. NRTs usually target more general language proficiency than CRTs, which means that students will not have studied for the test questions like they could for a unit-based CRT vocabulary test. NRTs focus on the differences in test takers' language proficiency. Only the most proficient can achieve high scores. CRTs, on the other hand, focus on test takers' abilities compared to a criterion. Importantly, while a line between pass and fail is part of Figure 2.4 for the CRT example, no such line exists in Figure 2.5, since there is no criterion for passing an NRT.

We use NTRs for many purposes, including for university admissions, since universities usually have a limited number of seats in classrooms. We also use them for selecting the most proficient person for a particular job. We will discuss NRTs in more detail in Chapters 7, 8, and 12.

Importantly, a true dichotomy between NRTs and CRTs does not always exist. While we interpret CRTs based on criteria, evaluators often make judgments about how well test takers meet these criteria based on (unintentional) comparisons to the performances of other test takers. Another way to think about this is to consider a situation where everyone passes a CRT. In such a situation, it is possible that evaluators would change the criterion to provide a pass rate that would better distinguish between the abilities of the students. Whether or not evaluators are aware of changes to the criterion, such changes would mean the CRT has become somewhat of an NRT.

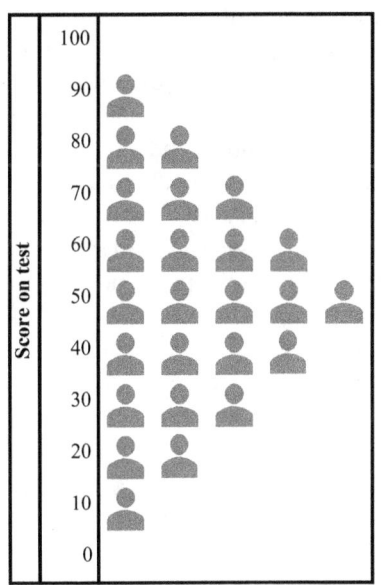

FIGURE 2.5 Normally distributed scores for an NRT. Most scores are near the average.

> **Time to Think 2.4**
> Describe an NRT that you have taken.

General Purposes of Language Assessments

There are many types of language assessments, and each serves a different general purpose. In this section, we will briefly discuss a few general types of purposes that are useful for understanding the language assessment principles that serve as the foundation for this book. In Chapter 3, we will discuss assessment purposes for specific contexts. We will begin the next section by exploring assessments that emphasize the promotion of learning, and then we will move on to ones that emphasize accurate measurement of proficiency or achievement. Importantly, however, all of these assessment types should aim to achieve both of these goals.

Dynamic Assessment

Dynamic assessment (DA) is an approach that emphasizes the relationship between learning and assessment. In DA, learning and assessment are fundamentally connected, and learning should always drive assessment. Vygotsky's (1934/1978) early twentieth-century thinking about the **Zone of Proximal Development (ZPD)** inspired the development of DA. The ZPD is the range of a person's abilities that are in the process of developing and may be most responsive to instruction. The aim of DA is to determine whether or not learners can identify and/or correct errors in their own language performances, the type and amount of mediation learners need for successful language performance, and how much the learners develop their language ability during the assessment. DA involves mediating a language learner's psychological processes by using prompts, suggestive questions, feedback, and examples when learners are not able to complete assessments by themselves.

Generally, teachers use one of two DA approaches in language classrooms. In the first, they attempt to quantify the type and amount of support they give to students during an assessment. Teachers follow systematic steps in determining what types of support to give students and then use this information to help determine what students can do individually and with various levels and types of support. For example, if a teacher wanted to assess a student's oral communication ability, the teacher might begin by asking a question at natural speed and intonation (5 points for a successful response). If the student does not respond, the teacher might systematically make the following accommodations: repeat the question at the same pace and with the same intonation (4 points for a successful response); repeat the question at a slower pace, emphasizing key words in the sentence (3 points for a successful response); and simplify the language in the question and ask again (2 points for a successful response). Each level of accommodation would be systematic, providing the student with more help in responding to the question. In such a situation, the score would also probably depend on the quality of the oral response. This approach makes it possible to compare both language and developing language ability across students. Another approach to DA is less standardized than the first. Teachers provide the learners with the support they need to be successful in completing the language activity. They base their support on their perception of the students' needs rather than a predetermined systematic support hierarchy.

Both of these approaches, along with various modifications of the two, can lead to individualized descriptions of learners' language strengths and weaknesses and the types of support they need to successfully complete specific language activities. Teachers can then use this information to group learners with others who have similar abilities and needs and to help learners create individualized learning plans (Poehner & Lantolf, 2023).

Learning-Oriented Assessment

Learning-oriented assessment (LOA) emphasizes the learning aspect of assessment by using teachers' judgments of student classroom performance to promote learning. Language teachers are constantly gathering evidence about their students' learning needs, progress, and achievement. Language learning activities, such as small group discussions, roleplays, reading aloud, grammar exercises, and vocabulary games can all be sources of this evidence.

We can see in Figure 2.6 that LOA has seven dimensions: contextual, elicitation, L2 proficiency, learning, instructional, interactional, and affective. These dimensions provide teachers with guidance for what to consider when evaluating students' language learning progress and/or language achievement (Turner & Purpura, 2016):

1. A contextual dimension underscores the fact that every classroom is different. Sociocultural and political forces and educational values, along with teachers' personalities, experiences, and expectations, are important.
2. An elicitation dimension stresses that language takes place in the classroom in various planned and instantaneous ways, including during formal tests and quizzes as well as practice activities, grammar exercises, and paired discussions. Each of the types of language activities that teachers use in the classroom is important when evaluating students.
3. An L2 proficiency dimension indicates that LOA adheres to alignment among the course objectives, curriculum, and assessment, and that learners should have a clear understanding

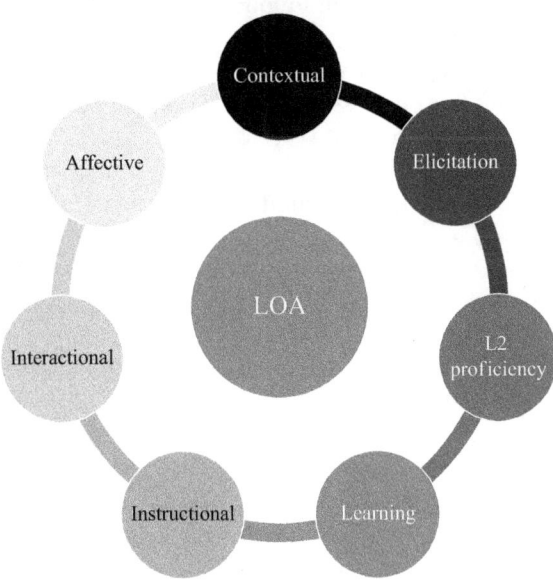

FIGURE 2.6 Seven dimensions of LOA.

of each of these. Teachers should constantly be ensuring that their evaluations of students' learning needs, progress, and achievement align with the course objectives and curriculum.
4. A learning dimension involves an understanding of how learning occurs and how this understanding impacts the conceptualization and implementation of learning and how teachers assess it. Teachers should be using effective learning techniques and connecting them to the assessment of their students.
5. An instructional dimension indicates the importance of a teacher's knowledge of the targeted language, subject matter (where appropriate), and teaching skills and how these elements can impact the learning and assessment. Teachers should be aware of their level of knowledge and skill in each of these areas and take this into consideration when evaluating students.
6. An interactional dimension emphasizes the importance of the interactive communication that takes place during spontaneous language use activities and how teachers should assess this communication. Teachers should use interactive activities in their classes and evaluate student progress and achievement based on students' abilities to effectively interact with others in the target language.
7. Finally, an affective dimension concerns how learners' attitudes, emotions, beliefs, and other personal characteristics impact the learning and performances that teachers assess. Teachers need to consider these student attributes when planning and teaching their classes. For instance, if one or more learners become overly anxious when they know teachers are evaluating them, the teacher may base evaluations on less formal activities that are less threatening to students.

Self-Assessment

In this form of assessment, learners themselves make judgments about their language abilities. **Self-assessment** is a process where individuals think about and assess the quality of their own work and ability (Andrade & Du, 2007). Language self-assessments often involve a list of can-do statements where individuals judge, for example, how well they believe they can complete a language activity, understand particular language input, or know some language features. An example of a can-do statement is: "I understood the newspaper article that we read." The individuals may then select their level of understanding from a list of options. For instance, they may be able to choose from five options, with the first option being less than 20 percent and then each option increasing by 20 percent.

Self-assessment can empower language learners by allowing them to judge their language ability and make decisions about the level of difficulty of the materials that they study. Research suggests that a relationship exists between self-assessments and other forms of assessment. However, this relationship depends on many factors, including the cultures of the individuals and the purposes and stakes of the assessments. For instance, people from some cultures commonly underestimate their language abilities, while individuals from other cultures commonly overestimate theirs. In addition, when the stakes of the assessment are high, many learners overestimate their abilities (Cox & Dewey, 2020).

Formative Assessment

Formative assessment aims to determine the learning a student achieves in a course and to provide an indication of how future learning should progress. For instance, formative assessments can help a teacher determine whether to teach more or less material in a course or what types of materials to use, so the students can meet the learning objectives. Teachers give formative language assessments to students while they are in the process of learning a language, such as at various points during a school term.

Portfolio Assessment

Portfolio assessment is a collection of examples of learners' language-related work. In a classroom situation, this process might include an ongoing collection of drafts of written papers and recordings of discussions or presentations that students create and select to be part of the portfolio. The portfolio aims to show learners' range and depth of language knowledge and their growth and development. It is common for universities to use portfolio assessment in writing courses. Students can write papers and then select the ones they want to revise and/or have the instructor evaluate. Instructors usually evaluate the students' work based on their writing development during the course and how well the writing meets the course criteria.

Portfolios emphasize the promotion of student learning through a process approach, but we also use them to provide indications of both proficiency and achievement. A portfolio that is widely used in many parts of Europe (and other countries) is the electronic European Language Portfolio (ELP). The electronic ELP consists of a record of the language learner's experiences (e.g., classwork, living in a country where the target language is the medium of communication) and achievements (e.g., a passing score on a language assessment), a self-assessment of what the learners believe they can do when using the target language, and products of work by the learners (e.g., video-taped presentations and writing samples) which aim to show ability, development, and motivation (Cummins & Davesne, 2009). Learners have used the ELP to showcase their language ability for prospective employers and places where they desire to study, and as proof of their general language proficiency and learning potential.

Diagnostic Tests

A **diagnostic test** aims to identify the strengths and weaknesses of a test taker with the purpose of guiding teaching and learning. Teachers usually give it at the beginning of a course. As an example, a test taker may take a diagnostic assessment at the beginning of an oral communication class. The test results can give test takers an indication of which areas of their oral communication abilities are strengths and which are weaknesses. For instance, students with low scores on pronunciation and high scores on fluency can focus on improving their pronunciation.

Placement Tests

We use placement tests to help determine the appropriate language support courses necessary for a student to be successful in a particular context, such as a university chemistry program. Placement tests usually align with the institution's language courses, meaning they assess the language learned in them. We will discuss alignment in some detail in Chapter 4. In a school setting, a team of teachers usually creates and administers placement tests, because they are the ones most knowledgeable about the curriculum.

> **Time to Think 2.5**
>
> Compare and contrast placement tests and diagnostic tests.
> Can we use the same test for both of these purposes? Defend your answer.

Proficiency Tests

A language **proficiency test** aims to provide a general indication of a test taker's language ability. This type of test can focus on specific abilities, such as biology vocabulary knowledge. We usually create proficiency tests from a general understanding of language rather than a specific course syllabus or set of objectives.

Summative Tests

A **summative test** provides an indication of a student's mastery of course criteria or objectives in school settings. Test developers, often teachers, create the assessments with the aim of determining which students have sufficiently learned the materials and met the objectives of the curriculum. School administrators or teachers administer summative assessments at the end of a course or program.

Standardized Tests

A **standardized test** requires all test takers to respond to equivalent questions, and test administrators must score this type of test in a highly consistent manner. We use standardized tests to provide an indication of test takers' language achievement or proficiency. Standardized tests grew from a desire to reduce favoritism, bias, and subjectivity in high-stakes decisions. Because they require a high degree of consistency, it usually takes test developers a long period of time to develop them. Before they use standardized tests, test developers carefully evaluate the content of the questions and use statistical procedures to further evaluate and modify them. We can see a bubble mark sheet for a traditional standardized test in Figure 2.7.

FIGURE 2.7 Traditional standardized test with bubble mark sheet.
Source: DrGrounds/E+/Getty Images.

We usually use standardized language tests for high-stakes purposes. We expect test developers to do everything they reasonably can to ensure that the tests will lead to effective indications of test takers' language proficiency or achievement and promote positive language learning practices. Examples of high-stakes standardized tests are the Test of English as a Foreign Language (TOEFL: www.ets.org/toefl) and the International English Language Testing System (IELTS: www.ielts.org/en-us). Both aim to identify individuals who have sufficient English to study in English-medium universities. The Test of English Language Learning (TELL: bit.ly/4baRK95), a tablet-based standardized English test, is an example of a test that aims to identify primary or secondary students in need of English support when studying in English-medium environments.

At first glance, we may think that standardized tests do not connect to learning. However, they play a critical role in promoting language learning practices. They have a washback effect, which refers to an assessment's effect on teaching and learning practices. For example, a standardized assessment that uses vocabulary recognition questions (where test takers identify whether a group of letters is or is not a word) may encourage test takers to memorize lists of vocabulary to prepare for the test. If the purpose of the assessment is to assess vocabulary knowledge and encourage the memorization of vocabulary, the test should have good washback. However, if the aim is to determine if test takers can function effectively in a university setting and promote learning that leads to effective university communication, vocabulary recognition questions could lead to negative washback. Learners may spend too much time memorizing vocabulary instead of communicating in university settings. Because of the prevalence of washback in high-stakes contexts, it is critical that we use standardized language tests that promote effective language learning practices. In Chapter 4, we will further discuss washback, since it is an important principle for all assessments, not just high-stakes ones.

> **Time to Think 2.6**
>
> Have you ever taken or given a standardized language test that you think promoted positive or negative washback?
>
> Why do you think the test had this effect?

Conclusion

In this chapter, we discussed various types of language assessments and ways we can describe and distinguish them. A major focus of the chapter is that language assessments should both promote effective language learning and provide an effective indication of proficiency or achievement. Of course, some assessments place more emphasis on one than the other, but completely ignoring either leads to poor-quality language assessment practice. Along with these two broad aims, we use language assessments for many different purposes, and we need to be sure we use ones that fit our desired purpose.

We began the chapter by discussing how a language program inappropriately used assessments for judging proficiency to measure language development and mastery of the curriculum. This test misuse resulted in negative impacts on the program and its instructors. The change to an assessment that assessed language development and mastery of the curriculum helped to solve the problem. This story is not at all unusual. Language assessments that are effective for one purpose are often harmful when we use them for another. Assessment users and developers need to carefully consider purpose and context when selecting or creating a language assessment. Another important lesson from this story is the need for language teachers to have sufficient language assessment literacy (LAL). Effective teachers and other language professionals need to understand language assessment principles, so they know when assessments are appropriate for their purpose.

Questions for Discussion

2.1 Have you ever used portfolio assessment as a learner or instructor? What are some strengths and weaknesses of portfolio assessment that we did not discuss in the chapter?

2.2 Do you think you would like to be a member of a placement test development and implementation team? What would be some of the pros and cons of such a role? What aspects of LAL (see Chapter 1) do you think you need to develop so you can effectively lead a team of teachers in creating and implementing a placement test?

2.3 What is the connection between a standardized test and learning? How can a standardized assessment promote good or bad language learning practices?

2.4 A car dealership needs to hire between three and five people to sell cars. There are thirty-two applicants and the dealership interviews each of them in the target language. Would you recommend that they use a CRT, an NRT, or both? Why?

2.5 Compare and contrast DA and LOA for a learning and assessment context of interest to your group.

Exercises

2.1 Identify each of the following assessments as criterion-referenced or norm-referenced, and provide justification for your decision:
  2.1.1 A vocabulary quiz on the words covered in a French reading chapter.
  2.1.2 A driver's license exam.
  2.1.3 An assessment for determining which person should get a job (only one position is available).
  2.1.4 A proficiency test.
  2.1.5 A portfolio assessment for a university writing class.
  2.1.6 A university Spanish placement test. The program has five courses, with preset course objectives and materials.
  2.1.7 A language immigration test. The test must determine if test takers have sufficient language ability to function effectively in the targeted country.

2.2 A third-grade elementary school teacher who is teaching English as a foreign language (EFL) believes that students learn best when their reading materials closely match their reading abilities. The teacher intends to have students work in groups and wants to create a quick way to determine how to put students into three ability groups.
  2.2.1 Of the assessment types introduced in this chapter (DA, LOA, self-assessment, formative assessment, portfolio assessment, diagnostic assessment, placement tests, proficiency tests, summative tests, and standardized tests), which would you recommend? Why?
  2.2.2 Would you recommend an NRT or CRT framework? Why?

EXERCISES

2.3 Using a search engine on the Internet, type in the name of any language followed by "Test". For example, type "English Test" and hit enter. Try to find a quick test that you can take.

    2.3.1 After answering a few questions on the test, indicate what type of assessment you think it is (DA, LOA, self-assessment, formative assessment, portfolio assessment, diagnostic assessment, placement test, proficiency test, summative test, standardized test, or none of these). Why do you think so?

    2.3.2 Is it a CRT or NRT?

    2.3.3 Does the assessment address the two major aims of language assessments? If so, how? If not, why not?

Be sure to provide the link to the test.

2.4 Now it is time to experience some types of assessments. Do not refer back to the chapter while completing the following assessments.

    2.4.1 Complete a formative self-assessment with can-do statements (Example 2.1):
Instructions. Use a 1–5 Likert scale to judge your understanding of the chapter (1 = Strongly disagree, 2 = Disagree, 3 = Neither agree nor disagree, 4 = Agree, and 5 = Strongly agree). Circle the number that best describes how you feel about each statement. When you have finished, add up your points. Your score should be between 10 and 50.

Example 2.1 A formative self-assessment with can-do statements.

Statements about Chapter 2:	1 = Low 5 = High
1. I can explain the two main purposes of language assessments.	1 2 3 4 5
2. I can explain the purpose of a diagnostic assessment.	1 2 3 4 5
3. I can explain the meaning of "stakes" in an assessment.	1 2 3 4 5
4. I can explain what an LOA is.	1 2 3 4 5
5. I can explain the purpose of a CRT.	1 2 3 4 5
6. I can draw the expected score distribution of an NRT.	1 2 3 4 5
7. I can explain what a self-assessment is.	1 2 3 4 5
8. I can explain what a portfolio assessment is.	1 2 3 4 5
9. I can explain what a summative assessment is.	1 2 3 4 5
10. I can provide examples of assessments that are highly subjective.	1 2 3 4 5

    2.4.2 Complete a true–false formative assessment.
Select either "True" or "False" for statements 11 to 15 in Example 2.2. Each correct answer is worth 10 points.

    2.4.3 Complete a short-answer formative assessment.
Write a short answer for questions 16 to 20 in Example 2.3. Each answer should be between 15 and 30 words. Correct answers are worth 10 points each.

Example 2.2 A true–false formative assessment.

Statements about Chapter 2:	True	False
11. The two main purposes of language assessments are to provide an indication of an individual's ability and/or achievement and to encourage effective learning practice.	☐	☐
12. Schools use a diagnostic assessment at the end of a term of study to determine whether or not a student has mastered the materials in a language course.	☐	☐
13. An example of a low-stakes assessment is a test to determine who is selected for a job.	☐	☐
14. In LOA, teachers use class activities to help them assess the language development of the learners.	☐	☐
15. When teachers use a CRT framework, they compare test takers' abilities.	☐	☐

Example 2.3 A short-answer formative assessment.

16. Give an example of an assessment that is highly objective. Explain why you think it is highly objective.
17. Draw and describe a score distribution of an NRT.
18. What is a high-stakes assessment?
19. How are standardized tests connected to learning?
20. Explain how a teacher could use a formative assessment in a reading class.

    2.4.4 Compare your scores on the three assessments. How do they compare? If they are different, discuss why you think you got a higher score on one assessment than in another.

    2.4.5 Which of the three assessments do you think was the most effective at measuring your knowledge of the information in Chapter 2? Which was the least effective? Why?

Additional Resources

Cambridge University Press (no date). *Learning-oriented assessment (LOA): The different stages of the LOA cycle (Video)*. YouTube. https://youtu.be/Dr0AtpfuIfQ

In this video, the presenter provides a brief description of the different stages of the learning-oriented cycle. The stages are easy to follow. Readers may attempt to apply the stages to their own teaching and assessment contexts.

Cummins, P., & Davesne, C. (2009). Using electronic portfolios for second language assessment. *Modern Language Journal* (Special Issue), *93*, 848–867.

This article introduces readers to portfolio assessments and discusses their strengths and weaknesses. It also introduces electronic portfolios and discusses how they connect to language criteria, such as the Common European Framework of Reference.

Galaczi, E. (no date). *Learning oriented assessment & technology. English with Cambridge (Video).* YouTube. https://youtu.be/coPm-qfkhcg. Cambridge University Press.

In this video, the presenter begins with a discussion of formative and summative assessment and then introduces LOA as a part of both of these types. The video emphasizes the importance of having a strong relationship between teaching and assessment.

Hamilton, M. (no date). How can assessment support learning? A learning oriented approach. *English with Cambridge (Video).* YouTube. https://youtu.be/UtSeNH9PvHw. Cambridge University Press.

In this video, similar to Galaczi's, the lecturer discusses summative and formative assessment along with LOA. It provides an accessible but somewhat detailed exploration of these topics.

Poehner, M., & Lantolf, P. (2023). Advancing L2 dynamic assessment: Innovations in Chinese contexts. *Language Assessment Quarterly* (Special Issue), *20*(1), 1–19.

This journal article provides an introduction to a special issue about DA. It provides an accessible introduction to the major concepts underlying DA. A particular feature of the article is a historical account of DA's origins and developments. It is worth noting that the special issue of the journal that the article introduces includes various examples of applications of DA in Chinese schools.

PART II

Gaining Knowledge of Language Assessment Principles

CHAPTER 3

Context, Purpose, and Impact: The Situation Matters

FIGURE 3.1 Cultural, sociopolitical, and educational backgrounds are important contextual variables for language assessments.
Source: Jon Feingersh Photography Inc/DigitalVision/Getty Images.

After I had taught in East Asia for a few years, I took a job teaching English as a Second Language (ESL) to college students living in the United States. At the beginning of each semester, students would take a placement test, which included an oral communication assessment. Each student individually met with an instructor and completed a few oral communication activities. One of them was to disagree with the teacher. An example would be for the student to try to convince the teacher to change a grade on an essay based on the student's belief that the teacher had made a mistake. I soon noticed that some teachers gave a lot of low test scores to students from certain cultures (for example, East Asian countries where I had taught) and high test scores to students from other cultures. Most students from cultural backgrounds with low test scores did not try hard to convince the teacher to change the grade on the essay. Their responses suggested that they were not comfortable disagreeing with a teacher and did not enjoy the assessment activity. On the other hand, students from other cultures seemed more comfortable and tried hard to get the teacher to change the grade.

Time to Think 3.1
What changes would you make to the assessment in the story to make it more appropriate for test takers from all cultures?

Introduction

The oral communication assessment in the introductory story provides an example of a test that was probably inappropriate for certain cultural groups, ones in which individuals are not comfortable challenging a teacher's authority. The team of teachers used an assessment design that they did not expect would influence test taker performance based on cultural background. However, most students had just arrived in the US to study English. Some had been in educational contexts where disagreeing with a teacher was appropriate, while others had not. The aim was to place students into English classes of appropriate levels – not to elicit responses based on cultural practices or educational experiences. As a result, the teachers probably placed students from some cultures into classes that were too high for their language abilities and students from other cultures into ones that were too low.

In Chapter 1, we discussed some potential uses and misuses of assessments. We learned that people have used language tests inappropriately in various contexts. In Chapter 2, we briefly considered the purposes and potential consequences of tests in terms of washback. In this chapter, we will discuss the importance of contextual factors and how they relate to the purposes and consequences of tests. We will see that these three factors directly connect with each other and are important for helping us to select, create, and use appropriate language assessments. We will begin by discussing some of the social influences that provide critical context for language assessments. We will consider the importance of context in relation to sociopolitical, cultural, and educational factors that can affect our language assessments. After we have gained some understanding of how social influences can affect language assessments, we will turn our attention to assessment purpose and impact. We will consider how language assessments' purposes and desired impacts closely relate to social influences and other contextual factors. We will conclude by recognizing the importance of the availability of resources in an assessment context.

Social Influences

Social influences are important contextual factors for language assessments. They include sociopolitical, cultural, and educational values and practices. In this section, we will discuss how these influences can affect assessments. We will also think about our own contexts and what social influences we need to consider when we select or design language assessments for our purposes.

Sociopolitical Factors

We as test users and developers need to be particularly aware that our values and beliefs can lead us to (unintentionally) select or develop inappropriate assessments. Whether we think about it or not, social values and political contexts influence what and how we choose to assess. This means that as a result of our values and beliefs, we might create assessments that favor some members of society over others (Zwick, 2022). To illustrate this point, let's begin by considering a challenge in many listening assessments. The decision about whether or not to use (only) native speakers (from certain countries, such as England and the US) for listening assessment inputs depends on social values. If we decide to create or select a test that requires listeners to comprehend the speech of native speakers only, we are valuing native-speaker competence and devaluing local speech varieties. By using this value when we make a listening assessment, we may be giving native speakers control over the language and any benefits related to passing our test. For instance, in a language test that a country uses to help select immigrants, native speakers of the language or language learners with access to the selected native variety may have an advantage. Many have argued against values that allow a particular group, often native speakers, to control a language. For example, to avoid valuing one type of speech variety over another, Levis (2020) has argued that instead of using the concept of nativeness, we should use **intelligibility**, which refers to how well we can understand a speaker. We need to consider these expert voices when we create or select language assessments for our purposes. We will discuss the use of speech varieties as listening assessment inputs in more detail in Chapter 6.

It is essential that we consider sociopolitical factors when we use language assessments. Norton and Stein (1998) report on a reading test that did not take into account sociopolitical factors; they remind us that when we do not consider these factors, we can upset, offend, or anger test takers. Causing such reactions in test takers is not ethical and may result in them not being able to demonstrate their language abilities effectively.

Norton and Stein were both white women who had helped in the development of a language test. They and others designed the test for Black African students who desired to enter an English-medium university in South Africa. Prior to using the test, Stein **piloted** – that is, tried out – the test to see if it worked acceptably well before using it. A group of Black high school students who were living in South Africa took the test in their home school. One part of the test required students to read and answer questions about an article from a South African newspaper. The article was about a family who reported to the police that some monkeys repeatedly came to their house and took fruit from their trees. The article reports that police went to the house to solve the problem, but when they tried to get the monkeys to leave, the monkeys attacked them. The police killed four monkeys before the others ran away.

After the Black high school students had taken the pilot test, Stein asked them, "What did you think about the passage?" (Norton & Stein, 1998, p. 238). Stein discovered that the content of the newspaper article upset many of the students. One student said the information was inappropriate because monkeys relate to witchcraft in South African culture. Another student felt the article was racist. The student thought that the monkeys were actually Black *people* trying to get food from white people's homes and that white people had killed Black *people*, rather than monkeys. A different student thought it was wrong to kill the monkeys. The student felt that monkeys had a right to the fruit, just as much as the humans did. Another student felt the article was too violent and felt upset when reading about killing monkeys.

Based on these students' reactions to the newspaper article about the police killing monkeys, the test administrators wisely chose not to use it as part of the actual university entrance exam. However, the example demonstrates how important the sociopolitical context can be for language assessment. In some contexts, this newspaper article may have been acceptable. For instance, if we gave the test to students studying in a context where people do not associate monkeys with witchcraft, belong to an oppressed group in society or think about monkeys differently than most people, the article might be effective for assessing reading comprehension.

Time to Think 3.2
Think of a context that is familiar to you. What sociopolitical values do you think we need to consider when preparing a test in this context?

Cultural Factors

When we create or select assessments, we need to be particularly aware of the potential influences of culture. We can define **culture** as "the values, beliefs, systems of language, communication, and practices that people share in common and that can be used to define them as a collective" (Cole, 2020). We must be careful when we use an assessment for test takers from diverse cultural backgrounds, such as ones who live in different parts of the world. However, we must also pay attention to less obvious cultural differences, such as ones that occur within a country, in a region of a country, or even within a town or school. For instance, individuals who grow up in rural environments may have different cultural knowledge than ones from large urban areas of the same country.

High- vs. Low-Context Cultures

We can find many different ways of thinking about culture, and we can use some of these approaches to consider its potential effect on language assessments. One framework that researchers have used (e.g., Fernández, 2021; Nishimura et al., 2008) originated with Edward Hall (1976), who placed countries on a cultural continuum from high to low context. While Hall discussed various aspects of high- and low-context cultures, two are particularly relevant to language assessment: communication style and privacy concerns.

COMMUNICATION STYLE

Let's begin by talking about communication style. According to Hall, in a high-context culture, much of what people want to communicate they do not state verbally. Listeners use contextual cues and background information to help them interpret what the speaker is saying. The non-verbal features of communication, such as facial gestures, may be more important than the verbal features. Speakers often take long turns without interrupting each other, and agreement is usually a feature of communication. On the other hand, in low-context cultures, information is mostly verbal. Contextual clues and background information are less important than in high-context cultures. Listeners rely mostly on verbal input and expect speakers to clarify unclear information. Hall and Hall (1990) classify Japan and Greece as high-context cultures, and German-speaking, Scandinavian, and North American countries as low-context cultures. We can see a comparison of communication styles in high- and low-context cultures in Figure 3.2.

While almost no group of people, in any particular country, is completely in the high- or low-context category, the framework reminds us that we need to pay attention to cultural values and practices. For instance, when we select or create an oral communication assessment, we must consider the type of assessment to use based on the culture of our test takers. Test takers from high-context cultures may perform differently on a group discussion than test takers from a low-context culture. In a **group oral (discussion task)**, two or more test takers discuss a topic with each other. The test takers control the discussion while a test administrator monitors (and rates) them. We will discuss group discussions in more detail in Chapter 11. Test takers from a high-context culture may use more body language and contextual cues to communicate with each other. They may take (long) turns without interrupting each other and

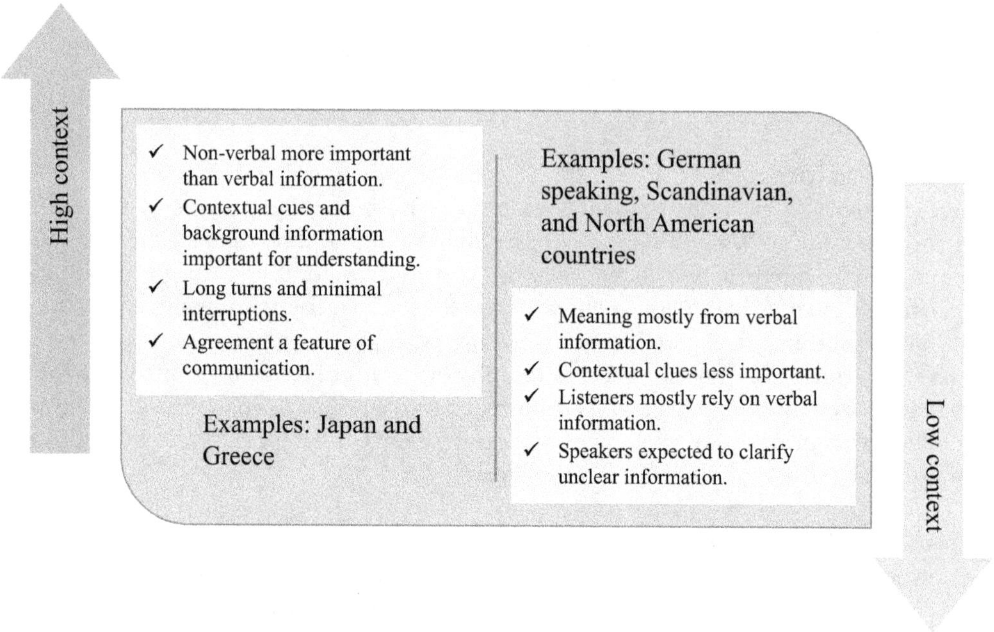

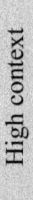

FIGURE 3.2 Comparison of communication styles in high- and low-context cultures.

avoid disagreement. As a result, a rater may not be able to determine whether the test takers are clearly communicating their ideas with each other, especially if the rater is from a low-context culture. On the other hand, test takers from a low-context culture may rely more on verbal information, interrupt more, and be more willing to disagree. Raters may assign these test takers a higher score for effective communication than ones from high-context cultures, even if both groups of test takers are communicating equally effectively.

PRIVACY VALUES

The value that cultural groups place on privacy is another aspect of Hall's framework that is highly relevant to language assessment. According to this framework, low-context cultures place high value on privacy, while high-context cultures may be less concerned about a person's right to privacy. How certain test takers choose to dress can be a cultural value related to privacy. For instance, some Muslim women wear a piece of cloth to cover the hair, neck, nose, mouth, or other parts of the head or upper body, called a hijab, burka, or scarf. For many Muslim women, it is not acceptable to remove these scarves in the presence of men. In some assessment contexts, test administrators ask test takers to show their ears, so they can check to see if they are wearing earbuds or another type of earpiece that would allow them to cheat. Following testing procedures to limit cheating might result in having a test administrator (who could be a man) check under a woman's scarf or use a camera to take pictures. These procedures would go against cultural values in such contexts.

Effects of Culture on Language Assessments in Local Contexts

People assessing test takers from the same country may wonder how cultural differences could impact their decisions about assessments. In fact, we can find many examples about test

Example 3.1 A culturally biased analogy question.

decoy: duck
a. net: butterfly   b. web: spider   c. lure: fish   d. lasso: rope   e. detour: shortcut

1977 SAT verbal test (Zwick, 2006)

questions that are appropriate for one cultural group within a country, region, or even town or school, but not another. For example, test developers designed a question to assess the intelligence test takers needed to study in an American university. To answer the question successfully, test takers had to identify a relationship between two words and then find the same relationship from five answer options. We can see a culturally biased question with this design in Example 3.1.

For the question in Example 3.1, test developers expected test takers to identify the relationship between "decoy" and "duck" (a decoy is a type of fake duck which we can use to trick actual ducks, as the ducks believe the decoys are real ducks). The test developers believed that answer option "c. lure: fish" best represented this relationship, because a lure is a type of fake fish we can use to trick actual fish, as the fish believe the lures are real fish. The purpose of the question was to assess test takers' abilities to identify relationships between words, but people from cultures that do not hunt and fish (for example, people from big cities) may have been unable to correctly answer the question – due to their cultural backgrounds, not an inability to identify relationships between words.

Time to Think 3.3

Think of a context that is familiar to you. What are some cultural values you think test developers should know in order to design an appropriate language assessment for this context?

Educational Factors

The educational systems that test takers have experienced can also affect how they perform on language assessments. Experiences with assessment design, equipment, and content are some examples of how test takers' educational backgrounds can impact their potential to demonstrate their abilities in language tests.

Assessment Design

Different educational systems value different approaches in teaching, learning, and assessing, and we must ensure that these differences do not negatively affect test takers' success in an assessment. For example, when we use a listening assessment, we need to decide how many times to present the spoken input. It is common in some learning and/or assessment contexts to present the input once, and in others twice. Moreover, sometimes we allow test takers to listen as many times as they desire. Test takers who are used to listening multiple times may have listening processes that are not effective when they can listen only once.

Of course, test takers who are used to a certain approach to learning or assessment may be able to complete an assessment with an unfamiliar design. However, they may not be able to demonstrate their abilities as effectively as they would with a more familiar design. We should therefore use familiar assessment designs whenever possible. However, as we will see in Chapter 6, other factors are also important when selecting the design of assessments, and it may not be possible to select ones that are equally familiar to all test takers.

Equipment

The way we use equipment to help us with our language assessments depends on our educational values. One of the ways that people from certain educational backgrounds use technology is to score test takers' writing and speaking abilities. Test takers can write an essay or tell a story, and then a computer scoring system can assign a score to the test taker for their writing or speaking ability. While people from some educational systems – ones that use electronic systems for various learning and assessment activities – may welcome the use of this technology for language assessment, others, who do not commonly use technology for learning and assessment, may not. For this reason, we need to consider carefully how we use technology and how it might impact test takers who have experience of different educational systems.

> **Time to Think 3.4**
>
> Are you for or against using a computer to score test takers' writing or speaking? Why or why not?
>
> Do you think your educational background influences your response to this question? If so, how?

Experience with equipment can impact test takers' potential to demonstrate their language abilities. In some educational contexts, computers, tablets, cell phones, and other technological devices are common. Students gain knowledge of how to use one or more of these devices and may prefer them to paper notepads, textbooks, pencils, pens, and other more traditional school supplies. On the other hand, some students may have very limited or no experience with or access to technological devices. They may be used to writing their work by hand and reading from a traditional paper-based textbook. We must also realize that test takers who are comfortable with one type of computer hardware, software, or keyboard may not be comfortable with another. Moreover, some test takers may be able to adapt quickly to unfamiliar equipment while others may not. We need to consider the experience of our test takers with different types of equipment when we administer assessments. Importantly, while we may be able to teach test takers how to use equipment with which they have little or no familiarity, their lack of comfort in using it may disadvantage them.

Managing Social Influences

Obviously, we must take into account social factors when we make decisions about whether or not to use language assessments – and, if so, how. The main way to account for social factors is simple. We include people who are most familiar with the sociopolitical, cultural, and educational values of the test takers in our language assessment decisions (Shohamy, 2005; Winke, 2020). For example, in classroom settings, we can involve teachers, parents, school administrators, classmates, and the test takers themselves. We can ask parents and school administrators to provide input on these factors. Teachers can help create or select assessments, and students who do not need to take the tests can help with piloting them – as Stein did with the so-called Monkey Passage. Parents and school administrators may be able to provide information about students' attitudes and concerns about certain content or test design. For other assessment contexts, such as employment, we can involve supervisors, coworkers, executives, members of the community, and, of course, the job applicants who are taking the tests. Critically, we need to involve individuals from any potential subgroup of test takers, so we can best ensure that our language assessments are appropriate for all who need to take them. By involving as many individuals from the local assessment context as possible, we increase our chances of using assessments that are context-appropriate.

Purposes and Impacts

We began this chapter by discussing the importance of context and values and how they relate to language assessments. These are important factors that will help us determine our aims in a particular context. Let's look at an example to see how contextual factors, purposes, and impacts relate to each other. Let's assume we have a hospital located in Bangkok, Thailand, and we need to hire twenty-five Thai nurses who can communicate with international English-speaking travelers. Based on contextual factors, we would determine what English-speaking (and other) characteristics we would expect from the nurses that we hire and how we would obtain this information. For instance, we would want to know if people in this context value formal language assessments and what speech variety is most desirable. Let's assume these contextual factors lead us to use an English proficiency assessment to help us select nurses for this purpose. We would need to consider the relationship between our assessment purpose and the potential assessment impacts.

As we have discussed in Chapters 1 and 2, the general purposes of language assessments should be to effectively measure test takers' language proficiency or progress and to support effective language learning practices. Our discussions in this chapter will help us to see the importance of using contextual factors to guide these aims. We can see the relationship among context, purposes, and impacts in Figure 3.3.

In Figure 3.3, our two assessment purposes directly relate to two assessment impacts: the effects of assessments and of the resulting decisions on stakeholders, and the effects of assessments and of the resulting decisions on language learning. Both of these depend on contextual factors.

Impact on Stakeholders

Our first assessment purpose relates to how the assessments and their resulting decisions affect **stakeholders** – that is, everyone that has an interest in the assessment or its results. When we use language assessments, a major aim is to effectively measure test takers' language abilities or achievements to help us make appropriate decisions. We want our language assessments to help us make decisions that will best serve the stakeholders. Who the stakeholders are and what their specific interests are depends on the particular context. Each may have a different goal or interest, and it is essential to consider all of them. Let's consider potential stakeholders for the scenario of our hospital in Bangkok, for which we need to hire nurses who can communicate with international travelers who speak English. Let's assume 125 Thai nurses apply for the positions.

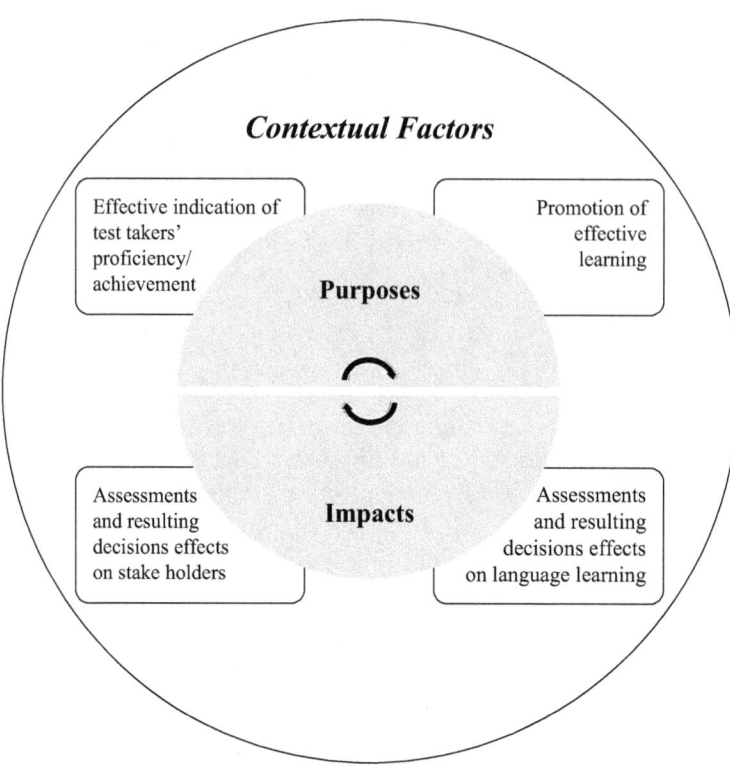

FIGURE 3.3 Relationship between contextual factors, test purposes, and test impacts.

Test Takers and Their Families

The test takers (our 125 Thai nurses, in this example) and their families are usually the individuals that language assessments affect the most. Impacts on these individuals can be positive or negative, and we, of course, want those impacts to be positive. In our example, 25 nurses pass the test and get the job, but the assessment would affect all 125 that applied. Let's discuss some of the potential impacts of the assessment. The 25 nurses who get the job may get a salary increase or other benefits from a new job. Their confidence, especially in using English, may increase as a result of getting the highly prized job. On the other hand, they may experience challenges in the new position and if not sufficiently proficient in English may struggle to succeed at the job. This could result in decreased job satisfaction and lowered self-confidence. The other 100 nurses would not get the benefits of a new job, and their self-confidence may decrease. However, they may be more comfortable in a job that does not require them to use a level of English above their abilities.

Obviously, language assessments can have important impacts on test takers' lives. Language assessments can also affect test takers' families and friends. In our example, the families of nurses who get the job may benefit financially and may need to relocate. Others may experience psychological effects associated with a family member failing to gain a position that they strongly desire.

People Who Have a Close Relationship with Test Takers

Language assessments can also affect people who work or study closely with test takers. In the example of the Thai nurses, these people would include English-speaking travelers and local doctors and other hospital staff and administrators. While test takers are often the stakeholders that assessments most affect, in this example the assessment might have the biggest impact on international travelers. Our language assessment will have a positive impact if the nurses who get the job can effectively use English to communicate with the international travelers. On the other hand, if their English is not good enough for this purpose, we may have some negative impacts, including potentially life-threatening outcomes. Our language assessment may also affect doctors and other hospital staff and administrators. The effects will be positive if the nurses who get the job are able to use English to do their jobs effectively. This will make it possible for doctors and other hospital staff to effectively care for English-speaking travelers.

People Who Do Not Have a Close Relationship with Test Takers

Language assessments can also affect people who do not have a close relationship with the test takers. In our example, the assessment could indirectly affect people such as staff in nearby hospitals, people in Thailand's travel industry, and even Thai society more generally. Successful English communication with international travelers at a particular hospital could increase its popularity, which may decrease the popularity of other hospitals. Our assessment may also have some impact on whether people choose to travel to Bangkok. If they believe they can communicate with medical staff in an emergency situation, they may choose to travel to Bangkok instead of to a country where medical staff are not as proficient in English.

Finally, our language assessment may have social impacts on Thai society. For instance, let's assume that all twenty-five of the nurses that pass our language assessment are from the same region or ethnic group, went to the same school, or were tall. People might associate such characteristics with successful English speakers in Thailand and select applicants with similar characteristics when they hire English users. Conversely, people from different regions or ethnic groups, ones who went to different schools, or who are short may have a harder time getting a job that requires English. We can see in Figure 3.4 some of the potential stakeholders in the example of the English-speaking Thai nurses.

> **Time to Think 3.5**
>
> What stakeholder roles have you played in relation to a language assessment?
>
> What positive and negative impacts have you felt in each of these roles?

Impact on Language Learning Practices

In addition to how assessments can impact stakeholders, we also need to pay attention to the impacts of our assessments on language learning and teaching practices. As we learned in Chapter 2, we refer to these impacts as washback. Assessments with positive washback lead to more effective learning and teaching practices, while ones with negative washback lead to less effective learning and teaching practices. For the example of the Thai nurses, we want the assessment to encourage nurses who desire future employment at the hospital to use language learning techniques that will help them be better English-speaking nurses. For example, we could have an assessment where a test administrator gives the nurse applicants an opportunity to demonstrate their ability to use English in a way similar to what they would use in a real

3 CONTEXT, PURPOSE, AND IMPACT: THE SITUATION MATTERS

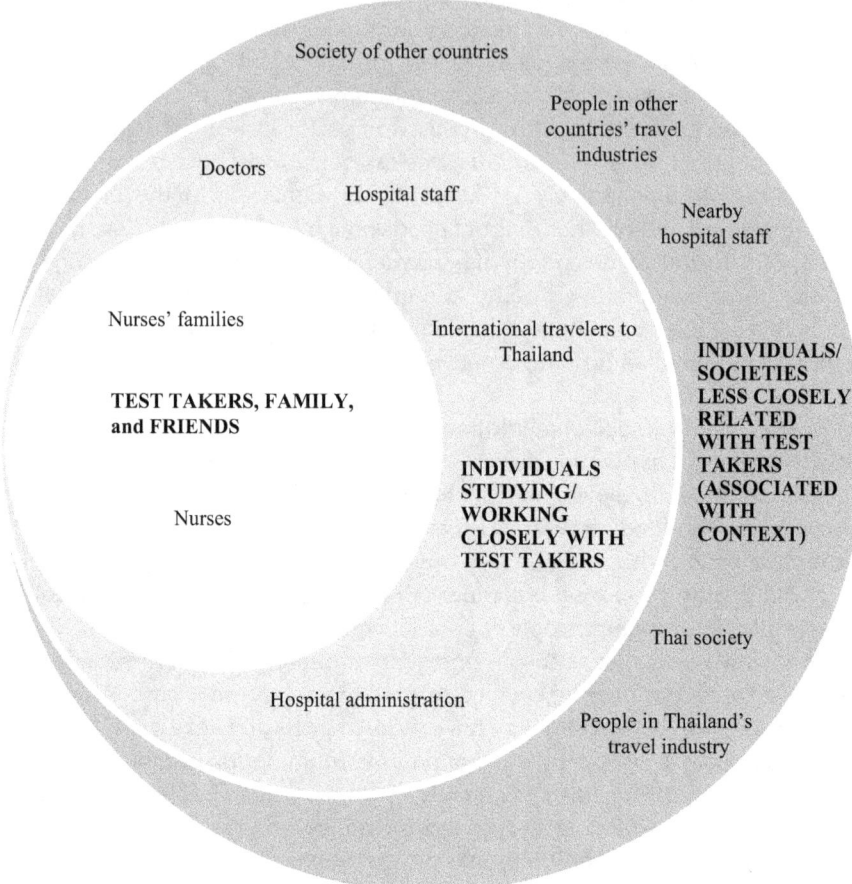

FIGURE 3.4 Potential stakeholders for our English-speaking Thai nurses example.

hospital setting. The test administrator could act like a patient and describe some symptoms to the nurse applicant. The nurse could ask for further information about the symptoms and take notes about them. Having this type of assessment may lead to future nurse applicants practicing similar situations. If this were to happen, we would consider this (increased) use of language learning practices to be positive washback on learning, since this is exactly the type of language activity that nurses do in hospitals. We will discuss the importance of selecting tasks from actual language situations further in Chapter 4. We can see the relationship between purpose(s) and impact(s) for our example about Thai nurses in Figure 3.5.

Availability of Resources

Our last topic in this chapter relates to the availability of resources for our assessments. The availability of resources is a critical factor in any assessment context. **Assessment resources** are materials we need to create or select and carry out assessments. The three types that we need to consider when we select or create language assessments are human resources, space, and material resources.

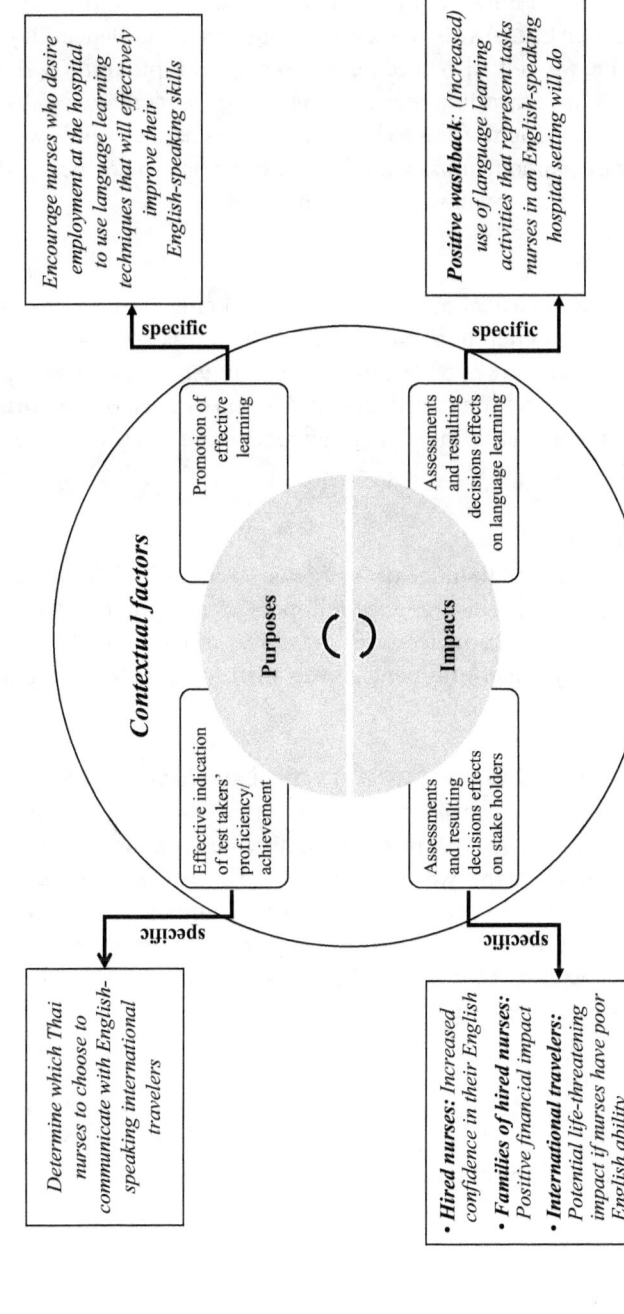

FIGURE 3.5 Relationship between contextual factors, purposes, and impacts in the English-speaking Thai nurses example.

Human Resources

Selecting, creating, planning, administering, scoring, and score reporting all require human resources. Importantly, we want someone who has sufficient language assessment literacy (LAL) (which readers should have after completing this book) to work with other stakeholders in the process. Others with LAL can also be of great value to a team. Depending on the assessment that we select or create, we may also need people to help with planning, writing test questions, administering, scoring and/or rating, and score reporting. For computer-delivered assessments, we need individuals with appropriate technological expertise. Teachers who decide to create formative end-of-week classroom quizzes may be able to manage all of these tasks independently. For larger-scale assessments, we will need more human resources.

Space

We will need appropriate space for our language assessments. First, we need space for creating them. Small-scale projects generally require little space for this purpose. Second, we need space for test administration. We may need one or more computer labs, a classroom, or office space. For large-scale assessments, we may need multiple testing centers. For **at-home assessments**, where test takers complete tests online at their homes or other internet-connected locations, test takers need a private, quiet space.

Material Resources

We will need materials for our language assessments. To create and deliver our assessments, we may need computers, special software, and/or paper. For computer-delivered assessments, we will need computers and possibly certain software, and a reliable internet connection. Obviously, for delivering paper-and-pencil assessments, we will need paper, pencils, and erasers, and possibly pictures or objects.

Balancing Assessment Goals and Available Resources

While we want to do as much as we reasonably can to make our language assessments effective, we usually do not have sufficient resources to make them perfect. As a result, whenever we select or create a language assessment, we must consider our context and balance our desire for a perfect assessment with the resources that are available. Importantly, however, we should not use poor language assessments simply because they are cheap options. If our resources are too limited to have an assessment that reasonably meets our aims, we should consider not using a language assessment for our purpose.

> ### Time to Think 3.6
> Think of a language assessment that you think requires additional resources to be effective. Which of the three types of resources would be most helpful for this assessment? Why?

Conclusion

In this chapter, we examined the importance of context in language assessment. We began by exploring sociopolitical, cultural, and educational factors and learned that they are central to successful language assessments. We also considered the importance of purpose and impact and how they relate to each other and the assessment context. We included a discussion of stakeholders and the importance of involving them when we use language assessments. Finally, we discussed the importance of having sufficient resources to help ensure the success of our language assessments.

This chapter began with a story about rating college students' oral communication proficiencies and how cultural background negatively influenced how students performed on the assessment. Students from certain cultures were much less comfortable with the assessment than ones from other cultures. As a result, teachers probably placed some students into inappropriate English language classes. As this story illustrates, and as we discussed in this chapter, considering contextual factors is critical when we use language assessments.

Questions for Discussion

3.1 Assume a teacher will give a listening assessment to help determine English grades for fourteen-year-olds in a Chinese public school. The students and parents believe that audio input should be from native English speakers. However, the teacher believes that the audio inputs should be from highly proficient Chinese speakers of English. Which type of audio input do you think they should use? Why?

3.2 Think of a real or hypothetical language assessment that has the potential for unintended social impacts. What contextual values contribute to these potential impacts?

3.3 What are some cultural values that could affect how we design and use language assessments? How can we include these cultural values in our language assessments?

3.4 Is it possible to create and/or use a language assessment in which the test developers and users do not introduce bias in some way? How can we limit potential test developer and user bias? Consider some language assessments that you know about in your discussion.

3.5 Assume you plan to use an English placement test to determine which classes fourteen-year-old middle school students should take. However, you do not have sufficient money to purchase an appropriate assessment. What would you do? Why?

Exercises

3.1 Think of a language assessment context that is relevant to your interests, such as a formative assessment in a university writing class. Briefly describe the context and then answer the following questions about factors that would guide your selection or creation of the assessment.
    3.1.1 How would sociopolitical factors affect your decisions?
    3.1.2 How would your cultural background affect your decisions?
    3.1.3 How would your educational background affect your decisions?
    3.1.4 What could you do to ensure that these three factors do not negatively affect your design or selection?

3.2 How much responsibility do you think test developers and users have for promoting positive social consequences? Think about the example we discussed in this chapter, about hiring English-speaking nurses in Thailand. Do you think the test developers would be responsible if an unexpected number of nurses who pass the assessment are from a certain region of the country? Justify your point of view.

3.3 Assume you are a high school language teacher who teaches a writing course. You want to create a summative assessment to determine how well students have mastered the course objectives and materials.
   3.3.1 Draw a figure like the one in Figure 3.4 and indicate potential stakeholders from each of the three levels.
   3.3.2 What would be the potential interests of each of these stakeholders?
   3.3.3 What could you do to best address the interests of each of the potential stakeholders?
   3.3.4 What are the potential positive and negative impacts on each of the potential stakeholders? Consider both intended and unintended impacts.
   3.3.5 Explain what washback is and how you could promote positive washback from your assessment.

Additional Resources

Mirhosseini, S-A., & De Costa, P. I. (Eds). (2020). *The Sociopolitics of English Language Testing*. Bloomsbury Academic.

This edited collection provides guidance on the types of sociopolitical considerations needed when creating language assessments. The book covers various contexts, including high-stakes and classroom-level language assessment. The prefaces are particularly valuable, as they provide an overview of the critical issues.

Sabbaghan, S., & Ismaeil, F. (2023). None of the above: Integrity concerns of standardized English proficiency tests. In S. E. Eaton, J. J. Carmichael, & H. Pethrick (Eds), *Fake Degrees and Fraudulent Credentials in Higher Education* (pp. 169–185). Springer.

The authors of this book chapter discuss concerns about standardized language assessments and their potential for containing bias against test takers from particular cultural backgrounds. The authors use examples that make their points clear and relevant to many people throughout the world. Readers may find other chapters in the book of interest as well.

Zwick, R. (2022). A century of testing controversies. In E. Clauser & M. Bunch (Eds), *The History of Educational Measurement: Key Advancements in Theory, Policy, and Practice* (pp. 136–154). Routledge.

This book chapter provides a discussion of the potential biases and discrimination that can be a part of standardized assessments. Of particular relevance is a review of a US court case in the 1970s that found some California public schools were intentionally discriminating against certain groups of people. They were using racially and culturally biased standardized assessments for placement into courses that many people felt were inappropriately stigmatizing.

CHAPTER 4

What and Who Are We Measuring? Validity and Alignment

FIGURE 4.1 Real-world language use on the playground.
Source: fstop123/E+/Getty Images.

Early in my career, I taught students who were preparing to be medical doctors in a Southeast Asian country. They were a select group who had achieved high scores on entrance exams, including English. The school had about four hundred and fifty medical students in a grade level, and teachers divided these students into fifteen class sections with about thirty students each. Extensive reading was the main focus of the class, and the students read a novel about a successful doctor who became ill and discovered how tough it is to be a patient. The students enjoyed the book, even though it was challenging for them. Each week, I gave the students comprehension questions about the book and helped them when they were unable to answer them. Then we discussed the doctor's challenges and how they might relate to the students' futures when they became doctors. Over the fifteen-week course, the students became much better at understanding the novel and relating it to their future careers.

I was expecting them to do well on the final exam. However, the final exam did not measure extensive reading, and as a result, my students did not do well on it. The assessment committee had created an exam by taking a page from the 221-page novel and deleting every seventh word. The students had to fill in the missing words. The assessment may have been a good measure of something, possibly vocabulary and grammar, but it was not a good measure of extensive reading, which was the main course objective.

> **Time to Think 4.1**
>
> What was wrong with the assessment that the assessment team created in the story at the beginning of the chapter?

Introduction

As we have discussed in previous chapters, the major aim of language assessments is to provide an indication of a test taker's language ability or achievement for a particular purpose and to promote effective language learning practices. Paying attention to the concept of **validity** is critical for achieving this goal. The concept of validity has evolved over the years and, as a result, we encounter various definitions, ways of thinking about it, and frameworks for helping us evaluate it. We will focus on one of these approaches and briefly discuss some of the others. We will begin the chapter by discussing some of the ways that people have thought about validity. Next, we will explore some techniques to identify what to measure with language assessments. After that, we will discuss the concept of **alignment** and how it helps us evaluate the validity of our assessments. Finally, we will briefly consider some other approaches to validity.

Validity

A common way to define validity is "the degree to which a test is measuring what it claims to measure" (Brown, 2022, p. 456). Let's see what this definition of validity would mean for assessing the Italian oral communication abilities of twelve-year-old immigrants that have lived and studied Italian in Italy for three months. The purpose of the assessment is to determine if the students are ready for promotion to a more advanced oral communication course. According to this definition of validity, the Italian oral communication assessment would be valid based on how well it measures oral communication. While this definition is accurate, it requires us to make many assumptions about the purpose of the assessment and the characteristics of the test takers. The definition also fails to tell us how we evaluate validity. For these reasons, the Standards for Educational and Psychological Testing (AERA et al., 2014, p. 11) define validity as "the degree to which evidence and theory support the interpretations of test scores for proposed uses of tests." This definition of validity makes it clear that we evaluate validity with evidence and theory and that validity depends on how we interpret and use test scores – not on the test itself.

Let's begin by talking about why it is important that we discuss validity in relation to how we interpret and use test scores – not the test itself. An assessment may be appropriate for one purpose and/or test taker group, but not for another. For instance, an assessment could effectively measure the Italian oral communication abilities of twelve-year-old immigrants who have lived in Italy for three months. However, the same assessment may not be effective for measuring the Italian oral communication abilities of nurses working in Italian hospitals. An oral communication assessment which produces scores that we can effectively use to determine whether or not we should promote the twelve-year-old beginner learners of Italian to a more advanced oral ability class may include some simple questions, such as "What is your hobby?," "Describe your favorite animal," or "Tell me about your hometown." However, these questions would not be appropriate for determining whether an adult nurse could effectively orally communicate in an Italian-speaking hospital. These questions do not target oral communication in a hospital, and they are probably too easy to be effective for this use. Even if individuals could answer all of these questions effectively, it would not mean they could successfully communicate with doctors, staff, and patients in an Italian hospital. We can see from this example that a test can be effective for one purpose and poor for another. For this reason, we do not refer to a test as valid or not valid. When we judge validity, we use the more detailed definition of validity, so we remember the importance of an assessment's purpose and test taker population when judging its effectiveness.

The second point that our expanded definition makes clear is that validity is a relative quality that we judge based on sources of theory and evidence. Decision makers need to make a judgment about whether or not the theory and evidence sufficiently supports or does not support the uses of the assessment scores. Judgments about validity require more theory and evidence in high- than low-stakes assessment contexts. For our low-stakes assessment of twelve-year-old learners of Italian, judgment about validity might rely mostly on how well we followed learning and assessment principles to design the assessment. On the other hand, validity judgments for a high-stakes assessment context, such as for immigration, may require a large amount of theory and evidence. Many stakeholders may decide whether the test scores are appropriate for making immigration decisions.

Throughout the book, we will think of validity as how confident we can be, considering theory and evidence, that the language test scores and their interpretations are effective indicators of test takers' abilities for the assessment's purpose.

When we think about validity in this way, we need to:

1. be clear about the assessment's purpose
2. clearly define what language abilities we want to measure
3. understand test takers' relevant personal characteristics
4. indicate the appropriate sources of theory and evidence for making an appropriate validity judgment.

In the chapters in Parts III and IV, we will discuss various assessment design principles that result from this way of thinking about validity. In the next section, we will explore some ways of defining what we want to measure.

> **Time to Think 4.2**
>
> Have you ever given or taken a/an (language) assessment that you felt had poor validity for its purpose? If so, why do you think so?
>
> If you have not given or taken such an assessment, talk about one that you feel was highly valid for its purpose.

Defining Constructs

At the heart of validity is knowing as precisely as possible what language ability it is that we want to assess. We cannot directly assess most language abilities. We refer to these unobservable abilities as **constructs**. An example of a language construct is the reading ability students need for success in university. We cannot directly observe test takers' abilities to comprehend a text. When we want to measure reading ability for this purpose, we can have test takers read a written passage and answer comprehension questions about it. Then we can judge their reading abilities for this purpose by how accurately they answer these questions.

We must have a clear definition of a construct if we want to measure it effectively. We can use various approaches to defining a construct, including language theory, language needs analysis, corpora, and curriculum objectives. Using one or more of these approaches provides us with important theoretical evidence about the validity of our interpretation of the test scores and their uses for a particular purpose.

Language Theory

One way to help us define a language construct is to use our understanding of how we use languages or how we learn them. We will consider an example from a test development project. This example will help us understand how we can use language theories and language learning theories to guide construct development. The aim of the project was to create a test that could place students learning English as a Second Language (ESL) into appropriate support courses for English-language oral communication at university.

The first step in the process is to select appropriate language or language learning theories or principles. **English as a Lingua Franca (ELF)** describes how English learners use English to communicate. Given that students at the university need to communicate in English with people from various cultural and language backgrounds, the test development team chose to use ELF principles to help create the construct for the test.

The second step is to review relevant literature about the theory or principles. The review of the ELF literature helped the development team to identify five ELF principles for creating the construct. The principles are international communicative competence, English rhetorical sensitivity, context sensitivity, motivation, and grammatical appropriacy.

The third step in the process is to use the theory and principles to create the construct. We can see this process in Figure 4.2.

FIGURE 4.2 Using language theory to create language constructs that we can assess.

When we use this approach, we usually think about how the theory or principles relate to the language abilities of the test takers. In the ELF assessment development project, the team thought about what abilities language users need based on these principles. We can see the five principles that the team identified in the ELF literature to guide the construct, along with a brief description of each, in Table 4.1. There is also a column that shows potential constructs for the English oral communication placement test, which describe individual abilities of the test takers.

We may find it useful to create a more specific construct. For example, for the first principle, international communicative competence, we might want to expand the construct to indicate

TABLE 4.1

Using theory to define a construct: ELF principles, description of principles, and constructs based on the principles.

ELF principle	Description of principle	Construct based on principle
International communicative competence	English users need to understand other English users, and other English users need to understand them. When communication breaks down, they need to be able to repair it.	The ability to understand advanced English speakers from many cultures, speak clearly enough that advanced English speakers can understand, and clarify meaning when misunderstandings occur.
English rhetorical sensitivity	Effective English use requires knowledge of linguistic and cultural differences to help the speaker select and use a suitable rhetorical style for communicating with people from different cultures and in various contexts.	The ability to use knowledge of linguistics and culture to determine and use a suitable rhetorical style to communicate with English users from different cultures in various contexts.
Context sensitivity	English users should show respect for local English varieties and use English to add to global knowledge.	The ability to show respect for local English varieties and add to global knowledge.
Motivation	English users should use English to achieve personal or cultural goals.	The ability to use English to help achieve personal or cultural goals.
Grammatical appropriacy	English users should achieve English communication through the use of grammar that is mutually understandable to advanced English users from diverse cultures.	The ability to communicate in a manner that is grammatically understandable to advanced English speakers from diverse cultures.

Source: Ockey & Hirch, 2020

what "understand" means. We might describe the listening skills individuals need to be able to understand others and the pronunciation features they need for others to understand them. These skills might include the ability to accommodate to unfamiliar speech varieties or pronunciation features important for understanding in a particular context. As this example shows, creating or selecting language constructs that align with language and/or language learning theories is important.

4 WHAT AND WHO ARE WE MEASURING? VALIDITY AND ALIGNMENT

> **Time to Think 4.3**
>
> Think of a context familiar to you. Would using ELF principles be appropriate for helping you select, evaluate, or create an assessment for this context? If so, why?
>
> If not, how might the principles be adapted for helping you select, evaluate, or create an assessment for this context?

Language Needs Analysis

We can use a language needs analysis to help us define our language construct. A **language needs analysis** refers to a collection of information about a language use situation and the language we need to function effectively in it. Language needs analyses are important because they help test developers identify the language a test taker needs for success in a particular situation. Test developers can use this information to define the constructs that they want to assess and create assessments that measure them. Individuals conducting language needs analyses for assessment purposes can use five steps to help ensure an effective process (see Figure 4.3).

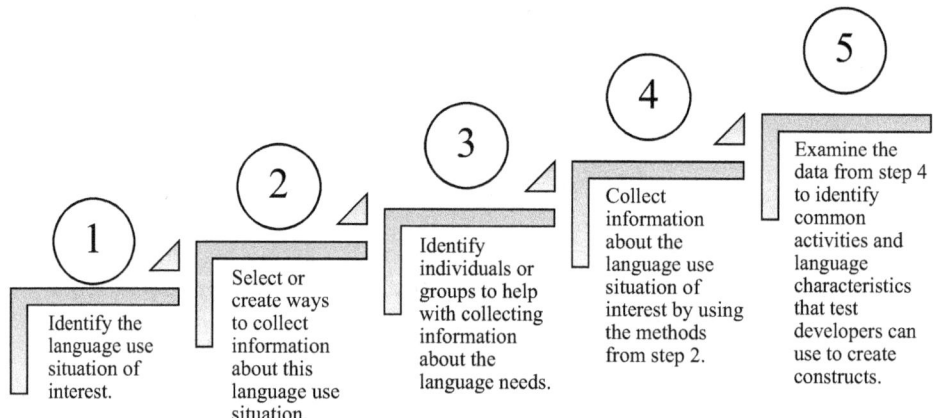

FIGURE 4.3 Steps in a language needs analysis for creating language constructs.

The first step is to identify the **target language use (TLU) situation** of interest. A TLU situation is a real-world place where test takers complete language use tasks (Bachman & Palmer, 2010). For instance, let's assume that we want to determine how well eight-year-old learners of English are able to communicate with others while playing games during school recess. Our TLU situation would be the school playground, where eight-year-old children use English while they play with one another.

The second step is to select or create appropriate ways to collect information about this TLU situation. Collecting information about the language children need to communicate on the playground could come from various sources. Teachers or others could observe and take notes about the language the students use or need to use. They might also record some interactions (with permission from the students and their parents) and examine the language the students use in the recordings. Teachers could ask the students and/or teachers to answer a questionnaire or interview them about the language students need for this context. Teachers could also review textbooks, research articles, and/or course materials for classes that aim to help similar children develop their social language skills.

The third step is to identify appropriate individuals or groups of individuals to help with collecting information about the language needs. Individuals who are using, teaching, or observing the language the children need in the TLU situation should help provide information. For the playground example, language-proficient eight-year-olds who play on a school playground and teachers who observe this behavior would be appropriate to observe or ask about the English they use during this activity. Parents with eight-year-old children may also be able to contribute information about the language these children need to communicate successfully on the playground.

The fourth step is to collect information about the TLU situation by using the methods from the second step. For the playground situation, a teacher may go to the playground and listen and take notes about the language they hear from English-proficient eight-year-olds. In other situations, such as for creating a curriculum-wide placement exam, the administration of questions to a large number of individuals and an examination of relevant research may be appropriate.

For the fifth step, test developers examine the data to identify common activities and language characteristics that they can use to create a construct. For the playground example, a teacher's notes may show that typical activities include playing hiding games and talking about which playground equipment to use. Teachers may notice that students use vocabulary for playground equipment, such as "slide," "seesaw," and "swing," and verbs for playing, such as "chase," "catch," and "run." Teachers may also notice that students' fluency and pronunciation are important for communication. Students who successfully communicate use more appropriate fluency and pronunciation than students who struggle to communicate with others. Test developers – in this case teachers – can then use these language situations and features to define or select an appropriate language construct for their purpose.

The language needs analysis for the playground example might lead teachers to define oral communication for this context and group of students as the ability to communicate orally with friends on a playground. Teachers might further subdivide this ability into more specific language features, such as interactional competence, fluency, pronunciation, grammar, and vocabulary that children need for communicating on the playground. Table 4.2 shows these abilities, along with a possible construct definition for this context.

TABLE 4.2

Using language needs analysis to guide construct development.

Construct	Definition
Interactional competence	The ability to understand other students and respond appropriately to them with language and/or physical actions.
Grammar	The ability to understand and use basic English structure to communicate, particularly sentences in the simple present and present progressive tenses.
Vocabulary	The ability to recognize and use vocabulary that children commonly use on a playground, such as action verbs and nouns referring to playground equipment.

TABLE 4.2 (cont.)

Construct	Definition
Fluency	The ability to speak at a speed that is appropriate for communicating information while playing with friends.
Pronunciation	The ability to pronounce simple words and phrases in a way that is understandable to English users from various cultural and language backgrounds.

> **Time to Think 4.4**
>
> What challenges do you think teachers would face when conducting a needs analysis for the playground situation?
>
> How could teachers overcome these challenges?

Corpora

Another approach to helping define a language construct is to use a **language corpus**. A language corpus is an organized electronic storage of language, usually written or spoken, that we can use for linguistic analysis (Barker, 2014). Corpora make it possible for test developers to determine the characteristics of language for particular spoken and written contexts. For instance, test developers could use a spoken academic corpus to identify the common types of words, sentence structures, and genres in an academic context. An example of a corpus that people have used to help define constructs for language assessments is the Corpus of Contemporary American English (COCA) (Davies, 2008–). COCA has more than one billion words from diverse genres, including spoken fiction, written fiction, magazines, newspapers, academic texts, TV and movie subtitles, internet blogs, and other internet webpages. COCA has various search options, including one that provides thousands of examples of how we commonly use academic vocabulary. We can see an example of a corpus of some uses of *strong argument* in Figure 4.4.

1	1990	ACAD	EnvirAffairs	A B C	not be reflected in purchase prices. Therefore, affected proprietors can make a strong argument that there is no inherent justice in requiring th
2	2009	ACAD	AmerIndianQ	A B C	, which is particularly based in theories of meaning, Craig Womack makes a strong argument that Native literature can not be studied simply as
3	1996	ACAD	SocialStudies	A B C	military prowess to guarantee them independence from potential subjugation. In fact, a strong argument could be made that the Comanches s
4	2000	ACAD	Mercury	A B C	contained one of the most read passages in all of science fiction and a strong argument to explore space. On the Moon an extraterrestrial beac
5	1991	ACAD	IntlAffairs	A B C	everyone and to no one. " # Hungarian-born economist Janos Kornai makes a strong argument in favor of selling firms to " flesh and blood " risi
6	1990	ACAD	ForeignAffairs	A B C	-- mounted by USSOCOM elements-were used with considerable effect during its course. A strong argument can be made, however, that it wou
7	2017	ACAD	Stanford Law Review	A B C	down the statute on First Amendment grounds and finding that there is a " strong argument that prescriber-identifying information is speech. "
8	2016	ACAD	Eighteenth - Century Studies	A B C	force behind fulfilling duties of justice across borders. Consequently, d'Holbach offers a strong argument for why fulfilling cosmopolitan duties
9	1994	ACAD	CanadaLaw	A B C	, the greater the outflow of payments for copyright works. There is a strong argument for a country with a relatively small economy to be a follo
10	2017	ACAD	Stanford Law Review	A B C	extend to prisoners.256 Calvin, anticipating this aspect of Evenwel, set forth a strong argument of its own, explaining that prisoners are differer
11	2014	ACAD	PolSciQuarterly	A B C	security issues, but so is the ability of the individual to discern a strong argument from a weak one. People who are better educated will probab
12	2014	ACAD	Ref&UserServQ	A B C	librarians. I recognize that this is not currently the case, thus your strong argument to maintain the OPAC. However, if nothing changes, we will
13	2001	ACAD	ArmedForces	A B C	local militia forces. He addresses religion only once, but he makes a strong argument for the importance that it played in his combat life, stating

FIGURE 4.4 COCA corpus example of *strong argument*.
Source: www.english-corpora.org/coca

When we define a language ability construct, we often rely on language theory or human judgment. We can use language corpora to confirm or disconfirm these judgments about the common structures, functions, and uses of language for a specific purpose. We can use language corpora for helping us develop general language constructs, such as the French language ability necessary for effectively functioning in a French-speaking country. We can also use corpora to help create more specific constructs, such as the Chinese language ability necessary to function effectively as a nurse in a Chinese hospital. Of course, it is important that we use corpora that are appropriate for each of these purposes. If we want to identify the language that Chinese nurses need, we must use corpora that contain the speech of Chinese-speaking nurses in a hospital setting.

An example of the use of language corpora to help define the constructs for a high-stakes assessment is the work of Biber and his colleagues (2004). They created the TOEFL 2000 Spoken and Written Academic Language Corpus (T2 K-SWAL) to help them identify patterns of language use in academic settings. TOEFL test developers could then use these common patterns to help them define the construct of academic English. This process would be similar to the one we discussed in the section about language theory to guide construct development. The difference is that instead of language principles, the common patterns of language use would guide construct development.

When we want to define a language construct, we can use more than one of the approaches that we have discussed. We might use more than one of them for designing a high-stakes assessment. On the other hand, for a low-stakes classroom quiz, teachers may use only their informal notes from observing students communicate in the language context of interest.

Curriculum Objectives

In educational contexts, we may not need to define our assessment constructs. People who have designed our courses may have already used an appropriate approach to defining a construct when they developed the learning objectives and course content. Learning objectives often closely relate to the student abilities or constructs that we want to assess in a classroom context. For instance, a learning objective might be, "When students write simple sentences, they can use simple past tense verb forms with 90% accuracy." This learning objective tells us that the construct we want to assess relates to students' abilities to use simple past tense verb forms correctly. Assuming the course objectives and curriculum are appropriate for our students, we can use them to guide our assessment constructs.

Time to Think 4.5

Have you ever used a textbook or other set of materials that included course objectives, teaching materials, and assessments that worked together to help students learn effectively? If so, describe what made this approach effective. If you feel the approach was not effective, please explain.

Alignment

When we create, select, or evaluate a language assessment, validity should be an important focus. Beginning by carefully defining the construct that we want to measure for our context and purpose is an important first step in this process. This step helps ensure that our test selection or development follows appropriate theory. After we clearly define the construct, we create or select an assessment that we can use to measure it for our context and purpose. We will discuss creation and selection of assessments in Chapters 6–12.

We judge validity by considering both theory and evidence. In some situations, we need a lot of theory and evidence, while in others we may require less. For instance, a low-stakes classroom quiz may require less evidence than a high-stakes assessment, such as one for immigration purposes. In the next section, we will discuss some of the sources of evidence that we can use to help us judge or ensure the validity of an assessment for a given purpose and context.

The Standards for Educational and Psychological Testing (AERA et al., 2014) define alignment in relation to how well **test content** and test takers' **response processes** match the test construct's content and response processes. Test content and test taker response processes are important sources of validity evidence.

Test Content

Test content refers to the test input, including the textual features of the passages and kinds of questions about them. We want the test content to align with the construct that we aim to measure. When we create or select a test for a particular purpose, we look at our construct definition and select content for the test that aligns with it. Let's consider the example of eight-year-old children who want to be able to communicate on a playground (see Language Needs Analysis) to better understand this concept. We decided that our construct is the ability to orally communicate with friends on a playground, with the subconstructs of interactional competence, fluency, pronunciation, grammar, and vocabulary that the children need for this purpose. In selecting content to assess this ability, we want to align the test content with the language children use in the TLU situation. To help us achieve this aim, we might decide to create a test that requires three students to talk with each other on a playground. We could provide pictures of playground equipment that we want students to discuss. We want the students to use the vocabulary and grammar structures that they would use on the playground. We also want them to use their ability to socially interact with each other. The better that the content of our test aligns with its construct, the more evidence we have that the assessment will lead to scores that we can interpret as effective indicators of the students' abilities to orally communicate on a playground. By following the principle of alignment, we are using theory to guide our creation or selection of an assessment for a particular context.

In addition to following theory to help us create or select the content of our assessment, we can ask experts for their advice about our assessment. They can advise us about selection of content and how well it aligns with the construct we want to measure for our context. For high-stakes assessments, we might hire a panel of experts to carefully judge how well our test content matches the construct that we want to measure. In lower-stakes assessment, such as our example of children on the playground, we may ask another teacher to look at the test content and tell us how well it aligns with our construct.

Figure 4.5 shows two ovals. The oval on the left represents the language construct that we have defined and are aiming to measure. The oval on the right represents the content of our assessment. Our goal is to have the construct and the content that the test measures align. Unfortunately, we are almost never lucky enough to have the two match exactly. Instead, our situation is usually like the one we can see in Figure 4.6.

Like Figure 4.5, in Figure 4.6 the oval on the left represents the construct that we are aiming to assess, and the oval on the right represents the content that the test measures. Where the ovals overlap in Figure 4.6, we have **construct-relevant content**. This is the content that we desire to measure with our assessment. For our playground example, this overlap might include vocabulary such as "slide" and "swing" and verbs in the simple present tense, because our

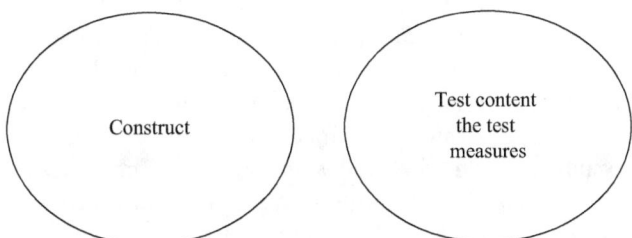

FIGURE 4.5 A language construct and the test content that the test measures.

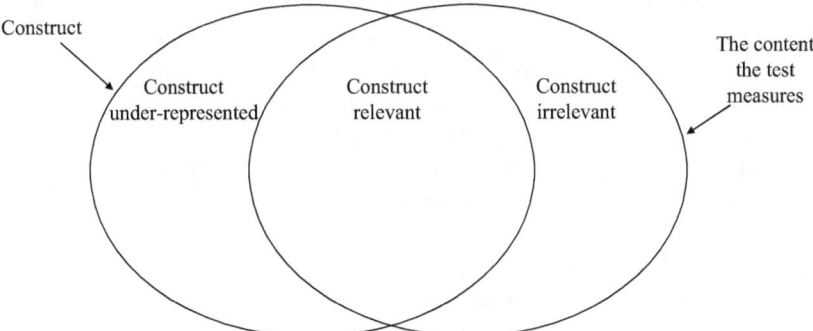

FIGURE 4.6 A test can measure some parts of a construct and not others.

roleplay task elicited the use of these parts of our construct. When the two ovals have high overlap, we have strong evidence in support of validity.

The part of the oval on the left that does not overlap with the oval on the right represents **construct under-represented content**. This represents the part of the construct we want to measure that the assessment does not measure. For our playground example, this might include vocabulary such as "chase" and "catch" and verbs in the present continuous tense, because our roleplay task did not effectively elicit these parts of our construct.

The part of the oval on the right that does not overlap with the oval on the left represents **construct-irrelevant content**. This represents content that does not relate with the construct that we are aiming to measure. For our playground example, our roleplay task might lead to students talking about what they would do if they were on a playground. Students' attempts to use conditional if-clauses would not align with the construct that we want to measure.

Response Processes

Another source of validity evidence for second language assessments is response processes. These refer to the techniques and procedures test takers use when completing an assessment. Just as we want the test content to match the construct, we want the test takers' response processes to match the language construct processes. As we did for test content, we can use Figures 4.5 and 4.6 to help us understand how the match between response processes and our test construct is a source of validity evidence.

Construct-relevant response processes are techniques and procedures that students use when taking the test that align with ones defined in the construct. Let's consider an example to help us understand construct relevance of response processes. Some tests that people design to assess global reading comprehension may not have a high level of construct-relevant response processes. If the aim of an assessment is to measure test takers' abilities to comprehend the main ideas in a newspaper article, we want test takers to read the article in the same way that people read newspaper articles for this purpose. We do not want them scanning for information, as they might when they read a train schedule. Therefore, if we have the test takers read a newspaper article and answer some questions about it to assess this ability, we do not want to give them the questions before they read the article. If we do, test takers may read the questions and then scan the article for the answers. As a result, the cognitive processes would not align with the cognitive processes of reading a newspaper article in the TLU situation. Evidence that test takers scan the article for answers (instead of reading the article before answering the questions) would suggest that the test scores might not provide a good indication of test takers' abilities to comprehend the main ideas in a newspaper article. We may be able to get test takers to use our targeted response processes by using a computer-based test that does not allow test takers to see the questions until they have read the passage. The first screen view could show only the passage, and a second screen view could show only the questions. We could program the computer to stop students from returning to the passage when they are answering the questions.

After we design an assessment, we can also collect evidence about the desired cognitive processes by observing students while they complete the task or by asking them what cognitive processes they used to complete it. Each of these approaches would provide evidence about the effectiveness of the test scores for making decisions about test takers' abilities to, for example, read a newspaper article.

Time to Think 4.6

Have you ever given or taken a language test that you thought was in poor alignment with the course content and/or response processes? If so, talk about it. If not, talk about an assessment you have taken that was in alignment with the course content and response processes.

How did the alignment or misalignment of the assessment you have just discussed affect you and/or the (other) students in the class?

Other Sources of Validity Evidence

We can use other sources of evidence to evaluate test score interpretations for a given purpose, including criterion-related evidence. While we do not usually think of this source of evidence as part of alignment, we will use the central thinking about alignment – that is, the degree that two things match – to understand it. **Criterion-related validity evidence** refers to how well the scores on our assessment match with scores on another established assessment that measures our targeted construct (Brown, 2022). For instance, to help us evaluate the reading assessment that we discussed in the previous section, we could find another reading assessment that someone designed for the same purpose and have a group of students take both tests. Then, we could **correlate** – that is, compare – the students' scores for the two tests to see to what extent their patterns match. If the students' scores on the two tests have a similar pattern, we have validity evidence for the appropriateness of the newspaper reading assessment scores and their interpretations. We will discuss correlation in Chapter 8.

Other Approaches to Validity

Researchers have developed many approaches to validity. In this final section, we will briefly discuss two more approaches to validity that we commonly encounter in language assessment.

The Socio-cognitive Framework

The Socio-cognitive Framework is a popular approach to validity (Weir, 2005). It divides validity into five aspects: context validity, cognitive validity, scoring validity, consequential validity, and criterion-related validity. **Context validity** refers to the relevance and representativeness of the assessment content, including language input, questions, and timing. Assessments with high context validity use language activities that align with real-world target language use tasks. **Cognitive validity** relates to how well the processes that test takers use to complete an assessment align with those they use to complete real-world tasks. The personal characteristics of the test takers, such as age, background knowledge, and personality, along with the context, affect the cognitive validity of an assessment. **Scoring validity** refers to the consistency and generalizability of the test scores. For instance, when two raters evaluate the same essay, how consistent are the scores that they assign? **Consequential validity** refers to the appropriateness of the interpretations or decisions that result from the scores. Impacts of the assessment, including washback on learning, are important indicators of consequential validity. Finally, the Socio-cognitive Framework also includes criterion-related validity, which refers to how well an assessment's scores correlate with scores on other assessments with the same construct. Test developers have used this approach to guide the development and evaluation of many large-scale assessments, including Taiwan's General English Proficiency Test (Wu, 2016).

Argument-Based Validation

Another approach to validity is argument-based validation (Chapelle, 2021; Kane, 1992). In this approach, we consider validity as a chain of claims and inferences. We evaluate the legitimacy of the chain with theory and evidence. Importantly, the types of theory and evidence necessary to support a particular assessment will depend on its context and purpose. Language assessment researchers have applied this approach to various language assessment contexts. For instance, Bachman and Dambock's (2017) argument-based validation model for classroom teachers (Figure 4.7) connects students' performances on assessment tasks to the assessment's consequences. The first link, or inference, in the argument chain connects students' performance on the language assessment to a language assessment record. The claim is that the desired assessment records are consistent. For example, students' answers on a true–false simple-present grammar assessment become scores out of 100. Evidence to support this link might include the finding that two teachers assigned the same scores for all students when checking the true–false questions. The second link in the chain connects the assessment record to an interpretation about students' language ability. For example, we interpret students' scores on the grammar test to indicate their ability to recognize the correct use of the simple present tense in short sentences. The third link connects the interpretation about the students' language abilities to decisions about them. For instance, we might decide to promote students to the next grammar level based on our interpretation about their mastery of the simple present tense. The

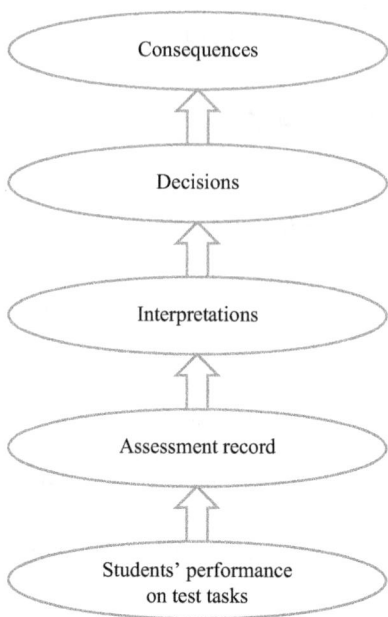

FIGURE 4.7 Bachman and Dambock's (2017) argument-based validation model for classroom teachers.

fourth and final link connects the decisions to the assessment's consequences. In our example, this would refer to the connection between our decision about promoting students to the effects it would have on them and others, such as teachers and classmates. For instance, we may accurately assign students to classes that fit their grammar abilities, leading to an effective learning environment for them.

Researchers have used this approach in many language assessment contexts, including classrooms (Bachman & Dambock, 2017) and high-stakes large-scale contexts, such as TOEFL iBT (Chapelle et al., 2008; Wu, 2016).

Conclusion

In this chapter, we have discussed the concept of validity and how it lies at the heart of language assessment. We defined validity as how confident we can be, considering theory and evidence, that the language test scores and their interpretations are effective indicators of test takers' abilities for the test's purpose. We discussed how this definition emphasizes the importance of clearly identifying the purpose of the assessment and defining the construct that we desire to measure. We learned about using theory, a language needs analysis, and corpora as ways to help us define our construct. We also discussed how to use course objectives and materials to help define the construct that we want to assess. We discussed the principle of alignment and how it closely relates to the concept of validity. We concluded by exploring some sources of validity evidence that we can use when evaluating a language assessment for a particular purpose. Importantly, people consider the concept of validity in many ways, including ones that we have not discussed in this chapter. Some of these ways might at first appear to be very different from what we have discussed.

However, almost all center around effectively assessing the construct of interest for a given purpose and context and the resulting consequences or impacts.

We began this chapter with a story about an extensive reading assessment for first-year university medical students that was not appropriate for its purpose. We will conclude the chapter by returning to this story and sharing what resulted from that testing practice. A stated objective of the course was for students to be able to read and understand an adult English novel in the field of medicine. However, the test developers did not define language ability based on global comprehension of a novel-length book. In fact, they did not even define what they wanted to assess. The test developers did not base the assessment on appropriate theory or evidence. They were experienced teachers, but they had limited knowledge about the concept of validity. Instead of thinking about the importance of validity and measuring the extensive reading ability of the first-year medical students, the committee simply created an assessment similar to one they had seen to assess reading in other contexts. As a result, we probably could not interpret scores on the test as effective indicators of the first-year medical students' abilities to understand an adult English novel about medicine. In addition, I suspect that the washback of this assessment practice was negative. Future students may not have focused on developing their extensive reading abilities. Instead, they may have practiced filling in deleted words on random pages of the text. This example provides a reminder about the importance of validity in language assessment.

Questions for Discussion

4.1 Talk with your group about the concept of validity.
    4.1.1 Discuss the meaning of validity based on what you have read in this chapter.
    4.1.2 Share an experience you have had with taking or giving a language test.
    4.1.3 Discuss with your group the experience in relation to the concept of validity.
4.2 Think of a language assessment that is familiar to everyone in your group.
    4.2.1 Decide on its purpose based on the characteristics of the learners and how you will use the scores.
    4.2.2 Discuss what your group believes the test's construct is (a sentence or two).
    4.2.3 Discuss how well the test content and response processes align with the construct.
    4.2.4 Use the five steps of a language needs analysis (see Language Needs Analysis in this chapter) to help you define a language construct for a context relevant to your interests.

Exercises

4.1 Talk about how you would explain the concept of validity to a group of senior high school language teachers who have not formally studied language assessment.
4.2 Explain how you might use corpora to help create an appropriate construct for a language assessment context relevant to your interests.
4.3 Find a definition of validity on the Internet. Then compare this definition to our use of validity in this chapter.
4.4 Discuss the relationship among validity, alignment, and washback. To help make your explanation clear, use an example for a language learning assessment context that relates to your interests.

4.5 Compare and contrast the approach to validity that we use in this book with the Socio-cognitive Framework and argument-based validation.
    4.5.1 What are the main similarities and differences?
    4.5.2 Which would you choose to use for a context of interest to you?
    4.5.3 Defend your choice of approaches.

Additional Resources

AERA (American Educational Research Association), APA (American Psychological Association), & NCME (National Council on Measurement in Education) (Eds). (2014). *Standards for Educational and Psychological Testing*. Retrieved April 20, 2022, from https://www.testingstandards.net/uploads/7/6/6/4/76643089/standards_2014edition.pdf

These standards provide excellent guidelines for analyzing and developing effective assessments. A large committee of experts continue to update these guidelines approximately every ten years. Many commercial and academic institutions in North America and throughout the world use the guidelines for evaluating the quality of an assessment.

Bachman, L. F., & Dambock, B. (2017). *Language Assessment for Classroom Teachers*. Oxford University Press.

This textbook provides an introduction for how classroom teachers can use an argument-based validation approach. It includes classroom-based examples and guidelines for applying the approach in typical classroom contexts.

O'Sullivan, B., & Weir, C. J. (2011). Test development and validation. In B. O'Sullivan (Ed.), *Language Testing: Theories and Practices* (pp. 13–32). Palgrave Macmillan.

This book chapter provides an accessible introduction to the Socio-cognitive Framework. The authors introduce each aspect of the framework with straightforward explanations and illustrative examples.

CHAPTER 5

Language Assessment Consistency: Uniformity and Reliability

FIGURE 5.1 Effective clocks are reliable. They keep time consistently.
Source: PM Images/DigitalVision/Getty Images.

I looked at the test scores again for at least the tenth time. Our university English program had administered an end-of-term writing assessment to nearly 1,000 students. We had planned to count scores toward final grades to help ensure fairness across thirty different sections of the course. Two teachers had independently assigned each student a score on a scale of one to twenty. I assumed that an average score by the two teachers would be a good measure of the quality of students' essays. However, when I looked at a few of the essays and their scores, it was clear that the teachers had not used uniform standards when rating. One of the teachers had given almost all of the students the maximum score of 20 points, while others had given few scores above 15 points. Students' scores depended on whether their ratings were from strict or lenient scoring teachers. In addition, teachers had used different criteria when they judged the essays, even though they all had the same scoring guidelines. Some focused on grammatical accuracy, while others focused on the strength of the argument. Our aim of making grades fair across classes failed because we did not pay enough attention to the uniformity of the scoring procedures.

5 ASSESSMENT CONSISTENCY: UNIFORMITY AND RELIABILITY

Time to Think 5.1

What could the team do to make the assessment in the story you have just read more effective?

Introduction

Uniformity and reliability are important qualities of language assessments. For **uniform** assessments, the setting, content, and scoring procedures are consistent. Uniform assessments usually lead to **reliable** scores – that is, scores that are consistent and stable. Uniformity and reliability are important for ensuring that language assessments provide a good indication of test takers' language proficiency or achievement and effectively promote language learning.

Language assessments are like clocks. We expect a clock to keep time consistently, and we expect language assessments to measure test takers' language abilities consistently. We prefer clocks that indicate one day as being just as many hours, minutes, and seconds as another. Companies make consistent clocks by carefully designing and then producing each part with high-quality materials, and users help ensure clocks' consistencies by keeping them clean, changing their batteries, and using them according to their design. As a clock's consistency in keeping time increases, its usefulness also increases.

Similarly, we expect language assessments to provide consistent measures of test takers' language abilities. If 100 students took a language proficiency test today, and then took the same test a few days later without further learning the test content, we would expect each student's score to be the same for the two tests. Test developers create consistent assessments by carefully designing and then producing each of their parts with high quality materials. Test users ensure an assessment's consistency by paying careful attention to its setting, content, and scoring. They maintain their consistency by keeping them up-to-date, for example, by retraining raters to score essays. As a test's uniformity increases, its score reliability usually increases, making it more useful for its purpose.

The chapter began with a story about a testing team that did not pay enough attention to uniformity. The team had not provided guidance to students about essay length and had used different questions of varying length and style in each of the classes. As a result, the students wrote for different audiences and purposes. The team did provide the raters with rating guidelines, but they failed to give them enough training to ensure that each rater would judge the essays in the same way. If the language testing team had paid more attention to the assessment instructions and uniformity of the rating procedures, they probably would have had a more useful assessment.

Time to Think 5.2

Have you taken or administered a language assessment that you thought was not uniform? If so, in what ways was it not uniform?

How might test administrators best ensure that assessments are uniform?

While uniformity is an important quality of an assessment, in certain circumstances complete uniformity may not be necessary. For example, test developers might be able to show that two different test administration procedures, such as computer-delivered and paper-and-pencil versions, lead to consistent scores. Although the delivery systems are not uniform, if the test takers' scores are stable, it may be appropriate to use different delivery systems. In other circumstances, giving all test takers an equal opportunity to demonstrate their language ability could require different assessment procedures for some of them. Test takers with disabilities may need **accommodations** to demonstrate their abilities effectively. For language assessments, accomodations are procedures or aids that help students demonstrate their language abilities despite their disabilities, without giving them any unfair advantage over students who do not have the disability.

An example of an appropriate test accommodation is a sound-level modification for a listening comprehension test. Increasing the volume of the listening input should help students who do not hear well to more effectively demonstrate their listening abilities. On the other hand, this accommodation should not give these test takers an unfair advantage over ones who have normal hearing. Because of these exceptions, language assessment experts use uniformity principles to create, administer, and score assessments. However, they rely on reliability measures to indicate their consistency and/or stability.

Uniformity

When creating or selecting language assessments or interpreting the scores from them, it is important to consider various aspects of their uniformity. In this section, we will discuss three aspects of an assessment's uniformity: setting, content, and scoring (Table 5.1). These factors stem from the work of Bachman and Palmer (1996) and Popham (1981). In Chapters 7 and 10, we will consider these aspects for particular types of assessments.

TABLE 5.1

Aspects important to the uniformity of language assessments.

Aspect of uniformity	Details to consider
Setting	Physical environment
	Equipment
	Administrative procedures
Content	Instructions
	Item type
	Language input: genre, topic accessibility, delivery, and length, grammatical complexity, and vocabulary difficulty
	Non-language input
Scoring	Types of scoring
	Avoidance of errors
	Reports and storage

Setting

An assessment's setting includes the physical environment, equipment, and administrative procedures. They are important contextual factors that we should consider when creating or judging the uniformity of an assessment.

Physical Environment

The uniformity of the physical environment of an assessment is important. If test takers take an assessment in different locations, the temperature in each should be similar. If some test takers take the assessment when it is extremely hot or cold, they may not be able to concentrate as well as test takers who take the assessment when the temperature is comfortable. Chairs, tables or desks, and personal space should be equally comfortable. Lighting, external noise, air drafts or ventilation, and even the color or designs and pictures on an assessment room's walls can have an effect on the assessment. All features of the physical environment that could have an effect on the performances of the test takers should be uniform.

It is worth noting that it may be difficult to control the physical environment of at-home assessments. For instance, some test takers could have a comfortable, quiet, private workspace, while others may be in a noisy public environment, such as a fast-food restaurant where the internet is available. This lack of a uniform physical environment can lead to unfair scores.

Equipment

We can use different types of equipment to aid in delivering an assessment. To help ensure uniformity, it is critical that the equipment functions as it should. Both low-tech equipment, such as pencils and paper, and high-tech equipment, such as computers, can lead to poor assessment uniformity. Checking the equipment before the assessment and having a back-up plan, such as extra pencils, if failures occur, are important steps to helping ensure uniformity.

We have used paper and pencils to help deliver assessments for a long time, and their use continues to be common in many contexts. People who administer paper-and-pencil assessments should ensure that there are enough sharpened pencils and that the paper form of the assessment is consistent for each test taker and test administration.

We can also deliver assessments through electronic devices, including computers, cell phones, and tablets. A completely uniform assessment would involve the same device with the same settings for all test takers. While it may not be necessary for such uniformity, test administrators should pay attention to the appearance of the test items across devices. The items and space to respond to the items should appear in a clear format that is the same on different devices.

Critical to assessment administration uniformity for internet-delivered assessments is the quality of the connection. Unclear sound or video quality can make it impossible for test takers to demonstrate their language abilities. The psychological effects of an inconsistent internet connection may also negatively affect test takers' performances. For instances, test takers may become more nervous or even angry when sound or audio quality are poor, and these emotions can negatively affect their performances.

> **Time to Think 5.3**
>
> Would you prefer to take an assessment delivered with paper and pencil or on an electronic device, such as a computer? Why?
>
> Which do you think has more potential for uniform test delivery? Why?

Administrative Procedures

We should have clear guidelines for the procedures to follow when we deliver an assessment. In a classroom context, these procedures may be much less formal than for a high-stakes assessment, but we should still have procedures and follow them. Even the way test administrators interact with test takers is important. Welcoming administrators can influence an assessment differently than unfriendly ones. When we involve more than one test administrator, we should train each one to treat test takers similarly. Teachers administering assessments to their own students need to be careful to treat each student equally. Other test delivery processes, such as the amount of time to complete a set of items, should also be uniform.

Content

Instructions, item type, language input, and non-language input are important features of content that test developers and users need to take into account when creating or judging the uniformity of an assessment. If the content is not uniform, the assessment can lead to inconsistent scores and unhappy test takers. For example, let's assume some students take a computer-delivered vocabulary test to help indicate their readiness for promotion to the next grade level. If most students get words that they studied during class time, while others get words that teachers have not introduced, input delivery would not be uniform.

One way to ensure that the content is uniform for test takers is to make it the same for all of them. Unfortunately, this is not always appropriate. For example, in a classroom situation, an instructor might be concerned about students sharing information with students in other classes who will be taking the assessment later. In addition, students in the same classroom may secretly share their responses with other students. Having multiple forms of an assessment is therefore critical in many language assessment situations. This section outlines some of the features of test content that need to be uniform when using different forms of an assessment.

Instructions

We should consider the instructions, both verbal and written, as important content for a language assessment. They should be uniform from one form to another. We should provide example questions if the assessment format is unfamiliar to test takers. Example questions help to ensure that test takers are able to understand what we expect them to do to successfully complete the assessment.

Item Type

Item type refers to the kinds of assessment activities that test takers must complete to demonstrate their language abilities. As we will see in Chapters 6 and 10, there are various item types for language assessments. Some of them require test takers to choose answers from a list of options, while others require them to produce answers. We maintain test uniformity by using types of questions that are familiar to test takers and by using clear instructions about how to respond to a question. We will discuss how to write clear instructions for particular types of questions in Chapters 7, 9, and 12.

Language Input

Some item types require test takers to read or listen to language input and then respond to questions or complete other tasks about this input. When test developers use different texts as input, it is important that the texts and their delivery are uniform across various features. These features include genre, topic accessibility, delivery, length, grammatical complexity, and vocabulary difficulty.

GENRE
We should use texts with similar style and organization to help ensure consistency across text passages. For instance, if we use a narrative to assess reading comprehension on one form of an assessment, we should use a narrative on another. Such passages should also have similar amounts of detail, inferencing, and other style features.

TOPIC ACCESSIBILITY
While it is important to use various topics for different forms of an assessment, these topics need to be equally accessible to all test takers. For instance, a university-level academic listening assessment should not be easier for students with some academic backgrounds than for ones with other academic backgrounds. Usually texts from early parts of an introductory course are appropriate for such contexts.

DELIVERY
The delivery of language input also needs to be uniform. For example, for oral assessments, it is important that each person administering the test deliver the tasks in the same way. If test administrators ask questions, they should use consistent speech rates and body language when talking with each test taker. One way to reduce the factors that lead to a lack of uniformity in an oral communication assessment is to use technology. Unlike humans, technology can deliver completely consistent assessments for each test taker. We will discuss some uses of technology for delivering assessments in Chapter 10.

LENGTH
The length of passages used should also be consistent across different forms of an assessment. Word-processing programs provide word counts that indicate the length of a passage. A good rule of thumb is for passages to be within 5 percent of the word count of equivalent passages. Thus, if one passage is 300 words, another should be between 285 and 315.

GRAMMATICAL COMPLEXITY
Grammatical complexity is also important for ensuring comparability of textual input. Texts should have clauses of comparable lengths and similar use of complex sentences, tense, voice, and other grammatical constructions. Software programs are available for judging the grammatical complexity or difficulty of a text (see Additional Resources for a list of free online software programs for this purpose). Usually, for low-stakes classroom assessments teachers can create or select passages based on their judgments of grammatical complexity.

VOCABULARY DIFFICULTY
Vocabulary difficulty is also important for creating or selecting consistent textual inputs. In low-stakes assessment contexts, teachers may be able to make appropriate judgments about the difficulty of vocabulary in a text. For higher-stakes assessments, teachers and other test developers can use software programs for judging the difficulty of vocabulary. (See Additional Resources for a list of free online vocabulary difficulty software programs for this purpose.)

Time to Think 5.4
What are some other ways you think texts should be consistent to help ensure a uniform assessment?

In classrooms with students who have a large range of language abilities, we may need to have test forms that are of differing difficulty levels. Test developers and users should assume that these are different assessments and score and interpret them accordingly.

Non-language Input
Sometimes we use non-language input on our assessments. For instance, classroom teachers may show their students a tennis ball or cricket bat to determine whether or not test takers know the vocabulary for these objects. We can also use pictures, graphs, and charts to give test takers a writing or speaking topic. When we use non-language input, we need to be sure that we use it in similar ways and that all test takers can recognize what it is. For instance, we do not want a graph on one form of an assessment to present information differently than on another.

Scoring
The way we score responses to questions can also influence the uniformity of an assessment. Uniformity in the way that we score, error avoidance, and accurate reporting and storage are important.

Types of Scoring
We can use **dichotomous scoring** or **polytomous scoring**. When we use dichotomous scoring, we mark an item either correct or incorrect. We do not assign test takers any points for partially correct answers. In contrast, when we use polytomous scoring, we can assign partial credit. For example, we could assign a score of between one and five depending on our judgment of the quality of an essay. We will discuss dichotomous scoring in Chapters 6, 7, 8, and 9 and polytomous scoring in Chapters 10, 11, and 12. We can use humans, computers, or a combination of the two to score language assessments.

Error Avoidance
Scoring errors can lower the uniformity of an assessment process. Errors for human-scored questions usually come from one of two sources. The first is inconsistent rating, for instance accidentally marking a response correct when it is wrong or assigning a high score to a poorly written essay. To help ensure consistency, we should check each response more than once. The second source of error is inaccurately totaling the points for each response. Individuals who are totaling scores by hand should double-check their calculations. For example, we can calculate a total test score by summing from the first score to the last, and then check the score by summing from the last score to the first. By changing the order of the calculations, we lower the chances of making an error. While neither of these errors is common for computer-scored assessments, using the wrong formulas can lead to inaccurate scoring. Therefore, it is important to carefully enter and check all formulas.

Reports and Storage
We also need to be careful to report and store scores accurately. Test takers and other score users must use the appropriate scores. Unfortunately, both human- and computer-scored

assessments often include many processes that can lead to the wrong score for a test taker. For instance, a human being or a computer program might enter a score into a spreadsheet on the wrong line. Score reporting errors are surprisingly common, even when we are very careful. Effective assessment requires a great deal of time and effort, and we make more errors when we are tired. In the box that follows you can read a true story of a score reporting error.

Given the importance of test takers receiving correct score reports, we should always check reports for accuracy. After they are ready, assessors should select a few reports and manually check them to see if they are accurate. Another way to check the accuracy of score reporting is to select a few of the test takers' score reports and see if they are reasonable. Teachers can sometimes predict the score a student might achieve on an assessment. Checking to see if the students who typically get high scores mostly do have high scores on their score reports can be a useful way to check scores.

Uses of Technology to Increase Uniformity

We have discussed some types of technology that we can use to help us develop or evaluate the language input that we use on assessments. We can also use **artificial intelligence (AI)** systems to help us for these purposes and more. AI is a technological system that can approximate human intelligence. For instance, we can use AI software, such as ChatGPT, which may be freely available on the Internet (https://openai.com/research/gpt-4), to help us create and evaluate language input. We specify the types of content we desire, and the AI will use large open-access databases (much of the language on the Internet) to create language texts (and non-language content). These types of systems create a response based on probabilities of successive words people have commonly used in language on the Internet. We can also use these types of AI to create questions for particular item types. By being specific about the features of the input that we desire, including type of genre, vocabulary difficulty, grammar difficulty, and type of visual input, we can use an AI to create assessment materials uniformly. Importantly, we need to understand the language assessment principles necessary for creating and then evaluating the materials that the AI creates. We will explore some applications of these types of AI in Chapters 7, 10, and 11 of the book.

A team of four of us had led the administration and scoring of a university placement test. About 120 students had taken a battery of performance-based assessments, and we had combined the scores to determine placement decisions. We put these decisions into a score sheet and sent it to an electronic database that would make the scores available to students.

The day after we reported the scores, a student who had taken the test came to my office. The student was surprised to have failed both tests completely. I was also surprised, because based on our short discussion, I judged the student's English to be quite proficient. I promised to check on the scores again. After looking at the scores in the combined spreadsheet and comparing them to the scores in the individual sheets, I noticed that somehow the scores of about ten students who had passed all of the assessments were in the cells indicating that they had failed all assessments. Fortunately, I was able to correct the error before it led to additional problems.

Reliability

By making an assessment uniform, we maximize the chances that our scores will be reliable. Reliability refers to how consistent and stable test scores are for a particular group of test takers and context. As we discussed at the beginning of the chapter, classroom teachers may not always need to calculate the reliability of every low-stakes quiz they give to students. Paying attention to the uniformity of these assessments may be all that they need to do. However, an understanding of the concept of reliability makes the importance of uniformity clearer. Additionally, when teachers use assessments for grading, placement, and other decisions, or need to interpret test reliability for high-stakes tests, they need to apply knowledge of this important concept.

The specific ways of checking reliability for particular purposes can be challenging to understand when we begin to learn about them. With this in mind, in this chapter we will consider reliability very generally, with the aim of providing background for when we encounter it in actual examples in Chapters 8, 9, and 12.

We consider the reliability of language assessments' test scores in various ways. Therefore, it is important when judging the effectiveness of a language assessment that we carefully select an appropriate approach to judging reliability. In this section, we will briefly discuss three types of reliability: test-retest reliability, parallel forms reliability, and internal reliability. As we will see in Chapters 8, 9, and 12 of the book, we need different ways of calculating reliability depending on our type of scores and the claims we want to make based on them. For now, we will only discuss these approaches to reliability based on whether we use the assessment as a criterion-referenced test (CRT) or as a norm-referenced test (NRT). As we learned in Chapter 2, we use NRTs to rank order test takers from most to least proficient, and CRTs to determine whether or not test takers have language proficiencies that meet certain criteria.

Test-Retest Reliability

Test-retest reliability provides an indication of how consistent test takers' scores on the same assessment are across different time periods. For example, if fifty students took a reading proficiency test on Thursday morning and then again two weeks later on Friday afternoon, assuming they did not learn some of the test content during this timeframe, we would expect the students to get equivalent scores on the test. We would judge reliability based on the consistency of the students' scores on the two test administrations. If students got the same or similar scores for the two test administrations, we would have evidence of reliability (See Figure 5.2).

An important consideration when using the test-retest approach to reliability is that the time periods cannot be so far apart that the language abilities of the test takers change. For instance, even if the students did not study for the reading test, if the tests were a few months apart, their language ability might improve enough for them to get a higher score the second time they take the test. On the other hand, the time periods need to be far enough apart that test takers' experiences of taking the assessment the first time do not impact their success when they take it the second time. For example, if the students took the test on Thursday and then again the following day, they might get a higher score on Friday because they remember some of the test content from Thursday. When deciding how long to have between the two tests, it is important to consider the intensiveness of language exposure and how much memory of information matters when students take the test a second time.

5 ASSESSMENT CONSISTENCY: UNIFORMITY AND RELIABILITY

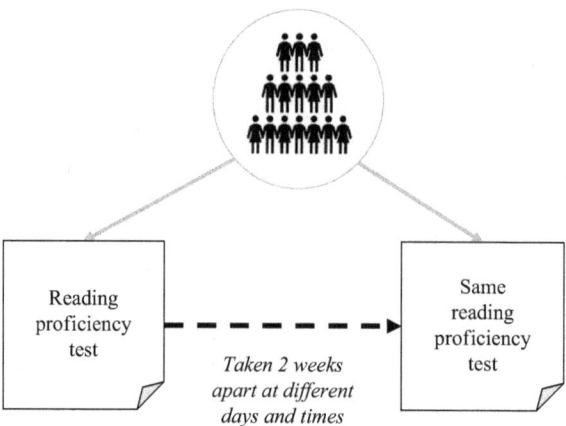

FIGURE 5.2 Design for assessing test-retest reliability.

> **Time to Think 5.5**
>
> Assume you want to determine how reliable an end-of-semester grammar test is. You have some students from another class take the assessment two times to see if it leads to reliable scores. How much time should you have between the first and second administrations? Why?

The concept of score reliability is a little different for CRTs and NRTs. For CRTs, we use the term **dependability** to distinguish it from reliability. Dependability refers to the consistency of the decision of whether or not the test takers' scores are above the cut-score of an assessment. For a dependable language assessment, test takers who passed the test on its first administration would pass it on its second administration too. For NRTs, reliability refers to how consistently the assessment ranks the test takers across the time periods. On a reliable test, test takers who got high scores on the first test administration would get high scores on the second too, while test takers who got low scores on the first test administration would also get low scores on the second. A perfectly reliable test would result in the same rank order of highest to lowest scoring test takers across the two test administrations.

Parallel Forms Reliability

We use **parallel forms reliability** to estimate how well two versions of an assessment provide consistent indications of test takers' abilities. We use this approach when we want to have more than one test version for the same purpose. For example, if we have six different sections of a listening class, and each section is at a different time of the day, we will need to give the test to students at different times. We may worry that students in earlier classes will share information about the test with students in later classes. In this situation, we could prepare multiple forms of the assessment with the aim of making them as uniform as possible for both context and content (although not containing the same passages and questions). This is a common practice among teachers who have multiple sections of the same class. When teachers need an estimate of the parallel forms reliability of a new test, they can give students the option of taking two versions of the test and getting the higher of the two scores. Teachers can then estimate the consistency of the scores for the students who took both test forms. For dependable CRTs, test takers who pass one form of the assessment also pass the other form of the assessment, and for reliable NRTs, the rank order of the test takers is consistent across the two forms of the assessment.

> **Time to Think 5.6**
>
> Think of a situation in which you have estimated, or might need to estimate, the parallel forms reliability of an assessment. Explain why this approach was or would be appropriate for this purpose.

Internal Reliability

Internal reliability provides an indication of how consistent scores are within one test administration. For example, a reading assessment with twenty-five comprehension questions that all consistently identify the same test takers as either proficient or non-proficient has high internal reliability.

There are a number of approaches for measuring internal reliability, including **split-half reliability**, where we divide the questions into two equal parts – for example, first half and second half, or odd and even. Then we compare the scores on the one half to the scores on the other half. For NRTs, we consider the assessment scores reliable if the test takers who get high scores on one half of the test also get high scores on the other half, while the test takers who get low scores on one half also get low scores on the other half. For CRTs, we consider the assessment scores dependable if test takers who pass one half of the test also pass the other, and test takers who do not pass one half do not pass the other.

In most situations, people use internal reliability rather than parallel forms reliability or test-retest reliability, because estimating internal reliability only requires one test and one test administration. In this book, we will focus on internal reliability because of its common use, particularly in small-scale assessment contexts such as classrooms.

Important Points about Reliability

Each type of reliability that we use gives us different information about an assessment for a group of test takers. The specific type of reliability we use is essential to understanding how an assessment's scores are consistent. This means it is not appropriate simply to report the reliability of an assessment. We need to report which type of reliability or dependability we used and provide a justification for the choice.

As we discussed in Chapter 4, tests are appropriate for a particular group of test takers. It could be that NRT scores are very reliable for one group but not reliable at all for another. For instance, an NRT might not consistently rank a group of highly advanced language users, because it may be too easy for them. They might all get perfect or near-perfect scores, and this would mean we could not rank order them. However, this same test might reliably rank a group of intermediate language users who have different levels of proficiency, because some might answer correctly and others incorrectly. As a result, the test takers may get a range of scores on the test. For this reason, we do not refer to the reliability of a test, but rather to the reliability of the scores of a particular group of test takers who take a test. This is less of a problem for CRTs, where the aim is to determine whether or not test takers meet a certain criterion or criteria. If all test takers meet or do not meet the criteria, it could still be dependable. We will discuss this issue further in Chapter 9.

Conclusion

In this chapter, we discussed the importance of uniformity in assessment. We learned about many ways that assessments need to be uniform to help ensure that they are fair for all test takers. Test users and developers should pay attention to the uniformity of the setting, content, and scoring. We also discussed the closely connected concept of reliability and explored some approaches to measuring it. Test-retest, parallel forms, and internal reliability are three basic approaches to reliability. Each of the aspects of uniformity and reliability depend on the stakes of the assessment. For instance, low-stakes end-of-class quizzes may not need to be highly reliable. Instead, the focus may be on delivering a uniform assessment that covers the class learning objectives effectively. On the other hand, for an end-of-term achievement test that teachers use to assign grades, the reliability of the scores is critical. Overall, tests should be reasonably uniform and reliable if they are to promote effective language learning practices and be effective tools for assessing test takers' language abilities and/or achievement.

We began the chapter with a story about the use of a writing assessment that aimed to make grading practices fairer across sections of the same class. In that situation we did not achieve our aim of increasing grading fairness, because we did not uniformly evaluate the essays. Fortunately, teachers paid more attention to test uniformity on future assessments, and teachers were happy about the increased fairness of grading practices.

Uniformity and reliability are important assessment principles that we need to consider when we evaluate test takers' language abilities. We need to make sure our assessments are uniform and lead to reliable scores. In the remaining chapters of the book, we will explore some specific language assessment contexts. We will apply the principles we have discussed in these first five chapters to these contexts.

Questions for Discussion

5.1 Imagine you are creating a writing assessment to place a class of thirty fifteen-year-old learners of English into five proficiency-based writing groups. What would you do to make your assessment acceptably uniform?
5.2 Share ideas about how you would explain the concept of reliability to a colleague.
5.3 How should teachers address uniformity for a teacher-made end-of-week classroom quiz?
5.4 How might cultural and educational practices affect the way we think about reliability for a particular context? Use examples to support your thinking.
5.5 Write a fifty-word text and use Text Inspector (see Additional Resources) to analyze it. Discuss how this measure of text difficulty could help you create uniform assessments when you give parallel assessments across four sections of the same reading class.
5.6 Compare and contrast test-retest reliability, parallel forms reliability, and internal reliability for NRTs and CRTs.

Exercises

5.1 Think of a language assessment context where you are/were a student or teacher.
    5.1.1 Describe the context.

5.1.2 What would you do to make the setting, content, and scoring as uniform as possible?

5.2 Find an assessment on the Internet (or another one that is available to you) and judge its level of uniformity. What further information would you like to have so you could better judge the assessment's uniformity?

5.3 Six teachers are teaching different class sections of twelve-year-old learners of French. They want the final examination to be uniform across classes. They know that students talk to each other about assessments, and they do not want students taking the test later in the day to have an advantage. Their plan is to create six forms of the assessment, one for each class.

5.3.1 What should the teachers do to ensure uniformity?

5.3.2 Which measure of reliability would be most appropriate to help judge the uniformity of the assessment?

5.4 Write a fifty-word reading passage for an assessment for a particular context.

5.4.1 Describe the context and test taker characteristics.

5.4.2 Use P_Lex (see Additional Resources) to identify words that may not be appropriate for the passage.

5.4.3 Based on the results from P_Lex would you change any of the words in the passage? Justify your decisions.

5.5 Explain why reliability and validity are both necessary for effective language assessment.

Additional Resources

Brown, J. D. (2021). Classical test theory. In G. Fulcher & L. Harding (Eds), *The Routledge Handbook of Language Testing* (pp. 447–461). Routledge.

This short chapter on reliability and related test analyses targets a non-technical audience. It introduces some theories and mathematics which underlie the concepts we have discussed in this chapter. Reading this chapter may also help prepare readers for Parts III and IV of this book.

Readability Scoring System. Readability formulas. https://readabilityformulas.com/free-readability-formula-tests.php

This readability checker, and others, provides information about a passage, including grammatical forms and vocabulary frequency in suggesting a particular level of readability.

Video Shorts #5 Validity, reliability, impact, and practicality. https://www.youtube.com/watch?v=DsgORIf2lDg

Lognostics: Free software from _lognostics. www.lognostics.co.uk/tools/index.htm

This page includes various tools for measuring vocabulary. The program P_Lex evaluates the vocabulary from texts and is appropriate for identifying words that may be too difficult for students in a reading passage, for example.

Text Inspector. https://textinspector.com/

This software, which is available on the Internet, provides over two hundred measures of the difficulty of an English text. These include grammar, vocabulary, and general readability.

PART III
Right or Wrong

CHAPTER 6

Assessing Comprehension and Knowledge with Dichotomously Scored Item Types

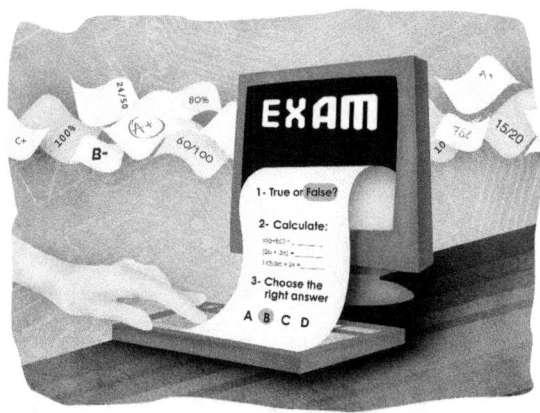

FIGURE 6.1 Selecting an answer.
Source: Fanatic Studio/Collection Mix: Subjects/Getty Images.

Many years ago, I was teaching English as a foreign language in an English-medium graduate university program in Japan. The purpose of the program was to prepare intermediate-level students for content courses taught in English. I was the coordinator of the listening courses and wanted teachers to help create the midterm listening test. As I began to discuss the creation of the test with the teachers, I discovered that they were in agreement about a few of them recording mini-lectures as input that was similar to listening activities students had heard in the classes. However, the teachers disagreed about the question format. Some felt they should use questions that allowed students to select an answer from a list of options. Others thought it would be better to use questions that required students to write an answer. They also disagreed about whether students should hear the input once or twice and if they should see the questions before they heard the input. The teachers asked students their opinions on these issues, but they did not agree, either.

> **Time to Think 6.1**
>
> What question format (types of questions) do you think the teachers should use in the scenario you have just read? Why?
>
> How many times do you think the teachers should play the audio input? Why?
>
> Do you think the students should see the questions before they hear the input? Why?

Introduction

When we select or create language assessments, we have many choices to make. One of these is deciding on an appropriate item type, which depends on the language abilities that we want to assess. When we want to assess the **receptive skills** of listening and reading, which we use to comprehend language, we may use different item types than when we want to assess the **productive skills** of speaking and writing, which we use to produce language. When we assess the receptive skills, we cannot see inside test takers' brains to know what they understand when they read or listen, so we usually assess their understanding indirectly. After test takers read or listen, we usually have them answer questions about the input to see how much they understood.

We also commonly have test takers answer questions when we want to assess components of language, including grammar and vocabulary knowledge. We use grammar and vocabulary knowledge assessments in classroom situations because developing this knowledge is an important part of the learning process, even though we would rarely use vocabulary and grammar in isolation in real-world contexts. As we discussed in Chapter 4, in classroom contexts, we want to align our assessments with the learning objectives and practices.

When we assess the receptive skills of listening and reading, and component parts of language, such as vocabulary and grammar, we must pay careful attention to the characteristics of the language input and the types of questions we use to assess understanding or knowledge of this input. We often use dichotomously scored items for this purpose.

In the first part of the chapter, we will discuss some dichotomously scored item types that we can use to assess listening skills, reading skills, and components of language, such as grammar and vocabulary. Next, we will discuss other design principles for assessing these skills and language components, with a focus on the characteristics of language input for listening and reading. In Chapter 7, we will discuss and use some techniques to determine how effective our dichotomously scored items are for a particular assessment. After we have gained some knowledge of this item type, we will practice creating and critiquing some in Chapter 8.

Dichotomously Scored Item Types

Selected Response Items

One type of dichotomously scored item is selected response. For **selected response items**, we expect test takers to choose a best answer from two or more options. Selected response items have two important advantages. First, many stakeholders appreciate that the scoring is highly objective (see Chapter 2) because this may limit unfairness in scoring. Second, selected response items are easy to score. Computers can score them automatically, or humans can score them

Multiple-Choice Items

Multiple-choice (MC) are popular selected response item types in many language assessment contexts. For MC items, we present test takers with a statement or question and ask them to choose the best answer from a list of options. We can see an example of a four-option MC vocabulary item in Example 6.1.

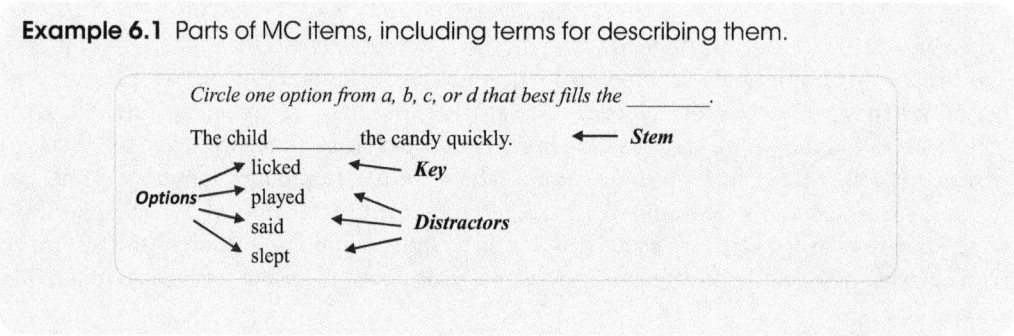

Example 6.1 Parts of MC items, including terms for describing them.

The **stem** is the word, phrase, sentence, or question that presents the item. In the example, the item stem is: *The child _____ the candy quickly.* The item has four answer **options** (*licked, played, said, slept*). We refer to them as options because a test taker can select one (or more) of them. The **key** is the response option that we consider correct. In our example, the key is *licked*. The **distractors** are the other options, ones that are less appropriate or incorrect. In our example, they are *played, said,* and *slept*.

The stem can take various forms in an MC item. In the example, we expect test takers to select the most correct option to fill the blank. We could also have the stem in the form of a question or a paragraph with more than one blank. Each of the blanks in the paragraph would have a list of options, so we may have more than one MC item in the paragraph. Grammar and vocabulary assessments sometimes use this approach to provide more context for an item. Importantly, MC items target test takers' abilities to recognize appropriate language, which is not the same as being able to produce it. For instance, if test takers correctly select *licked* in Example 6.1, this does not mean that they could use *licked* appropriately when they produce language by speaking or writing.

STRENGTHS

In addition to those of other selected response items, MC items have a number of advantages. First, people in many parts of the world use them and, as a result, most test takers are familiar with them. As we discussed in Chapter 3, when all of our test takers are familiar with an item type, we can be more confident that the items will successfully measure their language abilities. We can also use MC items to measure specific aspects of test takers' language abilities, such as the vocabulary item in Example 6.1. In this example, we can target test takers' specific knowledge of the word *licked*. If test takers know the meaning of the word, they should be able to select the correct option. Finally, the scoring of MC items is objective. As a result, MC items can be effective in contexts where stakeholders highly value reliability.

WEAKNESSES

Despite their popularity, MC items have some weaknesses. First, it can be very challenging to create effective ones. We will get first-hand experience of some of these challenges when we create our own items in Chapter 8. Second, construct-irrelevant differences in scores as a result of test taking strategies is common. Test takers may learn effective strategies for predicting what the correct answer is, and these strategies may not relate with the construct that the item aims to measure. For example, in Example 6.1, test takers may not know the word *licked*. However, they may be able to get the correct answer by knowing the other options are incorrect. As a result, we might wrongly believe that test takers know the meaning of *licked*.

This weakness relates to another one. Since test takers choose an answer, we usually cannot determine why they get answers right (or wrong) on MC items. They might get an item correct because they know the targeted information, know other options are wrong, or simply guess the correct answer.

Finally, and maybe most importantly, MC items do not represent the way we use language in real life. In an actual target language use (TLU) situation, we probably will not need to select from a list of options for what to comprehend, read, say, or write. As a result, it can be a challenge to create MC items that promote effective language learning practices.

> **Time to Think 6.2**
>
> Have you ever taken an MC test? If so, what strategies did you use to help you choose the right answer?
>
> If you have not taken an MC test, what strategies do you think you might use to do well on one?

True-False Items

True–false items are also popular in language assessment. Test takers read or hear a statement and select "True" if they believe the statement is correct or "False" to indicate that they believe it is wrong. We can see an example of a true–false item in Example 6.2. For this self-assessment, test takers select *True* if they believe they are familiar with washback in language assessment. If they do not feel that they are familiar with this concept, they would select *False*. In Example 6.2 a test taker chose *true*.

Example 6.2 A true-false item.

> *Circle True if the statement is correct or False if the statement is wrong.*
>
> True   False   I am familiar with the concept of washback in language assessment.

STRENGTHS

Like MC items, most test takers are familiar with true–false items. This familiarity helps to make them effective. Another advantage of true–false items is that we can use them to assess understanding when only two options are reasonable. For example, if we want to know if students know the vocabulary *right* and *left*, true–false items can be effective. Another advantage of true–false item types is that we can use them for self-assessments, especially in classroom environments. They can give us information about what content students believe they already know or have learned during the course. This can make it possible for teachers to focus on content that students need to learn.

WEAKNESSES

True–false items share many of the same weaknesses as MC items. They are difficult to create, test takers may get items correct without knowing the information that we aim to assess, and they are not representative of real-world language use tasks. Maybe of biggest concern is that test takers have a 50 percent chance of guessing the correct answer if they have no knowledge of the language we aim to assess. This high chance of guessing correctly can lead to inaccurate estimates of test takers' abilities.

Short-Answer Items

Another type of item that we can score dichotomously is **short-answer items**. For these items, test takers must write a response. They do not select from a list of responses like MC or true–false items. Short-answer items often have only one possible correct response. We can see in Example 6.3 a short-answer vocabulary item (assessing knowledge of the words *wheel* and *bicycle*). Test takers must write *two* (or *2*) to get the correct answer.

> **Example 6.3** A short-answer vocabulary item.
>
> Write one word to answer the question.
>
> 1. How many wheels does a bicycle have?

Short-answer items are not always limited to exact word (or number) responses. Some require test takers to provide the correct meaning to get the item right, which could be in the form of more than one word (but usually not more than one or two sentences). For these items, we can score them either dichotomously or polytomously. We will focus on dichotomously scored short-answer items in this section (and throughout Chapters 6, 7, 8, and 9). We can see an example of a reading comprehension short-answer item that requires a few words for a correct answer in Example 6.4.

> **Example 6.4** A reading comprehension short-answer item that requires a few words for an effective response.
>
> Read the story and answer the question about it.
>
> When I was a child, I decided I wanted to be a math teacher when I grew up. I was good at math until I got to calculus in college. I tried hard, but calculus did not make sense to me. I decided to change my major, and now I have discovered the amazing world of advertising.
>
> 1. Why did the person change to a different major?

A correct answer to the question might be: *Calculus was too hard*. However, test takers may use different words to provide this same meaning, and we would also score these responses as correct.

Strengths
Maybe the biggest advantage of short-answer questions as compared to MC or true–false questions is that test takers cannot simply recognize or even guess an answer by looking at a list of options. As a result, we limit lucky guessing and strategies for selecting a correct answer. Short-answer items also give us an indication of how well test takers can produce language rather than just recognize it. As we will discover in Chapter 8, short-answer items are also usually easier to write than MC items.

Weaknesses
Short-answer items that test takers can answer correctly with different words are harder to score. Partially correct answers and misspellings, for example, may require more time to effectively score. We will discuss these issues in some detail in Chapters 11 and 12 when we discuss polytomously scored items.

Variations of Item Types
In this chapter so far, we have discussed a few traditional dichotomously scored item types. We can find many variations of these item types as well as additional ones. Purpura (2004) discusses some variations of dichotomously scored grammar item types that aim to limit some of the weaknesses we have discussed in this section. Purpura also introduces other item types that we can use to assess grammar or other language components or skills.

> **Time to Think 6.3**
>
> Would you prefer to take an MC or short-answer second language reading test? Why?
>
> Which type do you think would provide a better indication of your reading ability? Why?

Assessing Receptive Language Understanding and Knowledge

In this section, we will discuss some principles for assessing receptive understanding and knowledge. We will focus on the assessment of listening and reading, but it is important to note that many of these same principles apply to the assessment of vocabulary and grammar. We will discuss vocabulary and grammar assessments in more detail in Chapters 8 and 9.

As we discussed in Chapter 4, after we determine our purpose and context, we identify or define our construct. An example reading construct for a university context is reading for basic comprehension, making inferences, reading to learn, and reading to find information (Chapelle et al., 2008; Schedl et al., 2021). If we determine that this is how we want to define reading, our items should all aim to assess these abilities. As we discussed at the beginning of this chapter, when we assess the receptive skills of listening and reading, we often provide test takers with either spoken input for listening or a written passage for reading. We can then have them respond to MC, true–false, short-answer, or other similar item types. We will use the content aspect of the uniformity framework in Chapter 5 (instructions, item type, language input, non-language input) to remind us of the important sources of validity evidence that we need to consider when we decide about the item types and their characteristics for reading and listening assessments.

Instructions

Clear instructions about what test takers should do are very important. Test takers need to know what to do, so they can effectively demonstrate their language abilities. The instructions for listening, reading, vocabulary, and grammar assessments that use dichotomously scored items can usually be quite short and simple. We can see an example in Example 6.1.

Item Type

Using an appropriate item type is important for assessing all language constructs. We discussed some of the strengths and weaknesses of common dichotomously scored item types earlier in this chapter. We need to consider each of these factors when we select an item type and its specific characteristics. In addition, we need to consider various other item characteristics.

Of particular importance when we select or create items for both reading and listening assessments is how much **item preview** we give to test takers. Item preview refers to showing test takers either the question stems or the answer options, or both, or neither, before they read or listen to a passage. When we discussed response processes in Chapter 4, we noted that we want test takers to use the same response processes when they read or listen during the assessment as they do when they read or listen in the TLU situation. In many TLU situations, our aim is general comprehension of the spoken or written information. We are not trying to find specific information. For instance, when students read a textbook or listen to a classroom lecture, teachers usually expect them to gain a general understanding of the information without telling them to skim or listen for specific information. If we aim to assess test takers' abilities to function in these situations, we probably should not provide question stems or answer options before students read or listen. On the other hand, if we want to know how well test takers can find targeted information, we may want to include question stems and answer options as an item preview. For instance, we may want to know if test takers can skim a movie advertisement and find out what times movies begin on a particular day. In other TLU reading or listening situations, where language users generally know what they are trying to find, it may be appropriate to give test takers only the question stems in an item preview (Koyama et al., 2016; Yanagawa & Green, 2008).

> **Time to Think 6.4**
>
> Have you taken an MC listening or reading test? If so, do you think it had an appropriate amount of item preview?
>
> If you have not taken an MC test, what is a situation where you think item stem preview (no answer option preview) would be appropriate?

An important issue for listening assessments is how many times we allow test takers to hear the input. As we discussed in Chapter 3, when we make this decision, we should account for the context. In some educational systems, it is common to provide the input two or more times. The rationale for this approach is that teachers often play an input multiple times during the teaching process, and the assessment process should be in alignment with this practice. Also, many real-world listening tasks, such as listening to an online blog, allow us to replay the input. On the other hand, in some situations, we may not be able to listen to information more than once, such as when we witness a crime. We need to consider our TLU situation and educational context when determining the number of times to provide the input.

For reading assessments, we need to consider how much time we want to give test takers to read the passage. When reading speed is part of the construct we want to measure, we use **speeded tests**, which we design to make the rate of the performance an important measurement criterion. For speeded norm-referenced tests (NRTs), we do not want all students to be able to finish responding to all items. When we do not consider rate of performance part of the construct, we use **power tests**, which we design to measure comprehension without concern about reading rate. When we use power tests, we want to provide test takers with enough time to respond to all of the items.

Language Input
Genre
We need to pay attention to the constructs we want to measure and how effectively we can use a particular input to assess them. For instance, if we want to measure test takers' abilities to find details in an input, the input must have details. Our listening and reading constructs often include the ability to infer meaning when something is not directly stated. If we want to assess this ability, we need to be sure that we can make inferences from the information in the input.

We also want the genre of our input to be similar to what test takers find in the TLU situation. For example, for a listening assessment in a university context, input may be a short lecture or two or more people discussing a topic. On the other hand, for a listening assessment in an aviation work context for pilots, input may be a weather announcement, flight recommendation, or flight emergency situation.

Topic Accessibility
The topics of our listening and reading inputs need to be accessible to test takers. As we discussed in Chapter 5, each test taker should be similarly familiar with the topic. We want test takers to have enough background knowledge to be able to comprehend new information, but we do not want test takers to know all of the information in the input. We need information that is unknown, so we can assess test takers' comprehension of it. For instance, if some of the test takers know the names of all of the planets, and their relationship to the sun, we do not want to have a reading passage that focuses on this topic. Otherwise, our assessment might assess previous knowledge in addition to reading ability. We need to pay special attention to this issue when we select or create listening or reading assessments based on factual inputs.

Delivery
Another important consideration for the input of listening and reading assessments is how we deliver it. When test developers create listening assessments inputs, they generally use scripted, authentic, or authenticated language.

SCRIPTED INPUT
For **scripted input**, test developers write the input based on their ideas or a corpus of what people often say in a particular situation. The test developers then have actors follow these scripts when they provide the inputs. When the test developers create a video-mediated assessment, the actors often memorize the script as they might if they were movie actors (Figure 6.2).

FIGURE 6.2 A scripted listening input. Actors memorize exactly what to say.
Source: Wayne Eastep/The Image Bank/Getty Images.

When we do not video-record the input, the actors often simply read the scripts, like voice actors do for some animation movies. The advantage of this approach is that we can use assessments that use language we expect test takers to know. For example, if we assume we are teaching a classroom unit about farm animals to beginning-level young learners, we may want to assess how well students can understand an oral story about the animals. We could create a story that uses the unit learning objectives, including word and sentence stress, vocabulary, and grammar structures. By creating our own script, we could ensure that we use language that we expect students to know. This approach might be most appropriate when we assess beginning-level learners in classroom situations.

AUTHENTIC INPUT

For **authentic input**, test developers find and use real-world spoken texts. They might record some students discussing a topic in class, find an oral blog on the Internet, or record an interaction between a supermarket clerk and a shopper (see Figure 6.3).

This approach recognizes the importance of using real-world inputs from the TLU domain. Using this approach helps to ensure that our listening inputs reflect the kind of listening test takers need to do in the real world. When actors read or memorize scripts, the speech often

FIGURE 6.3 An authentic listening input which comes from a real-world listening context.
Source: Tom Werner/DigitalVision/Getty Images.

differs from speech we commonly hear, especially in informal situations. For instance, researchers have found that listening texts that people write and then read aloud have different phonological, lexico-grammatical, and discursive features than authentic ones. They also differ based on the presence of hesitations and fillers (Ockey & Wagner, 2018). Let's take phonology as an example of how scripted and unscripted speech are usually different. The phonology of unscripted spoken discourse usually includes more features of connected speech, such as reductions and linking. Words like *want to* can become *wanna*, and sentences like *Did you eat yet?* can become *jeet yet?* Test takers may be able to understand clearly articulated speech, like *want to* but not connected speech like *wanna*. When one purpose of an assessment is to determine how well test takers can function in certain language use contexts, such as informal ones, we may need to include connected authentic speech in the listening inputs. Otherwise, our assessment scores may not provide an effective indication of our test takers' abilities to use language in these contexts.

AUTHENTICATED INPUT

Authenticated input is not scripted or authentic. It is somewhere between the two. In this approach, test developers create semi-scripted oral texts. They create the general outline of a speaking situation, and then actors construct discourse based on the situation (Wagner & Ockey, 2018). For instance, test developers might ask two speakers to discuss a subject they are studying in school (Figure 6.4).

FIGURE 6.4 An authenticated listening input. Actors follow a general outline but create the exact language while they speak,
Source: Klaus Vedfelt/DigitalVision/Getty Images.

The discussion would not come from a real-world text, but the language may be more like the oral inputs we could get from the real world than from actors reading scripts. For instance, it may have connected rather than carefully articulated speech. Because of the advantages of semi-structured oral texts as listening inputs, this approach continues to increase in popularity. In fact, we should probably use authenticated inputs in most situations where we do not use authentic inputs. Even for beginning-level students, we want to provide listening inputs that align with TLU situations. Most TLU listening situations include language fillers, connected speech, and other language features that are usually not in scripted input.

Most of the same issues associated with how authentic we want our listening assessments to be are also relevant for reading assessments. Our options are to:

1. create texts that include the topics, structural features, vocabulary, or other text features that we desire to assess
2. select texts from the TLU, such as first year textbooks when we want to determine readiness for university study
3. select texts from the TLU situation and then adapt them to be more appropriate for our assessment purposes.

Speaker Selection

We also need to consider the selection of speakers when we create or choose listening assessments. Generally, we want to follow two principles for our use of speakers:

1. We want them to be representative of ones that test takers might find in our TLU situation.
2. We want our test takers to be able to relate to at least one of them.

Let's assume we want to assess English listening comprehension of children on school playgrounds in the United States. We would probably want our speakers to include children with different ages, first languages, genders, races, sizes, and socioeconomic status. While it would not be possible to have speakers with every possible combination of these characteristics, we want speakers with a variety of the different characteristics we might find in this situation.

These characteristics, along with others, contribute to individuals' **speech varieties**. A speech variety is the pronunciation patterns of a particular group of people who speak a language. For instance, Received Pronunciation is a speech variety of English that many people in England, including the British royal family, speak. In our playground example, because of the varied backgrounds of individuals in the United States, we might expect to find children with different speech varieties.

For a number of reasons, we usually want to use multiple speech varieties in our listening assessments. First, in today's global world, even many local contexts include speakers with different speech varieties. We need to use multiple speech varieties to represent our TLU domain. Second, we want our test takers to be able to relate to one or more of the speakers in our assessment. By using speakers with different speech varieties, we have a better chance of making this happen. Third, research shows that familiarity with a speech variety can affect listening assessment scores. Test takers who are familiar with the speech variety of a speaker tend to get higher scores than ones that are not. By including multiple speech varieties, we are less likely to advantage or disadvantage any test takers. Finally, being able to understand speakers with different speech varieties is an important part of listening comprehension. Good listeners are able to understand unfamiliar speech varieties (Harding & McNamara, 2018; Ockey & Wagner, 2018).

> **Time to Think 6.5**
>
> Can you think of a situation where it may be appropriate to use speakers with only one speech variety for a listening input? If you can think of this type of situation, describe the context and defend your position. If you cannot think of such a situation, explain why you do not think you can think of a situation for this.

Length

The length of the input is an important consideration for both listening and reading assessments. Ideally, we should use text lengths similar to the ones that test takers listen to or read in the TLU situation. However, because it is usually not practical to have test takers listen to full-length university lectures or read complete novels, we often must use shorter inputs. When we use shorter inputs, we need to focus on including all of the features that are in the longer TLU situation texts. For instance, if the TLU reading situation is a university physics book, we want to have long enough inputs to include the genre, grammar structures, vocabulary, and other features that we might find in such a book.

Grammatical Complexity and Vocabulary Difficulty

We want the grammatical complexity and vocabulary difficulty of an assessment to be at an appropriate level for the test takers. It is better to use inputs that use vocabulary and grammar in the same ways we find them in the TLU situation. However, we have to be careful about this approach because it could make our inputs inaccessible to test takers.

We need to pay particular attention to the amount of low-frequency vocabulary in an input. The relationship between the comprehension of a reading passage and how many words people know is very strong. People who know more words have better reading comprehension (Qian, 2002). As we discussed in Chapter 5, we can use free online software programs to see how much low-frequency vocabulary we have in our input. For formative or summative classroom assessments, we can use inputs with grammar and vocabulary that test takers know from class. This helps us align our inputs with classroom activities and the TLU needs of the test takers.

Non-language Input

We also need to consider non-language input when we select or create listening and reading inputs and for vocabulary and grammar assessments. When we use listening or reading assessments, we need to decide whether or not to use charts, graphs, or pictures. We need to make these judgments based on our construct. If we are assessing a child's ability to understand a passage about some animals at the zoo, we may want to include pictures of the animals. However, if our purpose is to see how well children understand a description, we may not want to include a picture. Instead, we may ask the child to select a picture that best shows the description using MC format.

We need to pay special attention to how we use non-verbal input in listening assessments. Audio-only inputs provide test takers with only verbal information, while **multimodal inputs** provide test takers with both verbal and visual input. While audio-only inputs were popular for many years, due to technological developments and TLU situations that now include mostly multimodal input, this has changed. In most listening contexts, we experience visual information along with verbal input. We see people when we talk in face-to-face situations, and we commonly use video calls when we communicate online. We might also see slide decks or other visual information while listening to a classroom lecture. In addition to being more in line with the TLU domain, technology has made multimodal listening inputs for assessments increasingly available and easy to create. For these reasons, we usually want to use multimodal input when assessing listening.

> **Time to Think 6.6**
>
> Have you taken an audio-only and/or multimodal listening assessment?
>
> If you have used both, which do you think was more appropriate for the context in which you used them? Why?

Conclusion

In this chapter, we began by discussing some common dichotomously scored item types, including MC, true–false, and short-answer. We also learned that we can use these types of items to assess the receptive skills of listening and reading and components of language, such as grammar and vocabulary. We explored some of the issues that we need to consider when assessing these skills and components of language, particularly for listening and reading. We focused on the importance of selecting appropriate speakers for listening inputs, the authenticity of both listening and reading inputs, and the role of multimodal input for listening assessments.

This chapter began with a story about teaching English and trying to decide whether to use MC or short-answer items, whether to give test takers an item preview, and how many times to provide the input. The teachers decided to base their decisions on how the Test of English as a Foreign Language (TOEFL) and the International Language Testing System (IELTS) dealt with these issues at that time. While this was probably not a bad thing to do, it may have been better to begin with the purpose and context, then define the construct, and, finally, consider each of the factors important for listening assessments. This may have led to a more appropriate assessment for this situation.

In Chapter 7, we will learn some basic techniques for understanding how effective dichotomously scored items function for NRTs. Then, in Chapter 8, we will use information from this chapter and the techniques from Chapter 7 to help us evaluate and create some selected response items.

Questions for Discussion

6.1 Think of a listening assessment context.
    6.1.1 Describe the context, purpose, and general construct of the assessment.
    6.1.2 Discuss appropriate language and non-language characteristics of the input.
    6.1.3 Discuss whether or not you think an MC or short-answer item type would be more appropriate for the assessment.
6.2 What are some selected response item types (e.g., MC, true–false, short-answer) that you have used as a student or teacher?
    6.2.1 What was the context and purpose of the assessment?
    6.2.2 What were the strengths and weaknesses of these item types in this context?
6.3 In what situations do you think selected response item types would be appropriate and in what situations do you think they would be inappropriate? Provide reasons for your views.

Exercises

6.1 Watch the video "Select Response and Standardized Assessments" (https://youtu.be/oYF8Yr0QKQg; see Additional Resources for more information about the video).
    6.1.1 What strengths and weaknesses of selected response item types do the presenters mention?
    6.1.2 How do these compare with the strengths and weaknesses that we discussed in the chapter?

6.2 Think of a language assessment reading context where you are/were a student or teacher.
    6.2.1 Describe the context, purpose, and construct of the assessment.
    6.2.2 Discuss whether you think a selected response or short-answer item type would be more appropriate for the assessment.
    6.2.3 Discuss appropriate language and non-language characteristics of the input.

6.3 Describe a situation where you think authenticated language would be appropriate for a listening assessment. Explain why you think authenticated speech would be better for this context than scripted speech.

6.4 Evaluate three (or more) dichotomously scored item types. You can choose a test or take part of the Dialang test at https://dialangweb.lancaster.ac.uk/setals. Take a reading, listening, or structure test in one of the languages the test provides. The purpose of this test is diagnostic.
    6.4.1 Complete the vocabulary test. Explain the purpose of this test.
    6.4.2 Take the test that you selected (reading, listening, or structure). Select three item types from the test that we did not discuss in this chapter and write down an example item.
    6.4.3 Describe the strengths and weaknesses of each item type.

Additional Resources

Ockey, G. J., & French, R. (2016). From one to multiple accents on a test of L2 listening comprehension. *Applied Linguistics, 37*(5), 693–715.
This journal article discusses research on the effects of strength of an accent and familiarity with an accent on listening comprehension. It provides suggestions for how to judge the appropriateness of a speech variety for the input of a particular listening assessment.

Ockey, G. J., & Wagner, E. (2018). *Assessing L2 Listening: Moving Towards Authenticity*. John Benjamins.
This book provides discussion for selecting or creating listening inputs. Specifically, the authors discuss listening input authenticity, speech varieties, visual input, and integrated listening and speaking.

Purpura, J. E. (2004). *Assessing Grammar*. Cambridge University Press.
This book describes many types of grammar items and indicates their strengths and weaknesses. It is accessible to readers with little background in assessment. Although the examples focus on English, the item types are also generally appropriate for grammar in other languages.

Schedl, M., O'Reilly, T., Grabe, W., & Schoonen, R. (2021). Assessing academic reading. In X. Xi & J. M. Norris (Eds), *Assessing Academic English for Higher Education Admissions* (pp. 22–60). Routledge.

This book chapter provides a discussion about the construct of academic reading and some of the factors that test users and developers should consider when assessing reading.

"Advantages and Disadvantages of Multiple Choice." bit.ly/3Spgoum

This set of short videos provides some basic pros and cons of using MC item types. The instructor leads a discussion with students who are knowledgeable about the topic.

"Select Response and Standardized Assessments." Education at Illinois. https://youtu.be/oYF8Yr0QKQg

This nine-minute video introduces select(ed) response items. It discusses various approaches to this item type, including their use in computer adaptive tests. It also discusses some of the impacts on the effectiveness of test scores, educational practices, and test takers' and teachers' emotional states.

CHAPTER 7

Analyzing Dichotomously Scored Items for Selecting the Most Proficient Test Takers

FIGURE 7.1 A group listening to a person using statistics to explain an information pattern.
Source: andresr/E+/Getty Images.

When I was a young father, I attended a primary school parents' meeting. One of my children was beginning third grade (eight years old) and would soon be taking a standardized test for the first time. Some teachers introduced the test and shared an example of a score report. A few parents asked questions about the test, such as, "How did you create the test questions?"; "How do we know the questions are good?"; "Is the **mean** the same as the average?"; and "What is the **standard deviation** on this assessment?" The teachers did their best to answer the questions, but it was clear that they were not very knowledgeable about basic language assessment content and statistical analysis. This lack of knowledge made me question the teachers' abilities to effectively teach and assess my child, and I wondered how many other parents had the same concerns.

Time to Think 7.1

How important is it to you to expand your language assessment literacy (LAL) in the area of content analysis and statistical analysis? Why?

Introduction

As we discussed in Chapter 2, we use norm-referenced tests (NRTs) to help us compare the language abilities of test takers. Effective NRTs help us distinguish among test takers based on their language abilities. For example, if we assess reading, we expect the more proficient readers to get most items correct and our less proficient readers to get most items wrong. We want our test to lead to scores that spread test takers across a wide range of ability levels. We use content and statistical analysis to help us achieve this aim.

We will begin this chapter by examining how we can use content analysis to explore the sources of validity evidence for a reading passage for a ninth grade (14–15-year-olds) English as a Second Language (ESL) course. Next, we will use principles from earlier chapters to judge the effectiveness of dichotomously scored multiple-choice (MC) items in helping to assess reading ability for this group of test takers. Finally, we will discuss some test-level statistics that can help us determine the effectiveness of dichotomously scored items when we use NRTs. In Chapter 8, we will discuss how we can use content and statistical analysis together to help us decide which items to use for scoring a test and which items to revise or exclude for future test administrations. We will discuss the effectiveness of dichotomously scored items for criterion-referenced tests (CRTs) in Chapter 9.

Using Content Analysis to Evaluate Language Assessment Validity

Let's say a team is responsible for placing students into one of three reading levels in a ninth grade ESL program. They want an equal number of students in each group. Students come from many parts of the world and have English reading abilities ranging from intermediate to advanced. The team wants to assess students' abilities to read for general understanding, locate specific details, and make inferences (make a guess about something that is not stated) about content. Teachers will use this low-stakes assessment to make quick decisions that they can change later in the week if necessary. Because of a busy schedule, they can only use about fifteen minutes for the assessment. In Chapter 6, we discussed some considerations for selecting or creating reading assessments that we can use to help gather validity evidence based on a content analysis of input and item format. We will use these guidelines to help us evaluate, select, and revise reading passages and items that the team of teachers created. We can see in Guidelines 7.1 the list of content considerations for selecting or creating reading passages that we discussed in Chapter 6.

In this section, we will consider some examples of reading passages that teachers prepared for a reading assessment. We will evaluate them based on Guidelines 7.1.

Guidelines 7.1 Content guidelines for reading and listening input.

- The genre provides potential to assess the targeted construct.
- The topic is accessible to the test takers.
- Delivery is appropriately authentic.
- The length is sufficient to assess the targeted construct.
- The grammatical complexity and vocabulary difficulty are appropriate.
- The non-language input is appropriate.

Two teachers on the team provided one passage that they thought would be appropriate for the reading assessment. The team agreed that teachers could either write a passage or use artificial intelligence (AI) technology, such as ChatGPT. As we discussed in Chapter 5, these types of technology can create a text based on probabilities of the next words people have commonly used in large databases. One teacher brought a passage titled "How to score in football" (see Passage 1) and the other brought a passage titled "A difficult fishing trip" (Passage 2).

 See Appendix 7A for an example of how to use ChatGPT to create a reading passage.

Passage 1

How to score in football

A football field is 100 yards long, and each team has an end zone with goal posts on their end of the 100-yard field. Teams compete by trying to move the ball to their opponents' end zone without being tackled. There are many ways to score points. The first is a touchdown. You get a touchdown, worth six points, when you move the ball into the other team's end zone. Another way to score is to try to kick the ball between the field goal posts, a bar 10 feet above the ground with side posts 18.5 feet apart. You can kick from wherever someone tackles you. If you are successful, you get three points. A third way to score, a safety, is worth two points. To get a safety, you need to tackle an opponent who is holding the football in the opponent's end zone.

Passage 2

A difficult fishing trip

A few years ago, I encountered a mountain lion while I was fishing alone in a secluded mountain stream. The mountain lion growled at me, and I ran to my car. When I got to my car, the door was locked, and I realized that my car fob and cell phone were in my lunchbox. Unfortunately, I had left my lunchbox by the stream when I ran to the car. The mountain lion found the lunchbox, tore it open, ate my lunch, and completely destroyed everything else inside of it.

Time to Think 7.2

Which of the two passages do you think would be most appropriate for placing the ninth grade ESL students into reading groups? Why?

Content Analysis of Language Input
Genre Provides Potential to Assess Targeted Construct

Let's begin by judging the passages based on how effective they are for assessing the test takers' abilities of reading for general understanding, locating specific details, and making inferences about content. Both passages could assess general understanding of a reading input, and both have specific details. For example, Passage 1 has details about how to score and how many points you get for each of these ways to score. Passage 2 includes details about what was in the lunchbox and what the writer of the story was doing. However, the passages may not equally assess the ability to make inferences. Passage 1 is factual and may not provide much potential for assessing the ability to make inferences. On the other hand, Passage 2 may have the potential for measuring this ability. For instance, a question might ask how the person went home. The passage does not state how the person went home, but it does infer that the person could not drive the car, ride with a friend, or call someone with the cell phone.

Topic Is Accessible to Test Takers
Neither passage appears to provide content that is completely appropriate given the backgrounds of the test takers. Passage 1 is highly problematic. For most test takers, football is not the sport the authors describe in the passage. The passage is about American football, and people from most countries think of football as a completely different game. Test takers from countries where international football (called soccer in America) is popular may read the passage with the expectation that it is about international football. Their background knowledge about football may lead to lowered comprehension of the passage. On the other hand, test takers with knowledge of American football may already know some or all of the information in the passage. Passage 2 is probably less problematic, although test takers from low socioeconomic backgrounds may not be that familiar with a car fob.

Delivery Is Appropriately Authentic
Neither passage provides authentic input. The teachers chose to script them (possibly based on an initial draft from ChatGPT) instead of finding input from the real world. However, Passage 2 sounds more natural than the short choppy sentences found in Passage 1. As a result, although neither passage is ideal, Passage 2 may be more appropriate than Passage 1.

Length Is Sufficient to Assess Targeted Construct
Input should be long enough to assess the targeted construct. Both passages are short when we consider the amount of reading the students will do in the reading groups. However, they do require students to understand paragraph-level information that may require similar reading abilities to what they will need in the reading groups. Importantly, testing for phrase- or sentence-level reading may not be enough to place students into reading groups effectively, because these activities may not require higher-order comprehension skills that relate to general understanding, such as predicting and connecting ideas.

Grammatical Complexity and Vocabulary Difficulty Are Appropriate
The input should use grammar and vocabulary appropriate for the targeted construct. Passage 2 has a few low-frequency words, such as *encountered*, *secluded*, and *fob*, that students will probably not know. On the other hand, there are no low-frequency words in Passage 1 (although *yards* is not a common unit of measure in many countries). It may be better to have a few low-frequency words for this context, so that test takers need to infer meaning from context. The sentence structure in Passage 1 is less complex than in Passage 2. The sentences in Passage 1 are also shorter. Considering this information, Passage 2 may be more appropriate than Passage 1.

Non-language Input Is Appropriate

Neither passage has any non-verbal information, such as pictures or graphs. We would need to see the course reading materials to make a decision as to whether or not to add non-verbal language to the test. If the course syllabus states that students need to understand graphs, it would be better to include them.

> **Time to Think 7.3**
>
> Based on the content analysis, would you use Passage 1 or Passage 2 to help determine the ninth grade ESL reading groups? Why?
>
> Think of a context in which you work or study. What are the most important factors for a reading assessment input in this context?

Content Analysis of Selected Response Items

Once we have an appropriate passage, we need effective items to measure our targeted construct. The list in Guidelines 7.2 is useful for systematically evaluating MC and other selected response items. The list grew from the ones that Brown (2005) provides.

> **Guidelines 7.2** Systematically evaluating selected response items.
>
> 1. The items should assess only the targeted construct.
> 2. Information in one item should not influence responses to another.
> 3. The items should be straightforward.
> 4. The options should be syntactically parallel, similar in length, and concise.
> 5. The options should follow a systematic order.
> 6. The items should have only one best answer, with all the other options being reasonable.
> 7. Comprehension items should require test takers to understand the input.

Based on the content analysis, let's assume that the ninth grade reading assessment team decides to use Passage 2 for their reading placement test. The teacher who brought this passage for consideration also brought the two MC items in Example 7.1. It is not clear whether the teacher wrote the items or used a system like ChatGPT to create them.

 See Appendix 7B for an example of how to use ChatGPT to create MC reading items.

Let's evaluate Item 1 in Example 7.1 based on the list in Guidelines 7.1.

Items Should Assess Only the Targeted Construct

Item 1 targets the ability to make an inference about the content of the input. The input does not say how the writer of the story went home, but we can infer that the writer could not drive, because the mountain lion destroyed the fob. We also know that the writer was alone and could not call a friend, because the mountain lion had destroyed the story writer's cell phone. The

> **Example 7.1** Two MC items that a teacher brought to assess reading comprehension of Passage 2.
>
> 1. The person who wrote the story probably _____.
>   a. returned in a spaceship   b. returned on foot   c. returned in a friend's car
>   d. returned by driving the story writer's car
> 2. A mountain lion ate the _____
>   a. story writer's lunch   b. story writer's fob   c. story writer's friend
>   d. story writer's fish

option of a spaceship is impossible and not mentioned in the story. As a result, we can infer that the writer probably had to walk home. With any selected response item type, we cannot be sure from a content analysis whether or not some test takers can use strategies to answer questions that are not part of the construct that we want to measure. For Item 1, however, we cannot see any obvious ways for a test taker to answer the item correctly without a general understanding of the passage. Item 1 appears to measure the subconstruct of ability to infer meaning from the content well.

Information in One Item Should Not Influence Responses to Another
We do not want test takers to be able to use information from other items to help them answer an item. We can only see one other item, and it does not appear that any information in that question could help us answer Item 1.

Items Should Be Straightforward
We want to avoid writing items that can confuse or trick test takers. If test takers completely understand the input of a reading or listening passage, they should be able to answer every item about the input correctly. For instance, we do not want to use vocabulary in the item that is harder than vocabulary in the input (in this case the reading passage). Tricky items are problematic because they can lead to test takers with some knowledge getting the item wrong, while test takers who do not understand at all could randomly guess correctly. In other words, having some knowledge can lead to a wrong answer. With tricky items, we often incorrectly separate middle- from bottom-level test takers.

Item 1 is not completely straightforward. For instance, we have to infer where the story writer will return to. While we want to assess the ability to make inferences about content, we do not want test takers to have to infer what the question is asking. We probably should change the stem to, "The story writer probably returned home from the fishing trip _____".

Options Should Be Syntactically Parallel, Similar in Length, and Concise
Options that are not syntactically parallel – that is, they use different grammatical structures – can confuse test takers or give them unintended hints. For example, if the correct response begins with a preposition, the others should, too. For Item 1, the options are not syntactically parallel. It would probably be better if we replaced "by driving" with "in" for option d. A positive point is that our options are similar in length. This is desirable, because longer options commonly have more modifying words (such as "usually" and "generally") that test writers use to

make sure the answer is acceptable. Teachers sometimes teach test takers to select longer options when they do not know an answer. Our options are also not concise, meaning they repeat words that we should move to the question stem. In our example, instead of repeating the word *returned* in each option, we could add it to the stem.

Options Should Follow a Systematic Order

For selected response items, we want the options to follow a systematic order, to discourage test takers from trying to guess what the answer to the next question might be. For example, if test takers mark option *a* on questions 1, 2, and 3, they might guess that the next answer will not be *a*. We want test takers to select responses based entirely on their language abilities. When their language abilities are not sufficient to guide them to a response, we want them to randomly guess – not use strategies to get answers correct without knowing the answer. If we use a systematic order, such as alphabetical order, and we make test takers aware of this approach, they are less likely to use strategies that could negatively affect the effectiveness of their scores on the assessment. In our example, we could use alphabetical ordering of options to make the items more effective.

Items Should Have Only One Best Answer with All Other Options Reasonable

Items should have a correct or best option, but we want all of the distractors to attract test takers who do not have the language ability to answer the item correctly. Using unreasonable options increases the chances of test takers guessing the correct answer. In Item 1, option *a* (a spaceship) is unreasonable and probably would not function as an effective distractor, because test takers would know it is impossible to return by spaceship. It might be better to change this option to *by ambulance*.

Comprehension Items Should Require Test Takers to Understand the Input

When we assess comprehension of input (for reading or listening), we want to be sure test takers cannot answer the items based on their background knowledge. For example, if test takers read a passage about planets, we want to ask them information that is in the passage that they do not already know about planets. Ideally, the information that we assess should be surprising to them, so they are unlikely to guess the correct answer without comprehending the passage. For Item 1, test takers would not know how the person who wrote the story returned home, as it is a fictional story, so this item effectively meets this guideline.

Example 7.2 shows a revised version of Item 1 based on our content analysis.

Example 7.2 Revised item based on a content analysis.

The writer of the story probably returned home from the fishing trip _____.

a. by ambulance   b. in a friend's car   c. in the story writer's car   d. on foot

---

Time to Think 7.4

Use Guidelines 7.2 to complete a content analysis of Item 2 in Example 7.1. Explain what changes you would make to the item and why.

Using Descriptive Statistics to Evaluate a Test

We use content analysis to help us create or select test input and items for test takers. After we have given a test to our test takers, we can use statistical approaches to help us understand how effectively it functioned for them and how we might change it for future test administrations. We will evaluate a 25-item dichotomously scored MC NRT that a group of teachers created by following Guidelines 7.1. It is called the Grammar Tense Test. We will work with scores for only the first ten test takers, to make the manual calculations easier. (The scores of fifty test takers are in the online materials.) We will begin with summary statistics that provide information about how well the items work together at the test level. In Chapter 8, we will continue with the same example and explore the effectiveness of each item. We will see how we can use content and statistical analyses together to revise an assessment after we have given it to a group of test takers.

The Grammar Tense Test was part of an English language proficiency assessment that an English-medium university in the United States used to help determine whether or not upper-intermediate-level students needed English support courses. We can see the first three items of the test in Example 7.3.

Table 7.1 shows the responses of the first ten students who completed the Grammar Tense Test. (The entire test is available in the online materials.) We can see the students' names in the left column, the items across the top row, and the key (correct option) across the bottom row of the table. (The names are different than the ones of the actual test takers.)

The teachers assigned one point for each response that was the same as the answer key and zero points for all others. For example, for item 1, we would give a 1 to each student who selected the key option, which is d. This means we would give Ishan and Lula 1s, and we would give the other students 0s, because they selected a, b, or c.

Example 7.3 MC university-level Grammar Tense Test.

Instructions: The following items aim to assess your ability to identify correct grammar tense, such as simple past tense, in a sentence. Select the one option that most accurately completes the sentence by circling a, b, c, or d for each question.

1. We _____ a Gettysburg Address re-enactment during our visit to grandma's a year ago.

    a. had watched   b. watch   c. watched   d. were watching

2. When you drive up to Scenic Mountain tomorrow, you _____ how the earthquake changed the land.

    a. have seen   b. saw   c. see   d. will see

3. Lots of people _____ their way to the ancient Egyptian exhibit when I got out of the museum last night.

    a. had made   b. have made   c. were making   d. will make

TABLE 7.1

First ten students' selected options on the Grammar Tense Test.

	1	2	3	4	5	6	7	8	9	10	11	12	13	14	15	16	17	18	19	20	21	22	23	24	25
Pierre	c	d	c	d	d	d	a	a	c	b	c	d	c	b	c	c	b	c	b	d	b	a	d	c	a
Binna	a	d	c	d	d	a	a	a	a	c	d	d	b	b	d	c	c	c	c	d	b	d	d	c	a
Ishan	d	d	c	d	d	d	b	b	c	b	c	d	b	b	d	c	b	c	b	d	b	d	d	c	a
Kenji	c	d	b	d	d	d	a	c	c	c	d	d	c	b	d	c	b	c	b	d	b	a	d	c	a
Lena	c	d	a	b	d	d	b	d	a	a	c	d	c	b	a	b	b	c	c	d	b	b	c	c	a
Paulo	c	d	c	d	d	b	d	d	a	c	c	d	c	b	a	c	b	c	c	d	b	c	d	d	a
Chen	c	d	c	d	d	d	b	d	c	c	d	d	c	b	c	c	b	b	c	d	b	a	d	c	a
Jing	c	d	c	d	d	d	b	d	c	c	d	d	c	d	b	c	c	b	c	d	b	d	d	c	a
Lula	d	d	c	d	d	c	b	c	b	c	d	d	b	b	b	c	b	c	b	d	c	b	d	c	a
Anisa	c	d	a	d	d	b	b	a	b	c	d	d	c	b	d	c	b	c	b	d	b	a	d	c	d
KEY	d	d	d	d	d	d	d	c	d	c	d	d	c	b	d	c	b	b	b	d	b	c	d	c	a

7 ANALYZING DICHOTOMOUSLY SCORED ITEMS

 See Appendix 7C for instructions on how to use Excel to quickly score the responses (convert a, b, c, and d to 1 for correct or 0 for incorrect).

We can see the scored responses in Table 7.2 for the first ten students who took the test. We can also see a total score in the far right column, which is simply the sum of the items that a student got correct. For example, Pierre, the first student in Table 7.2, got nineteen items correct based on nineteen 1s, and six wrong based on six 0s.

Now that we have the scores for each test taker on each item, we can use some descriptive statistics to help us understand the general properties of the (first ten items of the) test.

Summary Statistics

We use summary statistics to give an overview of the scores on an assessment. They provide information about how well the test is working overall, and they indicate whether or not it is appropriate to use statistics that rely on scores that are normally distributed. Because understanding these statistics is fundamental to LAL, we will take a systematic approach to calculating them.

Minimum and Maximum

The **minimum** score, often abbreviated as min, is the lowest total score that any test taker gets on the test. By looking at the total column in Table 7.2, we can see that Lena got 14, which is the minimum score for the first ten test takers. The **maximum** score, often abbreviated as max, is the highest total score of any test taker on the test. We can see that Ishan got 21, which is the maximum score for the first ten test takers. The minimum and maximum help us know if the test is appropriately difficult. If the minimum is near the total possible score, our test is too easy, and if the maximum is near zero, it is too hard. Our minimum of 14 is not near 25, and our maximum of 20 is not near 0, meaning that our test is probably not too hard or too easy.

Range

The **range** is a measure of the difference between the minimum and maximum. To find the range for the first ten students on the Grammar Tense Test, we subtract 14, which is the minimum, from 21, which is the maximum, to get a range of 7. The range helps to tell us how well our test is separating test takers based on their abilities. For the first ten students on the Grammar Tense Test, we have a small range. We are only using 7 of a possible 25-point range, which means the test is not effectively separating test takers based on their grammar tense abilities.

Mean

The mean is a value that tells us the average score for an assessment. In fact, mean is just another word for average. We calculate the mean by adding up each test taker's total score and dividing that by the number of test takers (see Equation 7.1).

$$\text{Mean} = \frac{\text{Sum of the test takers' total scores}}{\text{Number of test takers}} \quad (7.1)$$

For the first ten test takers on the Grammar Tense Test, we would use the calculation in Equation 7.2 to find the mean:

TABLE 7.2

Scored responses for first ten students on first administration of the Grammar Tense Test.

	1	2	3	4	5	6	7	8	9	10	11	12	13	14	15	16	17	18	19	20	21	22	23	24	25	Total
Pierre	0	1	0	1	1	0	0	0	1	1	1	1	1	1	0	1	1	1	1	1	1	0	1	1	1	19
Binna	0	1	0	1	1	0	0	0	1	1	1	1	0	1	0	1	0	1	0	1	1	0	1	1	1	15
Ishan	1	1	1	1	1	1	1	0	1	1	1	1	0	1	1	1	1	1	0	1	1	0	1	1	1	21
Kenji	0	1	0	1	1	1	0	1	0	1	1	1	1	1	0	1	1	1	1	1	1	0	1	1	0	18
Lena	0	1	1	0	1	0	1	0	0	1	1	1	1	1	0	0	1	1	0	1	1	0	0	0	1	14
Paulo	0	1	0	1	1	1	0	1	0	1	1	1	1	1	1	1	1	1	1	1	1	1	1	1	1	20
Chen	0	1	0	1	1	1	0	1	0	1	1	1	1	1	0	1	1	0	1	1	1	0	1	1	1	18
Jing	0	1	0	1	1	1	1	0	1	1	1	0	0	0	0	1	0	1	1	1	1	0	1	1	0	15
Lula	1	1	0	1	1	0	0	0	1	1	1	1	1	1	0	1	1	1	1	0	0	0	1	1	1	19
Anisa	0	1	1	1	1	0	0	0	0	1	0	1	0	1	1	1	1	0	1	1	1	0	1	1	0	16

7 ANALYZING DICHOTOMOUSLY SCORED ITEMS

$$\text{Mean} = \frac{19 + 15 + 21 + 18 + 14 + 20 + 18 + 15 + 19 + 16}{10} \tag{7.2}$$

When we add the numbers on the top of the equation, we get a total of 175. We then divide 175 by 10, and we get a mean of 17.50 on the Grammar Tense Test for the first ten test takers.

Variance and Standard Deviation

We can learn more about how effectively a test separates a group of test takers on their language abilities by using **variance** and **standard deviation (SD)**. The variance of a set of test scores tells us how much the scores vary from the mean. The SD, which is the square root of the variance, is the average distance the scores are from the mean. To what extent scores vary from the mean is very important for NRTs. When we have little variance in test scores – that is, when all or most test takers get similar scores on the test – we cannot effectively rank order them from most to least proficient. Effective NRTs have sufficient score variance. We will discuss this topic further in Chapter 8.

We can see the formula for SD in Equation 7.3.

$$SD = \sqrt{\frac{Sum(each\ score - mean)^2}{Number\ of\ test\ takers}} \tag{7.3}$$

We can calculate the SD by following the steps in Guidelines 7.3.

Guidelines 7.3 Steps for calculating SD.

1. Find the mean.
2. Subtract the mean from each total test score. This gives the deviation scores.
3. Square each of the deviation scores.
4. Sum the squared deviation scores.
5. Divide the sum of the squared deviation scores by the number of test takers. This gives the variance.
6. Take the square root of the variance. This gives the SD.

Table 7.3 shows the test takers in the first column and their total scores in the second column. We will use the steps in Guidelines 7.3 to explain how we have calculated the values in each of the other columns.

The first step is to find the mean. We did this for the first ten students' scores of the Grammar Tense Test in Equation 7.1 and got a value of 17.50. We place the mean in the third column for each test taker.

Step 2 is to subtract the mean from each of the students' scores. Beginning with Pierre, we subtract the mean of 17.50 from 19 to get a deviation of 1.50. We can see the deviations for each of the students in the fourth column.

In Step 3, we square each of the deviation scores. For Pierre, we square 1.50 (1.50 multiplied by 1.50) to get a squared deviation of 2.25.

In Step 4, we sum all of the squared deviations to get a value of 50.50.

TABLE 7.3

Calculation of the variance and SD of the first ten students' scores on the Grammar Tense Test.

Test Taker	Total Score	Mean	Deviation Score	Squared deviation (x^2)
Pierre	19	17.50	1.50	2.25
Binna	15	17.50	−2.50	6.25
Ishan	21	17.50	3.50	12.25
Kenji	18	17.50	0.50	0.25
Lena	14	17.50	−3.50	12.25
Paulo	20	17.50	2.50	6.25
Chen	18	17.50	0.50	0.25
Jing	15	17.50	−2.50	6.25
Lula	19	17.50	1.50	2.25
Anisa	16	17.50	−1.50	2.25
Total				50.50

In Step 5, we divide the squared deviation by the number of test takers. We have ten test takers, so we divide 50.50 by 10 to get a variance of 5.05.

Finally, in Step 6, we take the square root of 5.05, which gives us an SD of 2.25.

We can interpret the SD to mean that our ten scores are, on average, 2.50 points above or below the mean of 17.50.

Time to Think 7.5

When we calculate the SD, why do you think we square the scores to calculate the average distance they are from the mean? (Hint: Add up the deviation scores.)

Score Distributions
Skewness

As we discussed in Chapter 2 (see Figure 2.5), we must have normally distributed scores to be able to use NRT statistics. In language assessment, we usually use **skewness** and **kurtosis** to help us determine if a set of test scores is normally distributed.

Skewness refers to how centered the scores are compared to the mean. We can have either positive or negative skewness. When most scores are to the left of the mean, the distribution is positively skewed, and when most scores are to the right of the mean, the distribution is negatively skewed.

Let's consider an example of fifty test takers' scores on a 20-item test. We can see positively and negatively skewed distributions for this example in Figure 7.2.

We refer to the figures in Figure 7.2 as **histograms**, a kind of chart that we use to represent how many test takers get a certain number of items correct. On the X-axis, we see Scores on Test and values from 0 to 20. On the Y-axis, we see the Number of Scores and values from 0 to 10.

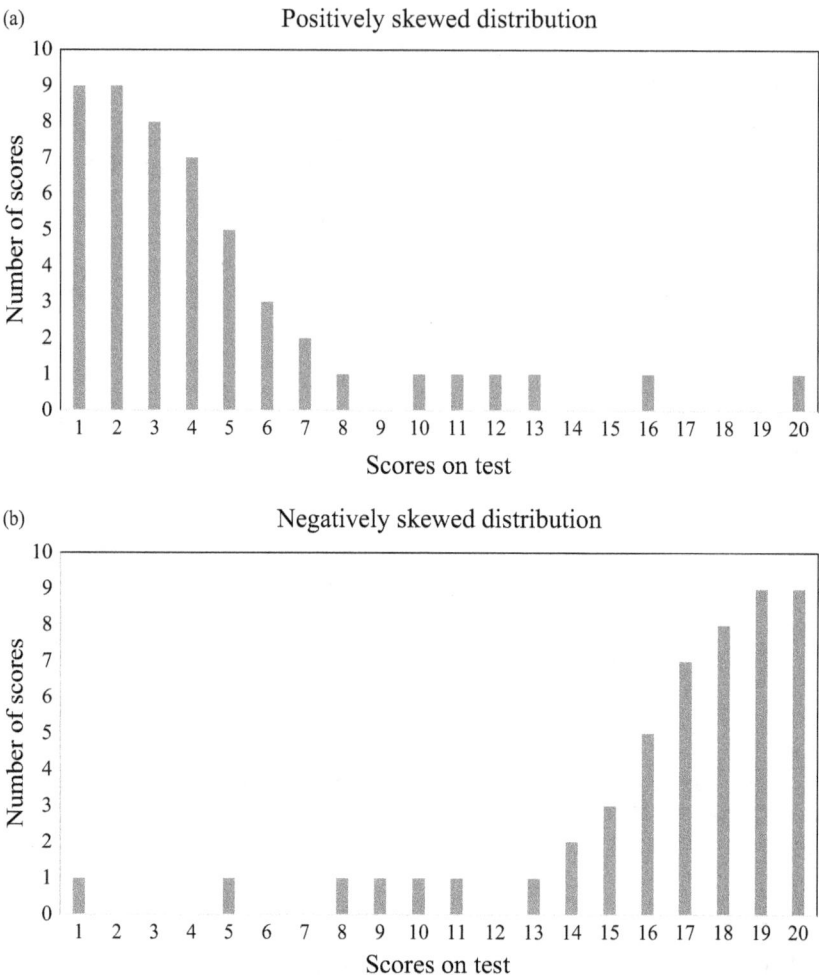

FIGURE 7.2 Positively and negatively skewed score distributions.

We can see how many test takers got a particular score by finding the number on the X-axis and seeing how high the bar is for that value. For example, in (a) (positively skewed distribution), we can see that nine test takers got one question correct by finding 1 on the X axis (Scores on Test) and seeing that the bar is nine high on the Y-axis (Number of Scores). The positively skewed distribution has a mean of 4.52, and thirty-three of the fifty test takers got below this value: nine got 1, nine got 2, eight got 3, and seven got 4. Only a few test takers got scores above 7. For the negatively skewed distribution, we see the opposite shape. The mean is 16.48, and most test takers got scores above this value. Only a few test takers got scores below 14.

Kurtosis

Kurtosis indicates a measure of how peaked a score distribution is. Like skewness, kurtosis can be positive or negative. Positive kurtosis indicates that the scores are too close to the mean, which means we do not have enough variance in our scores to effectively separate test takers according to their language abilities. Distributions with positive kurtosis are high and narrow. Negative kurtosis indicates that there are many high and low scores and not many near the mean. These score distributions are flat and wide when compared to a normal distribution. In Figure 7.3, we can see a score distribution with positive kurtosis (a) and one with negative kurtosis (b).

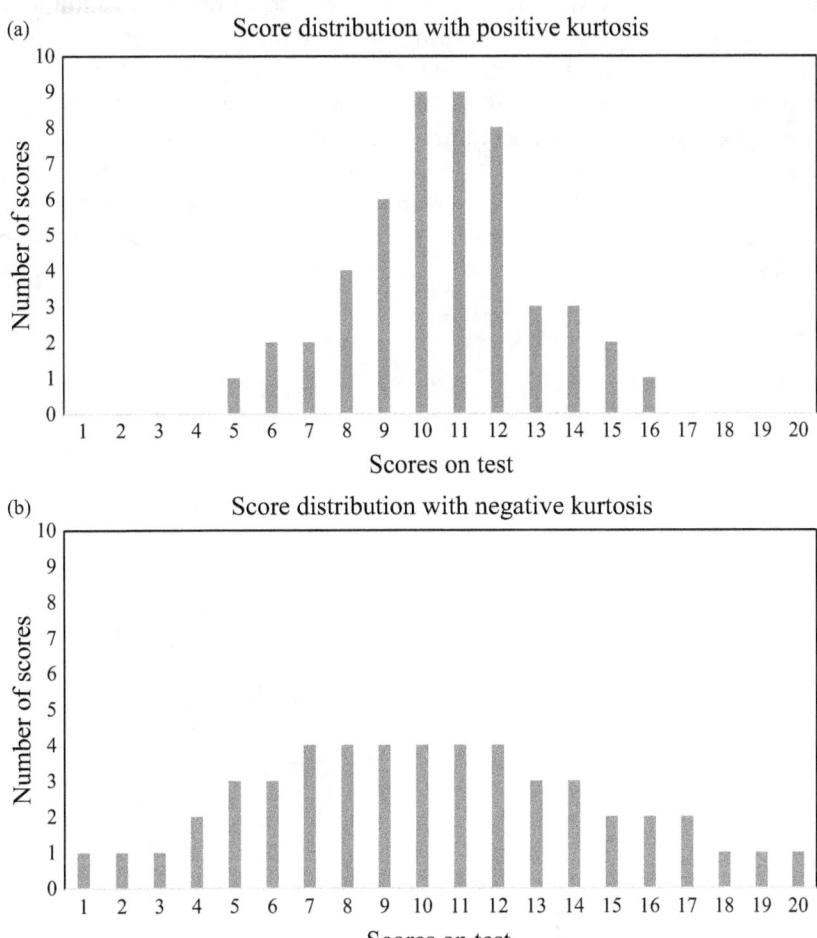

FIGURE 7.3 Score distributions with positive and negative kurtosis.

When both skewness and kurtosis values are 0.00, we have a perfectly normal distribution. In practice, we almost never have such values, and fortunately, we do not need such perfection. Research indicates that a set of scores with skewness and kurtosis values between −2.00 and +2.00 are distributed sufficiently normally for using NRT statistics (Larson-Hall, 2016).

 See Appendix 7D for how to use Excel to calculate the min, max, mean, variance, SD, skewness, and kurtosis for the fifty students in the first administration of the Grammar Tense Test. The online materials include the scores of all fifty test takers on this test.

Histogram of the Grammar Tense Test Scores

Let's consider the distribution of the Grammar Tense Test scores of all twenty-five items for all fifty test takers. We can see the distribution in Figure 7.4. The number of test takers who got a certain score is on the vertical axis, and the scores from 0 to 25 are on the horizontal axis. The columns or bars indicate how many test takers got a particular score. For example, we can see that eight test takers got a score of 18, by finding 18 on the horizontal axis and seeing that the column is eight high on the vertical axis. The black curved line indicates a perfectly normal distribution for this group of scores. We can see that the scores are quite normal for these fifty students, since most of the space under the normal curve line contains scores, and not much of the space above the normal curve line does. The skewness of these scores is –.55 and the kurtosis is –.12, both near the desired value of 0.00 and easily within the acceptable limits of –2.00 and +2.00. Larson-Hall (2016) shows how to create histograms in SPSS, the program that produced the histogram in Figure 7.4.

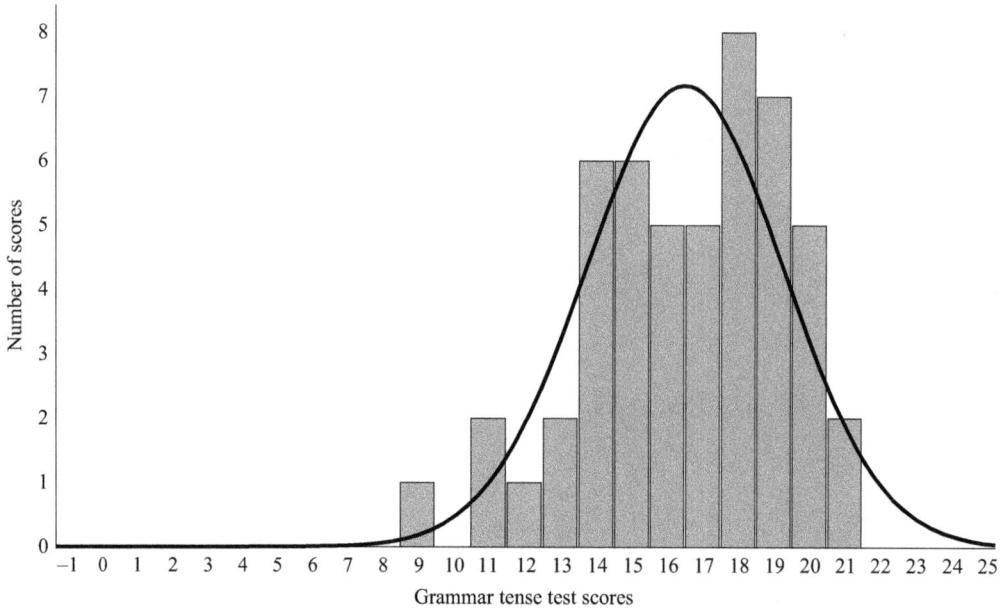

FIGURE 7.4 Histogram of the Grammar Tense Test. The scores are quite normally distributed.

Time to Think 7.6

Assume the scores for all fifty items of the Grammar Tense Test were very negatively skewed. Draw a picture to show how they would look.

Assume that the scores for all fifty items of the Grammar Tense Test were very positively kurtotic. Draw a picture to show how they would look.

Conclusion

In this chapter, we began by using the principles we learned in earlier chapters of the book to evaluate reading passage inputs and MC items for a ninth grade ESL reading placement test. By using a set of guidelines, we systematically identified problems with the passages and items. We can use these same principles to help us create passages and items. Next, we explored some basic descriptive statistics that we can use to evaluate the overall performance of a set of test items. These statistics included minimum and maximum, the lowest and highest test takers' scores. We also learned about range, which is the difference between the maximum and minimum scores, and the mean, which is the average of all the test takers' scores. We also discussed how to calculate the variance, SD, skewness, and kurtosis of a set of test scores. We learned that these statistics are important for judging the effectiveness of an NRT.

At the beginning of the chapter, I shared my experience of listening to a group of teachers who had limited statistical LAL. More knowledge about statistics may have increased their confidence and given the parents more faith in the teachers' abilities to teach their children. In the next two chapters, we will expand on our understanding of content and statistical analyses for language assessment. In Chapter 8, we will learn how to use statistical and content analyses of individual test items to determine their effectiveness and guide item revision. In Chapter 9, we will use content and statistical analyses to evaluate and revise CRT items.

Questions for Discussion

7.1 One of the teachers on the team creating the ninth grade ESL reading test created the following item to assess comprehension of Passage 1 (see the beginning of the chapter).

To get points for a field goal, the ball must _____ the field goal posts.
a. go through
b. be under
c. be kicked next to
d. kick by

7.1.1 Use Guidelines 7.2 to conduct a content analysis of the item.
7.1.2 Rewrite the item to make it more effective.

7.2 Use Guidelines 7.2 to help you create selected response items.
7.2.1 Write two true–false items for Passage 1.
7.2.2 Rewrite the two true–false items as MC items.
7.2.3 Discuss the advantages and disadvantages of MC items compared to true–false items and decide which type you think would be best for this test.

7.3 Take turns explaining the meaning and purpose of the following test statistics: max, min, range, mean, variance, SD, normal distribution, skewness, and kurtosis. Draw pictures to help with your explanations.

7 ANALYZING DICHOTOMOUSLY SCORED ITEMS

Exercises

7.1 Assume, the team creating the ninth grade ESL reading test decided to use Passage 1 for the test. One of the teachers created the following problematic item:

A _____ is worth one or two points.
a. touchdown
b. elephant
c. field goals
d. safety

    7.1.1 Use Guidelines 7.2 to conduct a content analysis of the item.
    7.1.2 Based on your content analysis, how would you adapt the item? Provide justification for your suggested changes.
    7.1.3 Write your revised item.

7.2 Use Guidelines 7.2 to help you conduct a content analysis of items 2 and 3 of the Grammar Tense Test (Example 7.3).
    7.2.1 Would you change either item? If so, which one and how?
    7.2.2 Provide justification for either not making any changes or the changes you recommend.

7.3 Use software like ChatGPT to create a passage and five MC passage comprehension items. Assume you want to create a 250-word narrative and five MC items to help assess the reading comprehension of ten-year-old students studying English in Japan (or another country of your choice). Your aim is to assess general comprehension, reading for details, and the ability to make inferences from a passage.
    7.3.1 Use software (e.g., ChatGPT) to create a passage (see Appendix 7A for guidance).
    7.3.2 Evaluate the reading passage with the help of Guidelines 7.1.
    7.3.3 Make any changes to the passage by using the software or by rewriting it until it is appropriate for its purpose.
    7.3.4 Use software (e.g., ChatGPT) to create three MC items (four answer options for each) to assess comprehension of the passage: one each for general comprehension, inferencing, and reading for details (see Appendix 7B for guidance).
    7.3.5 Evaluate the items with the help of Guidelines 7.2.
    7.3.6 Make any changes to the items by using the software or by rewriting them until they are appropriate for their purposes.

7.4 Manually calculate the maximum, minimum, range, mean, variance, and SD of test takers 11–20 of the first administration of the Grammar Tense Test. See Table 7.4 for the data, and see Appendix 7D for guidance on how to do the calculations with Excel.
    7.4.1 Show all steps and create a table like Table 7.3.
    7.4.2 Explain what the maximum, minimum, mean, range, variance, and SD tell us about the effectiveness of these twenty-five items for these ten test takers.

7.5 Calculate and interpret the descriptive statistics for the forty-six students who took the second administration of the Grammar Tense Test. (Access the online materials: ISLA. Ex.7.5)
    7.5.1 Use Excel to score the data (see Appendix 7C for guidance).
    7.5.2 Use Excel to calculate the maximum, minimum, mean, variance, SD, skewness, and kurtosis.

TABLE 7.4

Scores of test takers 11–20 on first administration of the Grammar Tense Test.

	1	2	3	4	5	6	7	8	9	10	11	12	13	14	15	16	17	18	19	20	21	22	23	24	25	Total
Ezra	0	1	1	1	1	0	0	0	0	1	0	1	0	0	1	1	1	0	1	1	1	0	1	1	0	16
Sonca	0	1	1	1	1	1	0	0	1	1	1	1	1	1	1	1	1	1	1	1	1	0	1	1	1	19
Leyla	0	1	1	1	1	1	1	1	0	1	0	0	1	0	0	0	1	1	0	1	1	0	1	0	1	14
Sal	1	1	1	1	1	0	0	0	0	1	0	0	1	0	0	1	0	0	0	1	1	0	1	1	1	14
Abdul	0	1	1	1	1	1	1	0	0	1	1	1	1	1	1	1	1	0	0	1	1	0	1	0	1	16
Juan	0	1	0	0	1	0	0	0	1	0	1	0	1	0	0	0	1	1	0	1	1	0	0	1	1	14
Maria	0	1	0	1	1	1	1	1	1	1	1	1	1	1	0	1	1	0	1	1	1	0	1	1	1	17
Emiko	0	1	1	0	1	0	0	1	0	0	0	1	1	1	0	0	0	0	0	1	0	1	0	0	1	12
Marty	1	0	1	1	1	1	0	0	0	0	1	1	1	1	1	1	1	1	0	1	1	0	1	1	1	16
Jing	0	1	0	0	1	1	1	0	1	1	1	1	0	0	0	0	0	1	1	1	1	0	0	1	0	13

7.5.3 Provide an interpretation of each of these statistics. What do they tell us about the effectiveness of the test?

Additional Resources

Brown, J. D. (2022). *Classical test theory*. In G. Fulcher & L. Harding (Eds.). *The Routledge Handbook of Language Testing*. Routledge.

This chapter introduces basic statistics for language assessment in a clear manner. Brown also provides a good reference list for readers interested in a more in-depth description of these statistics.

Carr, N. (2008). Using Microsoft Excel to calculate descriptive statistics and create graphs. *Language Assessment Quarterly*, 5(1), 43–62.

This journal article provides advice about how to use Excel to help understand statistics important to language assessment. Readers may find some tricks that will help them use Excel more effectively for this purpose.

Appendix 7A Using ChatGPT to Create Reading Passages

The following step-by-step instructions will help you create a reading passage using ChatGPT.

Starting ChatGPT

1. Open https://chat.openai.com/

After you have signed up for a new account, click on "ChatGPT" in the top left-hand corner of the screen. You will type your commands in the "Message" window at the bottom of the screen.

Prompting ChatGPT

> **Things to remember when prompting ChatGPT:**
> Prompting, in the context of ChatGPT, refers to the initial input or instruction provided by a user to start a conversation or request a specific response. A prompt can be a single sentence, a paragraph, or even a longer text. When prompting ChatGPT, remember:
> 1. Be clear and concise.
> 2. Be specific with your request.
> 3. Provide explicit constraints and guidelines.
> 4. Rephrase the prompt or add more context if output is not as expected.

We considered two reading passages in this chapter: "How to score in football" and "A difficult fishing trip." We will use the same topics. We will also limit the passage so that it is between 250 and 300 words. Finally, we need to make sure that the passage is appropriate for ninth grade students.

2. Knowing the information above, we can instruct ChatGPT to generate the first reading passage using the following prompt: "Create a reading passage on how to score in

football. The text must be between 250 and 300 words. The grammar and vocabulary that we use in the passage must be appropriate for ninth grade students (around fourteen years old)." Hit Enter or click on the "Send Message" icon.

Revising the Prompt When Output Is Not Appropriate

When we use these types of technology, we often do not get exactly what we desire. For instance, it is common to get bullet points instead of paragraphs. We may also get too many or too few words. Check the output to see if the passage is reasonable for its purpose.

3. Assuming we have bullet points instead of paragraphs and too long of a text, we might revise the prompt to: "Create a reading passage on how to score in football. The text should be in the form of paragraphs, no bullet points. Each paragraph should transition smoothly to the next one. The grammatical and vocabulary complexity in the text must be appropriate for ninth grade students or fourteen-year-old students. The minimum length of the output must be 250 words. The maximum length of the output must be 300 words." Hit Enter or click on the "Send Message" icon.
4. Let's assume the modifications resolved the bullet point issue. However, despite specifying the minimum and maximum word limit in the prompt, ChatGPT still produces a 400-word text. Let's try again. In the same chat thread, enter the following prompt: "The passage is too long. Cut the text so that it totals 300 words." Enter or click on the "Send Message" icon.
5. Another issue that you may notice is the complexity of the vocabulary in the text. There are many words that would be too difficult for ninth grade ESL students. Again, we need to instruct ChatGPT by reiterating the relevant part of the prompt. We can do so by entering the following prompt in the same chat thread: "The text you generated uses too many complex words. Please use vocabulary that 14-year-old students whose native language is not English can understand." Hit Enter or click on the "Send Message" icon.

It is usually necessary to go through multiple revisions to get an appropriate reading passage. Continue to give commands to ChatGPT until the passage is as close to what you desire as possible.

Appendix 7B Using ChatGPT to Create MC Reading Items

We have tried using ChatGPT to create a reading passage. Having revised the generated reading passage to meet our reading input guidelines, we will now create its corresponding MC reading items. The following step-by-step instructions will help you create MC reading items using ChatGPT.

Starting ChatGPT

1. Open https://chat.openai.com/ and click on "ChatGPT". Then type in your commands in the "Send a Message" window.

Prompting ChatGPT

Let's say we want to develop five MC reading items to assess test takers' abilities for global comprehension (one item), making inferences about content (one item), and locating specific details (three items). We will need to make sure that ChatGPT understands what each of these abilities entail. Each MC item should have four answer options.

2. Before we ask ChatGPT to generate the MC reading items, let's request ChatGPT to "remember" the reading passage it created (Appendix 7A) by using the following prompt: "Please remember the following text: [insert text here]".
3. Next, we ask ChatGPT to create a question targeting general understanding. We can use the following prompt: "Create a multiple-choice reading question with four answer options. The multiple-choice question should target a test taker's ability to generally understand the above reading passage."
4. Let's move on to the next item, the inferencing question. We can use the following prompt: "Create a multiple-choice reading question with four answer options. The multiple-choice question should target a test taker's ability to make inferences about the content of the above reading passage." We can continue creating additional items using similar commands.

Appendix 7C Guidelines for Scoring MC Items with Excel

This appendix will take us through the steps of converting MC answer options into right or wrong answers and getting a total score for each test taker. We will use the Grammar Tense Test MC Data for this purpose (online file: ISLA.Ap.7C). The online materials include a video that accompanies these instructions.

1. Open the ISLA.Ap.7C data file.
2. Complete the following steps to score the items as either right or wrong:

    a. Do this step to score item 1 for person 1.
    Select cell AC3 and type:

    = IF(C3=C$2,1,0)

    Press Enter. This command tells Excel that we want to assign a score of 1 if the number in cell C3 is equal to the number in cell C2, and if it is not equal to assign a score of 0. The $ symbol between C and 2 tells Excel to use the value in C2, which is the item key, to score all fifty of the test takers on the first item. After you press Enter, you should see 0 in this cell, since the first test taker got the first item wrong. The first test taker selected option c for Item 1, and the correct answer was option d.

    b. Do this step to score the rest of the items for the first test taker and all items for all other test takers.
    Copy the scoring command by clicking on cell AC3 and typing Control C. Hold the Shift key down and tap on the right arrow key twenty-four times (or hold it down until you get to column BA), so you can score the other twenty-four items. This should highlight cells AD3 to BA3. While continuing to hold the Shift key down, tap the down arrow forty-nine times (or hold it down until you get to row 52). Release the button. You should now see that you have highlighted cells AC3 to BA3 for rows 3 to 52.

c. Type Control V to paste the copied command into all of the highlighted cells. This should score all twenty-five items for all fifty test takers as either right, with a 1, or wrong, with a 0.

3. Do the following to find the total number of correct answers for each test taker:

   a. Select cell BB3 and type:

   =SUM(AC3:BA3)

   Press Enter. The total score of 19 for the first test taker should appear in cell BB3.
   b. Use this command to score the other test takers.
   Select cell BB3. Move the cursor to the bottom right-hand corner of this cell until a black cross appears. Click on the black cross and hold down while dragging down to cell BB52. Release the button. You should now see the total scores for each test taker.

Appendix 7D Calculating Descriptive Statistics in Excel

This appendix will take us through the steps for calculating the maximum, minimum, mean, variance, SD, skewness, and kurtosis of test scores with Excel. We will use the Grammar Tense Test scored data to complete the activity (online materials: ISLA.Ap.7D). The online materials include a video that accompanies these instructions.

1. Open the data file ISLA.Ap.7D.
2. Complete the following steps to identify the maximum:

   Select cell AB54 (you may have to scroll down and to the right to find this cell) and type:

   =MAX(AB3:AB52)

   Press Enter. This command tells Excel to find the maximum score for the scores from AB3 to AB52. You should see the maximum score of 21 for this data set in cell AB54.

3. Do the following to identify the minimum:

   Select cell AB55 and type:

   =MIN(AB3:AB52)

   Press Enter. This command tells Excel to calculate the minimum for the scores from AB3 to AB52. You should see the minimum score of 9 for this data set in cell AB55.

4. Calculate the mean, variance, SD, skewness, and kurtosis.
   We can use the same general process that we used to calculate the max and min to calculate the mean, variance, SD, skewness, kurtosis, and many other statistics in Excel. We simply change the command from Max or Min to the one we want. We can see the commands that we need in Table 7.D.1.

TABLE 7D.1

Excel commands for max, min, mean, variance, standard deviation, skewness, and kurtosis.

Statistic	Excel command	Grammar Tense Test, first administration
Max	=MAX(Data range)	21
Min	=MIN(Data range)	9
Mean	=AVERAGE(Data range)	16.54
Variance (population)	=VAR.P(Data range)	7.57
Standard deviation (population)	=STDEV.P(Data range)	2.75
Skewness	=SKEW(data range)	–.55
Kurtosis	=KURT(data range)	–.12

Note: We will use the variance and SD population estimates. An alternative is to use sample estimates. When we use sample estimates, we divide the sums of squares by the total number of test takers minus 1. Only when we use very small data sets will our result be meaningfully different if we use sample or population estimates, and we will not worry about this difference in this book. Larson-Hall (2016) discusses the use of sample vs. population estimates.

CHAPTER 8

Judging the Effectiveness of Dichotomously Scored Items

FIGURE 8.1 A person using statistics and figures to help understand test results.
Source: triloks/E+/Getty Images.

A team had created a multiple-choice (MC) listening assessment as part of a university placement exam. The assessment had five or six listening inputs, with about five comprehension questions for each and a total of thirty questions. The team had followed language assessment theory and guidelines, given each other feedback on items, and gone through numerous revisions. The team members were confident that their test would be effective. Before they used it, however, they piloted it to further evaluate the items.

Two teachers from another program agreed to let them pilot the test on their sixty students. Unfortunately, statistical analyses of the sixty test taker responses suggested many problems with the items. Some items did not have one clear answer, at least one item measured something different from listening, and others were not at an appropriate difficulty level. As experienced teachers who had language assessment training, we might expect they could make an effective listening assessment, but the statistical analyses suggested many problems. The assessment that the teachers created was not bad, but many items were not as effective as they should have been. The team discovered that information from statistical analyses can be helpful in creating an effective language assessment even when test developers are content experts with language assessment training.

Time to Think 8.1
In what types of assessment contexts do you think we should use statistical analyses? Provide reasons for your answer.

Introduction

In Chapter 7, we learned how we can use language assessment principles to help us select and create dichotomously scored items for receptive language assessments. We also explored some test-level statistical techniques to help us evaluate a test's effectiveness after we have administered it to a group of test takers. In this chapter, we will see how we can use statistical analysis to help us identify ineffective items on norm-referenced tests (NRTs), and then use content analyses to guide our decisions about what to do with these items.

We will begin with a discussion about item facility (IF) and point-biserials (PBs), two statistics that we can use to help us evaluate the effectiveness of individual test items. We will also explore correlational analysis, an important statistical technique that will help us understand PBs and reliability. After we have gained some knowledge of these statistics, we will see how we can apply content analysis and these statistical techniques to help us determine the effectiveness of each of the items on the Grammar Tense Test. Finally, we will expand our knowledge of reliability by discussing it in the context of this same test.

Item Analysis

In addition to considering test scores for all the items together, we can learn about the effectiveness of an assessment by exploring each item individually. Two statistics that will help us investigate the effectiveness of individual items are IFs and PBs.

Item Facility

Item Facility (IF) tells us how easy an item is for our group of test takers by indicating the percentage, on a proportion scale, of test takers who answer it correctly. To calculate IF, we sum up the number of test takers who got an item correct and divide by the number of test takers. For example, we can calculate the IF of our first item on the Grammar Tense Test by adding up the scores on this item. We can see in Table 7.2 (Chapter 7) that Ishan and Lula were the only two test takers who got the item correct. This means that the IF for the first ten items of the test would be .20. The math would be $(0+0+1+0+0+0+0+0+1+0)/10 = .20$. An IF of .20 indicates that 20 percent of test takers got the item correct.

 See Appendix 8A for how to calculate IFs in Excel.

With NRTs, we want the IFs to be near .50, meaning that about half of the test takers get each item correct. A general rule of thumb is that items with IFs between .30 and .70 are at an appropriate difficulty level for our test takers. Items with IFs below .30 may be too difficult, and items with IFs above .70 may be too easy. We should note, however, that an item with an IF a little outside of this range may be acceptable in low-stakes contexts, such as classrooms. We should also remember that an item with an IF of .70 is only slightly better than one with .71. In other words, we should not treat the rule of thumb as an absolute rule. We can see these general guidelines for judging IFs for NRTs in Guidelines 8.1.

Guidelines 8.1 Judging IF for NRTs.

Difficulty	IF
Too hard	Below .30
Appropriate	.30–.70
Too easy	Above .70

Time to Think 8.2

What is the item facility for the first ten test takers of Item 8 on the Grammar Tense Test? (See Table 7.2 for the scores.)

Is Item 8 harder or easier than Item 1, based on the scores of these ten test takers?

Point-Biserials

Point-biserials (PBs) are the **correlations** between the scores on each item and the total test scores. They tell us how effectively individual items distinguish among the ability levels of the test takers. Correlation is a statistical technique that we use to determine the degree of a relationship between two variables. In language assessment, we think of a **variable** as a characteristic that we can measure. Language assessment variables are usually item scores, test scores, or test taker characteristics, such as age and first language. We use correlation for many purposes in language assessment, including to calculate PBs and reliability and explore relationships among test takers' abilities.

Correlation: The Principle Underlying PBs

Because some knowledge of correlation will help us better understand PBs and reliability, we will discuss it briefly in this section. Let's begin by assuming we gave a group of students separate 15-item MC reading and listening quizzes. We can see some scores for ten students in Table 8.1.

SCATTER PLOTS

Since in our example students took both the reading and listening quizzes, we can compare to see how their scores relate with each other. We can investigate the relationship among the scores by putting them in a **scatter plot**, which is a graph where we plot the values of two variables. Figure 8.2 shows a scatter plot with reading on the X-axis and listening on the Y-axis. On each axis, we can see fifteen values that represent the number of items test takers answered correctly. We indicate each quiz score by placing a point where the two scores meet. For example, Student 1 got a score of 9 on reading and 7 on listening. We find this student's score by going to 9 on the X-axis (Reading) and then to 7 on the Y-axis (Listening). We can see a dot with a 1 next to it to represent our first student's scores on the two quizzes. Each dot represents the two scores for a test taker. We can see ten dots for the ten test takers.

TABLE 8.1
Assumed reading and listening quiz scores for ten students.

Student number	Reading quiz score	Listening quiz score
1	9	7
2	14	13
3	7	8
4	10	10
5	13	11
6	12	10
7	6	7
8	14	12
9	6	4
10	7	6

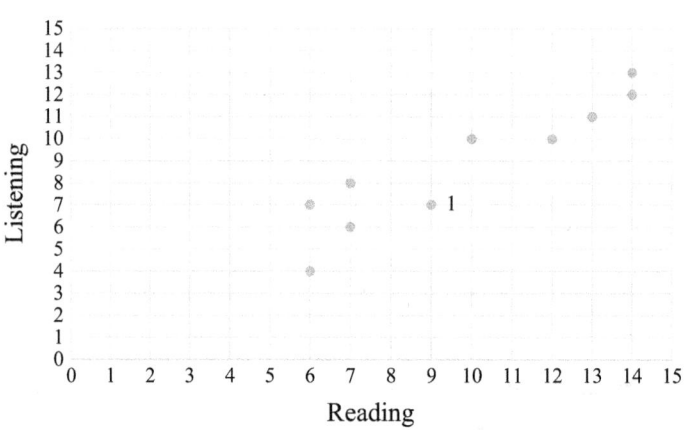

FIGURE 8.2 Scatter plot of reading and listening quiz scores.

Time to Think 8.3

Copy or draw Figure 8.2 and write student numbers 2 to 10 (from Table 8.1) next to the appropriate dot.

POSITIVE CORRELATIONS

We can see the relationship between reading and listening scores for the ten test takers in Figure 8.2. The data points go diagonally from the bottom left side to the top right side. In general, students who got low scores on the reading quiz got low scores on the listening quiz (students 3, 7, 9, and 10) and students who got high scores on the reading quiz got high scores on the listening quiz (students 2, 5, and 8). When high and low scores on one variable relate to high and low scores on another, we refer to the relationship as a positive correlation.

NEGATIVE CORRELATIONS

We can also have a negative correlation between two or more variables. Let's assume the same students who took the reading and listening quizzes also took a grammar error quiz, which we scored by counting the number of grammatical errors. We can see scores for this quiz for the same students as in Table 8.1, along with their reading quiz scores, in Table 8.2.

TABLE 8.2

Reading and grammar error quiz scores for ten students.

Student number	Reading quiz scores	Grammar error quiz scores
1	9	6
2	14	3
3	7	8
4	10	6
5	13	4
6	12	4
7	6	7
8	14	4
9	6	8
10	7	9

In Figure 8.3, we can see a scatter plot for the reading and grammar error scores. The pattern is the opposite of the one in Figure 8.2. The data points form a diagonal pattern from the upper left side to the bottom right side of the figure. Generally, students who got high scores on the reading quiz had a low number of grammar errors (students 2, 5, 6, and 8) while those who got low scores on the reading quiz generally had a high number of grammar errors (students 3, 7, 9, 10).

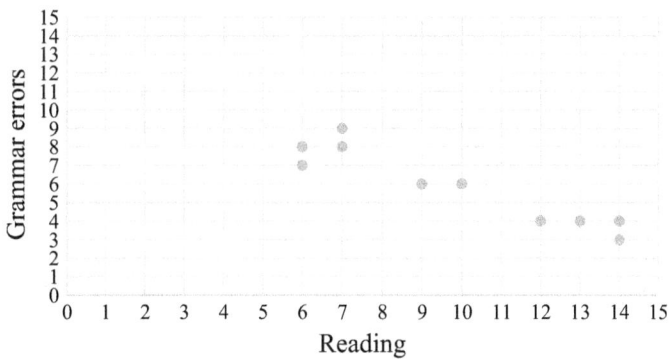

FIGURE 8.3 Scatter plot of reading and grammar error quiz scores.

When high scores on a variable relate to low scores on another variable, and low scores on one variable relate to high scores on the other variable, we refer to the relationship as a negative correlation.

ZERO CORRELATIONS

We can also have little or no relationship between two or more variables. When we have no relationship, the points do not form a pattern from top left to bottom right or from bottom left to top right. They form a rectangular pattern. When there is no relationship (correlation), we cannot predict how a test taker would perform on one test based on their score on another.

In Chapter 7, we discussed the importance of sufficient score variance for effective NRTs. We learned that when all test takers get similar scores, we cannot effectively rank order them. We can see from the scatter plot in Figure 8.2 that our correlation depends on the amount of score variance. If all students got the same scores, we would have no score variance and no correlation. For example, if all test takers got 6 on the reading quiz, we would see a vertical line of dots. This would indicate no correlation between reading and listening scores. If all students got 6 on the listening quiz, we would see a horizontal line of dots. This would also indicate no correlation between the scores on the two variables. Score variance is therefore an important property of an NRT.

> **Time to Think 8.4**
>
> Draw a scatter plot of ten imaginary reading and listening scores with (near) zero correlation. Explain why the correlation is (near) zero.

STRENGTH OF CORRELATIONS

In addition to telling us about the type of relationship (positive or negative), correlations also tell us about the strength of the relationship. Correlations can have values between positive 1.0 (1.00) and negative 1.0 (–1.00). A correlation of 1.00 tells us that the rankings of the scores on one variable perfectly align with the rankings of the scores on another. For example, if the correlation between our reading and listening test scores was 1.00, we would know that the student ranking from highest to lowest on the reading test would be exactly the same as on the listening test. If the correlation was –1.00, we would know that the student rankings are opposite of each other. The test taker with the highest score on reading would have the lowest score on listening, and the test taker with the lowest score on listening would have the highest score on reading. All other scores would also be exactly reversed.

Uses of PBs

Now that we know a little about correlation, we can further discuss how we can use PBs to help us evaluate the effectiveness of individual items on an NRT. We calculate the PB for an item by correlating the scores of the test takers on the item with their total scores on the test.

POSITIVE PBS

For an effective item, we expect the PB, which is the correlation between scores on an item and the test scores, to be positive and high. Items with high **positive point-biserials** rank order the test takers in a similar way that the total scores rank them. Most of the students who get high scores on the test get the item correct, and most of the students who get low scores on the test answer the item incorrectly. When we have an item with a high positive PB, we say that it has good **item**

discrimination. Items with good discrimination effectively distinguish among high- and low-scoring test takers. Importantly, when we have little score variance, such as when most test takers answer an item correctly, we cannot have high PBs, because the item scores cannot highly correlate with the total scores.

NEGATIVE PBS

Items with **negative point-biserials** correlate negatively with the total score. Item scores that correlate negatively or not at all with the overall test scores do not effectively distinguish among more and less proficient test takers. In fact, items with negative PBs decrease the test's potential to discriminate among test takers. Items with negative PBs indicate that most test takers who answer an item correctly got low scores on the test, and most test takers who answer the item incorrectly got high scores on the test. This means that the item goes against the test's general score pattern, reducing its consistency.

ZERO PBS

An item with a (near) zero PB indicates that there is (almost) no relationship between how test takers perform on the item and the test. Some test takers who get the item correct get high scores while others get low scores. Similarly, some test takers who get the item wrong get high scores while others get low scores. As a result, items with zero PBs do not help us separate more and less proficient test takers. While these items do not negatively influence the effectiveness of the test, they are not useful, because they waste valuable test taker time with little or no benefit.

JUDGING PB VALUES

We cannot rely on an exact PB value to judge the effectiveness of an item. We have to take into account the assessment context, including the construct that we want to measure and how high the stakes are for the test. That said, we generally consider items with PBs of .30 and above (the higher the better) to be effective for almost any context. Items with PBs of between .20 and .30 are generally acceptable in low-stakes contexts, and items with PBs of below .20 tend to be ineffective. Importantly, however, we need to keep in mind that there is almost no difference between .29 and .30. We should not judge one item as better than another based on small differences in PBs. Items that have negative PBs are always problematic for an NRT and we should exclude them from scoring. If we use the test in the future, we should remove or revise these items. We can see general guidelines for judging items based on PBs in Guidelines 8.2.

Guidelines 8.2 Judging items based on PBs.

	Below .00	Between .00 and .20	Between .20 and .30	.30 and higher
Quality of item	Very poor	Poor	Okay	Excellent
Exclude item from scores?	Yes	No	No	No
Remove item from test or revise for next test administration?	Yes	Yes	Maybe (depends on context)	No

Importantly, when we use PBs, we assume that all of the test items measure the same ability. When we use PBs to help us analyze the effectiveness of an assessment with subsections that measure different abilities, we need to separate these sections in our analyses. For instance, if we had listening and reading sections, we would calculate their PBs separately. We would correlate each listening item with the total score for all listening items, and separately correlate each reading item with the total score for all of the reading items.

 See Appendix 8A for how to calculate PBs in Excel.

Content Analysis, PBs, and IFs to Judge the Effectiveness of Test Items

In Chapter 7, we discussed how to use content analysis to help us select and judge the effectiveness of test items before we administer a test. After we administer a test, we can use the test takers' responses to help us further evaluate the effectiveness of the items. This step will help us determine which item scores to include in a total score and which items to exclude or revise for future test administrations. In high-stakes assessments, we usually have a group of test takers pilot the test items, so we can use their responses to help us evaluate the test's effectiveness. When we have test taker responses to test items (either from a pilot or test administration), we can use a combination of content and statistical analyses to evaluate and best ensure the test's quality.

We will analyze the Grammar Tense Test (the complete test is available in online materials) to explore how we can use content analysis, PBs, and IFs to help us judge the effectiveness of dichotomously scored items after a group of test takers has completed an NRT. We can see the items, answer key, IFs, and PBs of the Grammar Tense Test in Table 8.3.

 See Appendix 8A for how to calculate these values.

TABLE 8.3

Items, answer key, IFs, and PBs for the Grammar Tense Test.

Item	Key	IF	PB
1	d	.30	.24
2	d	.98	.03
3	a	.28	−.19
4	d	.84	.56
5	d	.94	.26

TABLE 8.3 (cont.)

Item	Key	IF	PB
6	d	.72	.22
7	d	.10	−.26
8	c	.64	.33
9	b	.40	.51
10	c	.88	.36
11	d	.82	.57
12	d	.84	.20
13	c	.72	.03
14	b	.78	.35
15	d	.32	.30
16	c	.94	.39
17	b	.72	.54
18	c	.64	.40
19	b	.76	.40
20	d	.96	.30
21	b	.90	.31
22	c	.10	−.40
23	d	.70	.59
24	c	.60	.43
25	a	.66	.23

Time to Think 8.5
Based on the data in Table 8.3, select the three best and three worst items. Provide justification for your decisions.

Evaluating IFs for the Grammar Tense Test

We will begin by considering the IFs. We want IFs for an NRT to be between .30 and .70, but for our low- to medium-stakes Grammar Tense Test, we may accept a little higher or lower values. In Table 8.3 we can see that items 3 and 7 are too hard. Only 28 percent and 10 percent of the test takers answered these items correctly. A bigger concern is that fourteen of the twenty-five items are too easy. More than 70 percent of test takers correctly answered items 2, 4, 5, 6, 10, 11, 12, 13, 14, 16, 17, 19, 20, and 21. However, it is worth noting that items 3, 6, 13, and 17 are only slightly outside of the .30 to .70 range and may be acceptable for the Grammar Tense Test context. It is okay to use the scores from items with high IFs when we make decisions about test takers. They may actually help us a little to distinguish among more and less proficient test takers. However, if we plan to use the test for future administrations, we should revise or exclude these items because answering them is not an effective use of the test takers' time.

Evaluating PBs for the Grammar Tense Test

Our PBs in Table 8.3 suggest that most of our test items are effectively separating more and less proficient test takers. Most of the items have PBs above .30, and these high positive PBs indicate that most test takers who answered an item correctly got a high score on the test while most test takers who answered the item incorrectly got a low score on the test. We want to see many items with PBs above .30 because this means that most items are effectively distinguishing among the proficiencies of the test takers. However, the PBs suggest that we do have a few problematic items. Our biggest concerns are items 3, 7, and 22. These items have negative PBs, which means that more test takers who got low test scores answered them correctly than test takers who got high test scores. We should not include these three items when scoring the test for our Grammar Tense Test's placement decisions, and we should either exclude them or revise them for future test administrations.

After we have used PBs and IFs to help us identify poorly performing items, we can use content analysis to try to see why they are problematic. Based on our content analysis, we can decide about possible revisions or whether or not to use them at all on future test administrations. We can see the three worst items (all had negative PBs) on the Grammar Tense Test in Example 8.1.

Example 8.1 Items 3, 7, and 22 of the Grammar Tense Test.

3. Lots of people _____ their way to the ancient Egyptian exhibit when I got out of the museum last night.

    a. had made   b. have made   c. were making   d. will make

7. The Gallery worker _____ whether a piece of art is authentic or a forgery nearly every day this week.

    a. has investigated   b. investigates   c. investigating   d. will investigating

22. The property management company _____ the rent on your apartment when you sign the new lease.

    a. has raised   b. raised   c. will be raised   d. will have raised

---

Analyzing Item 3 of the Grammar Tense Test

Let's begin with Item 3. If we conduct a content analysis using Guidelines 7.2, we discover that the item does not satisfy Guideline 6. It appears to have two options, *a* and *c*, that could be correct. Option *a*, *had made* is acceptable because people could have already gotten to the exhibit when the writer got out of the museum. Option *c* is also acceptable because people could have been in the process of getting to the museum when the author got out of the museum. Our PB suggests that many of the highly proficient test takers may have chosen option *c* instead of *a*. In fact, we can see that this is what happened if we look at Table 7.1. Based on our negative PB, low IF, and content analysis, we should exclude the scores on Item 3 when we make decisions about test takers' grammar tense knowledge. Moreover, if we use this test in the future, we should revise or exclude this item by replacing either *a* or *c* with an incorrect option.

Analyzing Item 7 of the Grammar Tense Test
Next, let's use content analysis to see if we can discover why Item 7 has a negative PB. Again, it looks like this item does not follow Guideline 6 (Guidelines 7.2). The best answer, *a*, is not the key option. In addition, option *d*, which is the key, is not reasonable. It is not grammatically possible to have *will investigating* in Standard English. We learn more about this item by considering the IF. Only 10 percent of test takers selected the key option, when we would expect 25 percent of test takers to select the correct option by chance alone on a four-option MC item. Like Item 3, we should not use the scores from Item 7 to place students into English as a Second Language (ESL) classes, and we should revise or exclude the item if we use the test again. Scoring the test with the correct key would help to solve this problem.

Analyzing Other Items of the Grammar Tense Test
Items 2 and 13 have near zero PBs. They do not negatively affect our test results, but they only slightly (because they are a little greater than 0.00) help us separate more and less proficient test takers. They waste test takers' valuable time. We can use these scores when we make decisions about ESL class placement, but we should revise or exclude them if we use the test again.

Overall, our MC Grammar Tense Test is poor. Only items 8, 9, 15, 18, 23, and 24 are very effective. Items 3, 7, and 22 decrease the test's effectiveness, and the other items are not as effective as we would desire. It is worth noting, however, that they do help us to a small degree (because they have positive PBs) to separate our test takers based on their grammar tense knowledge. If we use this test again, we should revise or replace all items except 8, 9, 15, 18, 23, and 24.

> **Time to Think 8.6**
> Based on the IFs and PBs of the Grammar Tense Test, what would you do for this test administration? Would you exclude any items from the scoring? If so, which ones? Provide justification for your answer.

Reliability

In Chapter 5, we learned that reliability estimates give us information about the consistency of our language assessment scores. For NRTs, high reliability indicates that our test scores rank order test takers consistently. As we discussed in Chapter 5, we often estimate reliability based on the internal consistency of test scores. When each of our items leads to similar rankings of test takers, we have evidence of a test's internal reliability.

Cronbach's Alpha
Cronbach's Alpha is a measure of internal reliability that we often use in language assessment. The logic that underlies Cronbach's Alpha is similar to the logic that underlies PBs. For PBs, we correlate item scores with total test scores to see if test takers who perform well on an item also perform well on the test, and test takers who perform poorly on the item also perform poorly on the test. When we have this relationship, we have large positive PBs.

When we use Cronbach's Alpha to assess a test's internal reliability, we consider the correlations of the scores of all the items with each other to see how similarly they rank order the test takers. When the high-scoring test takers consistently answer items correctly, and the low-scoring test takers consistently answer items incorrectly, Cronbach's Alpha will be high. When Cronbach's Alpha is high, each of the items have high positive correlations with each other, which means they provide similar rank ordering of most proficient to least proficient test takers. Once we have a better conceptual understanding of Cronbach's Alpha, we will explore its mathematical formula and discuss it in more detail in Chapter 12.

The reliability of the scores for the fifty students who took the Grammar Tense Test depends on the correlations among the scores of all twenty-five items. However, to help us better understand the concept of reliability, we will only consider the correlations among items 21, 22, 23, and 24. We chose these four items because items 21, 23, and 24 had good PBs (moderate to high positive), and Item 22 had the worst PB (high negative) of all the test items. This will make it possible for us to compare the effects of items with good and bad PBs on the reliability of a set of assessment scores. We can see these correlations in Table 8.4.

TABLE 8.4

Correlations among items of the Grammar Tense Test.

	Item 21	Item 22	Item 23	Item 24
Item 21	1.00	-.56	.22	.14
Item 22	**-.56**	1.00	**-.22**	**-.27**
Item 23	.22	-.22	1.00	.18
Item 24	.14	-.27	.18	1.00

We can see the correlation between two items by finding the value in Table 8.4 where a column and a row meet. For example, the correlation between Item 21 and Item 22 is –.56. Actually we see this value twice in the table, once when we see where the column and the row meet and once when we see where the row and the column meet. We can also see that, unsurprisingly, the scores on each item correlate perfectly with themselves. All values on the diagonal from the top left to the bottom right are 1.00. We can see that with the exception of the correlations between Item 22 and the other item scores, all correlations are positive and either near or above .20. This means that items 21, 23, and 24 are reasonably consistent in their measurement. They rank order test takers in a similar manner. Item 22, on the other hand, takes away from the consistency of the scores. It rank orders test takers completely differently than the other items. Its negative values indicate that students who got high scores on the other items got low scores on Item 22, and students who got low scores on the other items got high scores on Item 22. As a result, Item 22 lowers the reliability of the test scores. For a set of highly reliable test scores, we would see all high positive correlations in the table.

This discussion of internal reliability for NRTs, where we measure the consistency of item scores by correlating them, also applies to test-retest and parallel forms reliability. The difference is that we correlate scores across two test administrations in the test-retest approach and across different forms of a test in the parallel forms test. High positive correlations indicate score reliability across the test administrations or test forms.

Interpreting Cronbach's Alpha and Other Reliability Estimates

We interpret Cronbach's Alpha to indicate the amount of variance in the scores that is consistent. We estimate consistent score variance by considering how much of the scores' differences for all the items correlate. Cronbach's Alpha, like other reliability estimates, can be as low as .00, meaning the test is not reliable at all (no positive pattern of correlation among the items), and as high as 1.00, meaning the test is completely reliable (a perfect pattern of positive correlation among the items) for the test takers. An appropriate reliability depends on the test context. In high-stakes contexts, reliabilities should be near .90 or higher. In low-stakes contexts, we might be satisfied with values near .70 or higher.

A reliability of .70 indicates that 70 percent of the score variance is consistent in separating the more and less proficient test takers. Importantly, we need to remember that a reliability estimate does not indicate what we are measuring. It only tells us how consistently we are measuring something. This is why we always use content analysis (which will help us to know what we are measuring) along with statistical analysis to help ensure that we are assessing our targeted construct.

Cronbach's Alpha for the Grammar Tense Test

We will now consider the reliability of the Grammar Tense Test scores.

 See Appendix 8B for how to calculate Cronbach's Alpha's reliability for the Grammar Tense Test scores.

For our twenty-five-item test, our reliability estimate is .50 for the fifty test takers' scores. This suggests that only 50 percent of the differences in the scores relate to grammar tense knowledge. Half of the differences in scores relates to something else, such as guessing, test-taking strategies, tricky items, or unclear answers. We should not be surprised to see this low reliability estimate, since three items (3, 7, and 22) had negative PBs, and many items had poor IFs.

Following typical scoring procedures, we excluded the three items with negative PBs and rescored the test. This revised scoring increased the reliability to .66, which is much better, although we still have not reached our target of .70 for a low-stakes assessment.

What to Consider When Using Cronbach's Alpha

When we use Cronbach's Alpha, we need to consider some assumptions about this approach. First, we assume that every item measures the same (or similar) construct. Cronbach's Alpha estimates the consistency of the items for measuring an ability. If the items measure different abilities, the scores for each item will not be consistent. One test taker may have more ability on a skill measured by one item, while another may have more ability on a skill measured by another. This difference will decrease the estimate of reliability.

Second, scores on each item must be independent of scores on another. If getting one item correct increases the chances of getting another right or wrong, we cannot use this approach. Finally, when we use Cronbach's Alpha, we assume that each item is equally difficult and that about half of our test takers get it right and half get it wrong. When we have very high IFs (near or above .90) or very low IFs (near or below .10), our reliability estimates will indicate that our test is less consistent than it actually is.

Ways to Increase the Reliability of Test Scores

Given the importance of reliable test scores, we will conclude this section by discussing how to increase reliability of test scores. We have discussed IFs and PBs, two important statistics for helping judge an item's effectiveness. First, by using items with PBs above .30 and IFs between .30 and .70, we increase our chances of having sufficiently reliable test scores.

Second, having more items increases the reliability of test scores. More items leads to increased opportunities for more proficient test takers to outperform less proficient test takers. Let's consider an MC test with only one item. Based on the results, it would be difficult to rank order a group of test takers, since we would only have two possible scores, zero or one, and luck may have a huge impact on the results. On the other hand, if we have 100 items, we have many possible scores for ranking test takers, and luck should not be a big factor.

Third, it is easier to measure a simple construct reliably than a complex one. For instance, we can usually be more consistent in measuring test takers' ability to determine whether to use a period or a question mark than in judging their overall speaking abilities.

Finally, it is easier to get high reliability when we have test takers with a wide range of proficiencies. When test takers have similar ability levels, they may get the same (number of) items right, making it difficult to rank order them according to proficiency. While we usually are not able to change our test takers' proficiency, we should remember this principle when we consider the reliability of a set of scores for particular test takers.

Conclusion

In this chapter, we discussed how we can use IFs and PBs to help evaluate the effectiveness of dichotomously scored test items after we have administered a test. We saw that we can use these statistics together with content analysis to help us increase the quality of our tests. We also discussed how we can use reliability to evaluate the overall effectiveness of test items to separate more and less proficient test takers.

At the beginning of the chapter, we learned about a team of language teachers who created an assessment. The team was very happy when the changes they made based on information from the IFs, PBs, and content analysis from the pilot data resulted in a more useful test. They discovered that they could learn and use these techniques, which are helpful for understanding and increasing the quality of language assessments.

Questions for Discussion

8.1 Discuss why you think Item 22 on the Grammar Tense Test (see Example 8.1) is not effective at separating more and less proficient test takers who took the test on grammar tense knowledge.
    8.1.1 Based on a content analysis, why do you think Item 22 has a negative PB?
    8.1.2 Would you use the scores on Item 22 to place test takers into ESL classes? Why or why not?
    8.1.3 Revise Item 22 with the aim of making it more effective.
    8.1.4 Provide justification for the changes that you would make to the item.

8.2 Assume your group will explain what IF, correlation, and PBs are to a group of high school language teachers who need to explain these concepts to parents.
    8.2.1 Explain the logic that underlies each of the three concepts.
    8.2.2 Explain how language experts can use these three concepts to help evaluate and increase the effectiveness of dichotomously scored NRTs.

Exercises

8.1 Revise items 2, 3, 7, and 13 of the Grammar Tense Test (all items are available in the online materials).
    8.1.1 Use content analysis, IFs, and PBs to guide item revision.
    8.1.2 Provide justification for any changes that you make.

8.2 Based on the analyses discussed in this chapter, the teachers decided to make some changes to the scoring when they administered the Grammar Tense Test the following year to a different group of students. They excluded items 3 and 7 and corrected the scoring key for Item 22 from option c to d. They kept the same numbering, so they could easily compare the IFs and PBs to the previous year's results. The revised 23-item test does not have an Item 3 or an Item 7. Use Excel to analyze the results of this test administration. Use the Revised Grammar Tense Test data (online materials: ISLA.Ex.8.2).
    8.2.1 Calculate the IFs.
    8.2.2 Calculate the PBs.
    8.2.3 Use the IFs, PBs, and a content analysis to evaluate the items. Identify the five best items and the five worst items. Justify your decisions.
    8.2.4 Calculate Cronbach's Alpha and indicate whether or not the test scores are sufficiently reliable for placing these test takers into ESL classes. Provide justification for your decision.

Additional Resources

Bachman, L. F. (2004). *Statistical Analyses for Language Assessment*. Cambridge University Press.
The book provides a comprehensive introduction to how to use statistics to analyze language tests, including PBs, IFs, and Cronbach's Alpha. It provides detailed examples and explanations for how to analyze both criterion-referenced tests (CRTs) and NRTs, at both the item and test levels.

Green, R. (2013). *Statistical Analyses for Language Testers*. Palgrave Macmillan.
The first four chapters of this book introduce readers to entering data into various software packages; checking and correcting data files; item-level analysis, including IF and PBs; and descriptive statistics. It comes with data files that readers can use to practice analyzing language tests.

Appendix 8A Calculating IFs and PBs in Excel

This appendix will take us through the steps for calculating IFs and PBs in Excel. There is also an online video that demonstrates the steps. We will use the Grammar Tense Test scored data (Online materials: ISLA.Ap.8) to complete the activity.

1. Open the Excel data file ISLA.Ap.8.
2. Do the following to calculate the IFs:

   a. Select cell C54 and type:

   =AVERAGE(C3:C52)

   Press Enter. This command asks for the mean of the scores from C3 to C52. The IF of .30 for the first item should appear in the cell.

   b. Select cell C54. Then put the mouse over the bottom right corner of the cell until the cursor becomes a small black cross. Click and hold down while dragging the mouse to the right until you have selected all the cells in this row up to and including cell AA54, which is the column for the last item. Release the mouse button. The IFs for the other twenty-four items should appear.

3. We will now use Excel to correlate the scores on each item to the total scores on the test. This will give us a PB for each item. Do the following to calculate the PBs:

   a. Select cell C55 and type:

   =PEARSON(C3:C52,$AB$3:$AB$52)

   Then press Enter. The value .24 should appear in the cell. This command requests the use of a Pearson correlation between column C (the scores for item 1) and column AB (the total score) for rows 3 to 52 (all fifty test takers). The four $ symbols prepare us for the next step by telling Excel to correlate other columns to Column AB (the total score) too.

   b. Select cell C55. Then put the mouse over the bottom right corner of the cell until the cursor becomes a small black cross. Click and hold down while dragging the mouse to the right until you have selected all the cells in this row up to and including cell AA55, which is the column for the last item. Release the mouse button. The PBs for the other twenty-four items should appear.

   c. Check the IF values and the PB values. The IFs should be between 0.00 and 1.00, and the PBs should be between −1.00 and 1.00. If any values fall outside of this range, there is an error in the calculations. Note, however, that if all test takers got an item right or all test takers got an item wrong, the PB value for the item will indicate an error message, because it is not possible to calculate a correlation with no score variance. When an error message appears, we need to insert a 0.00 into the cell.

Appendix 8B Calculating Cronbach's Alpha in Excel

This appendix will take readers through the steps for calculating Cronbach's Alpha reliability with Excel. There are online videos that demonstrate how to complete this activity. We will use the Grammar Tense Test data (online materials ISLA.Ap.8) to complete the activity. We will calculate and discuss the formula for Cronbach's Alpha in Chapter 12, but we will use the following shortcut formula for calculating Cronbach's Alpha (Brown, 2022):

$$Cronbach's\ Alpha = \frac{Number\ of\ items}{Number\ of\ items - 1}\left(1 - \frac{Sum\ of\ the\ item\ variances}{Total\ score\ variance}\right)$$

1. Open the Excel data file ISLA.Ap.8.
2. Complete the following steps to calculate Cronbach's Alpha:

   a. Do the following to calculate the variance for Item 1.
      Select cell C56 and type:

      =VAR.P(C3:C52)

      Press Enter. The variance of .21 for the first item should appear.

   b. Do the following to calculate the item variance for items 2 to 25 and the total score variance:

      Select cell C56. Then put the mouse over the bottom right corner of the cell until the cursor becomes a small black cross. Click and hold down while dragging the mouse to the right until you have selected all the cells in this row up to and including cell AB56, which is the total score column. Release the mouse button. The twenty-six cells from column C (the first item) to AB (the total score) in this row should be active, and the variances for the other twenty-four items and the total score should appear.

   c. Do the following to sum the variances of the twenty-five items:
      Select cell C57 and type:

      =SUM(C56:AA56)

      Press Enter. This will give the sum of the item variances, which is 3.93 in this data set.

   d. For the remaining steps, you can use Excel or a calculator. We will use Excel, but you may find it easier to use a (cell phone) calculator.
      Do the following to divide the sum of the item variance by the total score variance.
      Select cell C58 and type:

      =C57/AB56

      Press Enter. This tells Excel to divide cell C57, which is the sum of the item variances, by cell AB56, which is the total score variance. You should get a value of 0.52.

   e. Subtract the value in d (0.52) from 1.
      Select cell C59 and type:

      =1-C58

Press Enter. This tells Excel to subtract the contents of cell C58, which is .52, from 1. The value should be 0.48.

f. Divide the number of items on the test by the number of items on the test minus 1. Since the Grammar Tense Test has twenty-five items, divide 25 by 24.
Select cell C60 and type:

=25/24

Press Enter. You should get a value of 1.04.

g. Multiply the values from steps e and f.
Select cell C61 and type:

=C59*C60

Press Enter. You should get a value of .50. The reliability on the Grammar Tense Test is .50.

CHAPTER 9

Identifying the Masters: Evaluating Criterion-Referenced Assessments

FIGURE 9.1 A panel of teachers setting standards for an assessment.
Source: SDI Productions/E+/Getty Images.

One day, I had a graduate student instructor who came to my office to ask me an assessment question. The instructor was excited that most students had gotten high scores on the semester summative assessment. The instructor had created the assessment based on the course objectives and materials and was excited to see how effective it would be. Unfortunately, the reliability estimate was very low. While we were talking, I discovered that the instructor had used a norm-referenced test (NRT) approach to assessing reliability (Cronbach's Alpha). We looked at the test scores together and discovered that most students had gotten high scores, while a few had very low scores.

Time to Think 9.1

In the story you have just read, the teacher used an NRT approach for assessing reliability. Why was this a problem and what type of approach should the teacher have used?

Introduction

As we learned in Chapter 2, we use criterion-referenced tests (CRTs) and NRTs for different purposes. The aim of NRTs is to help us rank order test takers, so we can select the ones with the highest language proficiency. On the other hand, we use CRTs to determine whether or not test takers have particular language knowledge or have mastered language proficiency criteria. We use CRTs in many situations, such as to determine whether or not students have achieved language course objectives, to place test takers into appropriate language level courses, and to identify workers who have sufficient language skills to be successful in a particular job. In each of these situations, we need to determine what language knowledge test takers have or what test takers can do with the language and at what criterion level (Sawaki, 2016).

In the story at the beginning of the chapter, an instructor incorrectly used an NRT framework to determine the reliability of scores for a CRT. The instructor did not want to rank order test takers in this situation. Instead, the instructor wanted to determine whether or not the students had particular language knowledge or ability. In this CRT situation, using an NRT will not give a good indication of the test's effectiveness. In this chapter, we will discuss appropriate uses of CRTs and how to evaluate them. We will discover that we can rely on some of the knowledge we learned about NRTs, but because we use CRTs and NRTs for different purposes, we will also need to gain knowledge specific to CRTs. To help us understand CRT concepts, we will discuss the use of Vocabulary Test 1 in an English as a Second Language (ESL) classroom setting for assessing vocabulary achievement.

We will begin this chapter by learning about a language program and a vocabulary assessment that instructors used in this program. We will use the vocabulary test, Vocabulary Test 1, as an example of a CRT throughout the chapter. Next, we will discuss how we use content analysis to help us analyze, select, or create items for a CRT. After that, we will discuss how to identify a score that appropriately separates test takers who show mastery of the criterion from those who do not. We will then discuss how we can use statistics to help analyze, select, or create items for CRTs. After we have discussed important content and statistical procedures for analyzing, selecting, and creating items for CRTs, we will use this knowledge to analyze Vocabulary Test 1. Finally, we will discuss dependability and calculate it for our Vocabulary Test 1 test scores.

Vocabulary Test 1

We will consider a real example of a midterm vocabulary test to help us understand how to determine whether or not students have mastery over certain language skills. A university in the United States offers an oral communication English as a second language course to students who need language support when they begin their studies at an English-medium university. Each semester there are multiple classes, and each has about fifteen students. One course objective is for students to be able to recognize and understand academic vocabulary and short phrases that they encounter in the course. The students use a book and videos that include communicative activities to help them learn how people use the vocabulary in real-world contexts. The teachers do not provide the students with a list of these important vocabulary items, because this may result in the students focusing only on lists of words and ignoring others. Instead, they introduce important vocabulary during class activities and encourage students to learn them.

Teachers who had taught the class followed the principles in Chapters 3, 4, 6, and 7 to create a multiple-choice (MC) vocabulary test. Their aim was to determine whether or not students had sufficient mastery of the academic vocabulary and to motivate them to study it. They chose to use an MC item type because the vocabulary objective was recognition and understanding, and the students were all familiar with this test format. Example 9.1 presents four of the twenty-five items in Vocabulary Test 1. The full test is in the online materials accompanying this book.

Example 9.1 Items 1, 2, 24, and 25 of Vocabulary Test 1.

Based on the materials you studied in the class, select the one best vocabulary option to complete the sentence. Circle either a, b, c, or d.

1. Usually people use _____ to indicate a question.

    a. eye contact   b. head movements   c. inflection   d. voice fillers

2. You can guess how someone feels by the _____ that the person uses.

    a. idioms   b. repetition   c. synonym   d. tone

24. The new international student wasn't quite sure how to _____ in with American students.

    a. blend   b. engage   c. participate   d. work

25. While working on the group project, I noticed that Sam was _____ many of my ideas from the final draft.

    a. excluding   b. leaving   c. preparing   d. taking

Time to Think 9.2

What do you think are some strengths and weaknesses of criterion-referenced formative assessments, like Vocabulary Test 1?

Content Analysis for CRTs

We can use the same guidelines for judging the content effectiveness of CRT items as we do for NRT items. We discussed these considerations in Chapter 6 and saw examples of their application in Chapters 7 and 8. Like NRTs, content analysis for CRTs focuses on judgments of how effectively the input (when we have comprehension tests) and items measure the targeted test construct. Because we define our construct as a criterion for CRTs, we create and analyze our items by considering each criterion or achievement objective. In high-stakes assessments, we provide judges with detailed guidelines to evaluate the content of each item and the test format. In low-stakes contexts, such as classroom settings, we usually rely on systematic teacher judgments of each item.

Judging the Test Format, Overall Construct Representation, and Relationship among Items

One approach to judging the content of CRT items is for judges to begin by considering the test format, overall construct representation, and relationship among the items. Next, they can evaluate each item individually. Guidelines 9.1 presents a rating scale for judging a CRT with selected response items.

Guidelines 9.1 Rating scale for judging a CRT with selected response items.

Instructions:
1. Judge how appropriate you think the test format (multiple-choice for this test) is for the test takers. Will it be unfair or unclear for any of the test takers?
2. Judge the overall test's construct representation: how well it assesses all aspects of the construct as defined by the criteria or course objectives. List any aspect of the construct/objective that you think the test does not sufficiently assess in the comments.
3. Consider whether information on one item could lead to success on another.

	Strongly disagree	Disagree	Agree	Strongly agree
A. The item format is appropriate for this group of test takers.	1	2	3	4
Comments				
B. The items measure all aspects of the construct.	1	2	3	4
Comments (please mention what aspects of the construct the items do not measure or aspects that they measure which they should not)				
C. Information from one item does not lead to success on another item.	1	2	3	4
Comments (please mention which items affect each other and how)				

We can use the rating scale in Guidelines 9.1 to judge the test format, overall construct representation, and relationship among the items of Vocabulary Test 1. Let's begin with question A. The item format is probably appropriate. All of the students in the classes have taken MC tests with four options, and the targeted construct relates to understanding vocabulary when listening to a classroom lecture rather than the ability to produce them in spoken or written form. As we learned in Chapter 7, MC items are appropriate for assessing receptive knowledge. We cannot answer question B with the information we have. To judge how well items measure all aspects of the construct, we would need to see the course objectives and the materials that instructors teach in the course. To answer question C, we look to see if any vocabulary words in an item might help students answer another item correctly.

> **Time to Think 9.3**
>
> Look at the four items from Vocabulary Test 1 in Example 9.1. Would any information from an item help students to answer another item correctly? Defend your answer.

Evaluating Item Content

After we have judged the test format, overall construct representation, and relationship among the items, we evaluate each item individually. Guidelines 9.2 provides a rating scale for this purpose.

Guidelines 9.2 Rating scale for judging MC item content on CRTs.

Instructions:
1. Write the item number in the space next to Item.
2. Write the most relevant criterion in the space next to Relevant criterion/objective if there is more than one criterion or objective.
3. Judge the item number you wrote in 1 for each of the selected response guidelines and provide comments for why you gave each rating.

Item _____ Relevant criterion/objective _____

	Not at all	Somewhat	Well	Very well
1. The content of the item aligns with the criteria.	1	2	3	4
Comments				
2. The item is straightforward.	1	2	3	4
Comments				
3. Options are syntactically parallel, similar in length, and concise.	1	2	3	4
Comments				
4. Options follow an appropriate systematic order.	1	2	3	4
Comments				
5. Items have only one best answer, with other options reasonable.	1	2	3	4
Comments				

> **Time to Think 9.4**
>
> Use the rating scale in Guidelines 9.2 to evaluate items 1 and 2 of Vocabulary Test 1 in Example 9.1.
>
> What was the most challenging thing about evaluating these two items?

As we can see in Guidelines 9.1 and 9.2, the rating lists for CRTs cover the same information as the ones for NRTs (see Guidelines 7.2). The major difference in the process is the way the judges rate how well the items measure the construct. When judging how well an item measures a criterion for a CRT, the judge needs to pay attention to each one and make sure that the items align with at least one of them. An important consideration in this judgment is that the difficulty of the item aligns with the course expectations. It is also important that judges consider how well the test measures all aspects of the criteria. In a classroom setting, the judges need to be familiar with the course objectives and materials to make these judgments successfully.

Importantly, as Brown and Hudson (2002) point out, content analysis for CRTs is more central to a test's effectiveness than it is for an NRT. Because the aim of an NRT is to rank order test takers on their language abilities, we can rely to a great degree on statistical analysis. Assuming the content of an item looks like it would reasonably assess the targeted construct, we can generally trust PB estimates to help us identify items that effectively rank order test takers on NRTs. With CRTs, we must depend less on statistics and more on careful judgment of the content of the item and how well the content appears to assess the construct.

Selecting Content Judges

When we use CRTs to assess how well students meet course objectives, we have to choose our content judges carefully. On one hand, we want to involve instructors who are currently teaching the course. They know the course objectives and the teaching materials and methods they use to achieve these aims. We also want them to feel involved in the assessment process. Their involvement helps to ensure they will support the use of the test and encourage and prepare their students appropriately. On the other hand, when we involve current teachers, we may unintentionally narrow the curriculum. When teachers know what items will be on an assessment, they may prepare their students to answer the items without them understanding the targeted concepts. Moreover, since there is almost never enough time for a test to measure every aspect of language important to a course, teachers may teach only information which focuses on specific language knowledge that they know will be on the test and ignore other equally important information.

When we make decisions about who should be our content judges or item writers for CRTs in classroom contexts, we need to consider the stakes of the test, our available resources, and the attitudes of the teachers toward the assessments. For higher-stakes assessments, we should increasingly consider excluding current teachers as content judges or item writers. In such cases, when available, teachers who have previously taught the course may take on this role. We may also be able to have two forms of an assessment where teachers judge or create a form that they will not use for their students. We also need to consider the teachers' attitudes toward the test. When we do not include teachers in making judgments about test items for their students, we may unintentionally create a feeling of mistrust. In such situations, it may be best to discuss this concern with them and trust that they will teach the course content without focusing on items they know are on the test.

Standard Setting

After we have done our best to ensure appropriate content for a test, we need to set or evaluate a particular criterion for our assessment purpose. A **cut score** is the score that determines whether or not a test taker passes or fails a CRT. We assign passing scores to test takers who score at or above the cut score and failing scores to ones who score below it. We interpret passing scores as indications that test takers have sufficient mastery of the target language knowledge or ability criteria. Cut scores provide test takers with a goal that does not depend on how others perform on the assessment.

We refer to the process of setting cut scores as **standard setting** (Davies et al., 1999). Standard setting approaches rely on a panel of experts who make judgments about appropriate cut scores. This means that it is important to select appropriate individuals for this purpose. Each context will require a different set of experts, and the ones we choose are critical to standard setting success. For classroom settings, such as for a summative vocabulary test, a panel of judges may be two or three of the course instructors. For high-stakes assessments, the panel may include ten or more language, assessment, and content experts. For example, we may include Japanese teachers, assessment experts, and successful Japanese police officers when setting language standards for becoming a Japanese police officer.

Test-centered and test-taker-centered are two general approaches for setting cut scores in standard setting studies. In **test-centered approaches**, a panel of experts judge the difficulty of the test input and items. The experts' aim is to determine which items a minimally competent test taker could answer correctly. We define a minimally competent test taker as a test taker who has the lowest level of ability necessary in order for us to consider that person acceptably proficient. In **test-taker-centered approaches**, a panel of expert judges who are familiar with the test takers' ability levels select test takers that they believe do and do not have sufficient language knowledge or ability to meet the targeted criteria. Then, they create the cut score from the score that best separates these two groups of test takers (Shulruf, 2018).

The Angoff Method

The Angoff (1971) method is a popular test-centered approach to standard setting. Its popularity comes from its long history, its simplicity, and its appropriateness for various contexts. It is appropriate both when we want to assess language proficiency (e.g., reading comprehension) or language knowledge (e.g., mastery of specific vocabulary that we teach in a course).

When we use the Angoff method, we begin by giving expert judges our test and asking them to estimate the chances that a minimally competent test taker would respond to each item correctly. In contexts where the experts may not have a clear idea about the ability of a minimally competent test taker, the panel can discuss their views with the aim of arriving at general agreement. For classroom settings, teachers can rely on the course objectives and their experience teaching the course when making their judgments. Next, the expert judges go through the items one at a time and write a value between 0 and 100 percent for each. A value of 100 percent indicates that the judge believes a minimally competent test taker would have a 100 percent chance of answering an item correctly. After a judge has provided an estimate for each item, we average the percentages for all of the items. If we have more than one judge, we average the judges' average percentages for all test items to get the cut score.

The cut score from the Angoff method is in the form of a percentage correct for the assessment (between 0 and 100 percent). When using the Angoff method, having multiple expert judges usually results in more accurate cut scores. However, this method can be effective in low-stakes classroom assessments even when only the course instructor is available to be an expert judge.

We will now discuss how a course coordinator used the Angoff method to set a cut score for Vocabulary Test 1. The first step was to select an appropriate panel of judges. Since Vocabulary Test 1 is a low-stakes classroom assessment, one teacher who was also involved in curriculum development judged the percentage chance that a minimally competent test taker should be able to answer each item successfully. We can see the judge's responses in Table 9.1.

We would expect a student with no knowledge to have about a 25 percent chance of answering a four-option MC item correctly, and the judge did not give any ratings below 25 percent. When we sum the percentages for the twenty-five items, we get 1,620. We then divide this number by 25 (the number of items) to get a value of 64.8 percent. We can calculate the raw cut score by multiplying 25 by 64.8 percent. Our result is 16.20, so we can decide to set our cut score at 16 (about 65 percent). We classify students who get 16 or higher as masters, and ones who get 15 or lower as non-masters.

The Contrasting Groups Method

The **contrasting groups method** is a popular test-taker-centered approach to setting cut scores (Livingston & Zieky, 1982). The first step in the contrasting groups method is for a panel of expert judges to identify a group that they believe to be masters of the criterion and another that they believe to be non-masters. In a classroom setting, teachers often identify the master group based on successful completion of a course of study. This group may not be all of the students who finished a class. Rather, it is usually students that the teachers judge to have completed the course successfully. The other group includes students that the teachers judge as not having mastered the language knowledge or ability criterion. In a classroom setting, this is often students who unsuccessfully finish a course or ones who have not taken the class, yet.

In the second step, the two contrasting groups take the test, and we place the cut score at the score where most of the masters would pass and most of the non-masters would fail. Depending on whether it is better to make the error of passing non-masters or that of failing masters, we can adjust the cut score slightly up or down. For instance, in classroom situations, we may be willing to allow a student who may not be completely ready for the next class level to pass the test and try the next class. In this case, we would set the cut score toward the bottom of where the teachers judged the separation between masters and non-masters. On the other hand, in situations where passing a test taker who does not have enough language knowledge or ability could lead to a serious problem, we may set the cut scores a little higher. An example would be a test for airline pilots, who need to speak a certain language to communicate successfully with other pilots and air traffic controllers.

TABLE 9.1

A teacher's judgment of the percentage chance that a minimally competent student would have of answering an item correctly.

Item	%
1	80
2	90
3	90
4	80
5	90
6	70
7	60
8	70
9	60
10	40
11	50
12	90
13	40
14	60
15	50
16	80
17	40
18	80
19	50
20	70
21	60
22	50
23	90
24	40
25	40

> **Time to Think 9.5**
>
> Think of a context where you have used or taken a CRT. Do you think the Angoff method or contrasting groups method would be more appropriate for this context? Justify your answer.

Multiple Cut Scores

In some contexts, CRTs need more than one cut score. For instance, we might want to use Vocabulary Test 1 to help us assign vocabulary grades to students, and we might have three grading categories: advanced, proficient, and developing. When we have more than two score categorizations, we need more than one cut score. In fact, we need one less cut score than score categorizations (for example, four cut scores for five categorizations). We use the same procedures as when we use one cut score. The difference is that we need to repeat the process for each cut score.

To create advanced, proficient, and developing categorizations for Vocabulary Test 1, we could use the Angoff method twice. For setting the first cut score, we would have the judges estimate the percentage chance that students that they consider minimally proficient could answer each item correctly. We would use that data to set the cut score between proficient and developing. Then, we would have the judges estimate the percentage chance for students that they consider minimally advanced answering each item correctly. We could use this data to help set the cut score between proficient and advanced.

Descriptive Statistics

When we use CRTs, we usually report three descriptive statistics: the mean, median, and mastery rate. We have already discussed the mean in Chapter 7. In the next sections, we will consider the median and mastery rate.

The Median

When we report descriptive statistics for CRTs, we often report the mean as we do with NRTs. However, because CRTs may not have a normal distribution, we also report a statistic that we refer to as the **median**. When we line up the scores from highest to lowest, the median is the score at the midpoint.

We can see the scores for the highest thirteen test takers on Vocabulary Test 1 in Table 9.2. Importantly, these are not the first thirteen test takers. These are the thirteen with the highest scores, and we have ordered them from highest to lowest. To calculate the median, we find the score at the midpoint, which is 20 (the seventh score from both the top and bottom). Note that if we have an even number of test takers, our median will be halfway between the two middle test takers.

Mastery Rate

We also report the cut score along with the **mastery rate**, which is the percentage of test takers who pass the test. For Vocabulary Test 1, twenty-nine of the fifty-four test takers got scores of 16 (the cut score) or higher. To calculate the mastery rate, we divide 29 by 54 to arrive

TABLE 9.2

Scores of the thirteen most proficient test takers on Vocabulary Test 1.

Name	Total score
Vahit	23
Luca	22
Jongsu	21
Chen	20
Marisa	20
Jiwoo	20
Mohamed	20
Emiliano	19
Nova	19
Arthur	19
Abubakar	19
Nicholas	19
Alexis	19

Note: We considered thirteen scores to avoid dividing among students who got the same score (19) on the test.

at a mastery rate of 54 percent. This means that 54 percent of our students in the oral communication class demonstrated mastery of the vocabulary items studied in the first half of the course.

 See Appendix 9A for how to use Excel to calculate the median and mastery rate for Vocabulary Test 1.

Assuming the content analysis indicated that the items were at an appropriate difficulty level, we would probably consider this as a low mastery rate in most classroom contexts. Depending on how important vocabulary development is, we may decide to encourage students and instructors to place more emphasis on vocabulary in the second half of the semester.

Statistical Item Analysis

In addition to content analysis, we can use statistical techniques to help us evaluate the effectiveness of CRT items for a particular test. We usually use two item-level statistics for this purpose: item facility (IF) and the B-Index.

Item Facility

We calculate IF for CRTs in the same way as for NRTs. For each item, we sum the number of correct responses and divide by the number of test takers. IFs range from 0.0 (no test takers answered correctly) to 1.00 (all test takers answered correctly). However, for CRTs, we do not have any targets or guidelines for IFs. For CRTs, we do not aim to have half of the test takers respond to items correctly, and we do not expect a normal score distribution as we do for NRTs. We use IFs to help us understand which aspects of our constructs test takers best understand. When items have high IFs for classroom contexts, we have an indication that students have mastered the content the item measures.

The B-Index

We use the **B-Index** to help determine how well scores on individual items contribute to the master vs. non-master decision on the test. The B-Index compares the IFs of masters and non-masters. For each item, we compare the IF for test takers who showed mastery on the test with the IF for test takers who did not. Then, to obtain the B-Index, we subtract the IF of the test takers who did not show mastery from the IF of those who did.

 See Appendix 9B for how to calculate the B-Index for Vocabulary Test 1.

A B-Index can be a number between –1.00 and 1.00, the same range as point-biserials (PBs). Brown and Hudson (2002) indicate that items with B-Indexes of .20 and higher can be appropriate for CRTs. Items with negative B-Indexes are problematic. However, Brown and Hudson (2002) emphasize that the assessment context, the relative importance of the content of an item, and IFs are also important when judging an item's effectiveness.

The logic underlying the B-Index is that test takers who show mastery on a test will correctly answer effective items, while those who do not show mastery will incorrectly answer effective items. For Vocabulary Test 1, the logic would be that students who studied vocabulary diligently would demonstrate test mastery and would answer effective vocabulary items correctly. On the other hand, less diligent students would not demonstrate test mastery and would answer effective items incorrectly.

Using Content Analysis and Statistical Analysis to Judge Item Quality

When we judge the effectiveness of a CRT item, we consider its content, IF, and B-Index. In this section, we will judge items 25 and 2 of Vocabulary Test 1. We can see the item numbers, the answer key, IFs for masters and non-masters, and the B-Index for Vocabulary Test 1 in Table 9.3.

When we judge the effectiveness of a CRT item, we can begin by looking at the B-Index. Seventeen of the twenty-five items have a B-Index above 0.20 (3, 4, 5, 6, 8, 9, 11, 12, 13, 15, 17, 19, 20, 21, 22, 23, 24), which suggests that they function effectively. Of the other eight, Item 25 is the one that appears the most problematic. It has a B-Index of –.18, which indicates that more students who answered the item incorrectly showed mastery on the test than students who answered the item correctly.

TABLE 9.3

Item numbers, answer key, IFs for masters and non-masters, and B-Index for Vocabulary Test 1.

Item	1	2	3	4	5	6	7	8	9	10	11	12	13	14	15	16	17	18	19	20	21	22	23	24	25
Key	d	d	b	c	c	a	c	a	b	c	b	b	c	a	b	a	d	b	d	a	a	a	b	a	d
IF	.44	1.0	.85	.52	.80	.74	.50	.80	.54	.35	.50	.89	.35	.70	.56	.78	.22	.93	.57	.61	.69	.65	.87	.39	.43
IF masters	.48	1.0	.97	.69	.93	.97	.55	.90	.72	.41	.66	1.0	.45	.79	.66	.79	.34	.97	.72	.76	.86	.86	1.0	.59	.34
IF non-masters	.40	1.0	.72	.32	.64	.48	.44	.68	.32	.28	.32	.76	.24	.60	.44	.76	.08	.88	.40	.44	.48	.40	.72	.16	.52
B-Index	.08	.00	.25	.37	.29	.49	.11	.22	.40	.13	.34	.24	.21	.19	.22	.03	.26	.09	.32	.32	.38	.46	.28	.43	−.18

When we look at a content analysis of this item (see Example 9.1 for the item and Guidelines 9.2 for the content analysis rating scale), we might judge that the content of the item aligns with the criteria. The item stem came almost directly from an activity in the textbook, and all of the vocabulary were ones teachers expected students to know. The item is at an appropriate difficulty level (Question 1). The item appears to be straightforward, because it does not seem like it contains any tricks (Question 2). The options are all syntactically parallel (verb + ing) (Question 3). The options follow a systematic order, as they are in alphabetical order (Question 4). As a result, for this item, we would provide ratings of 4 out of 4 on the rating scale for Questions 1–4. However, Question 5 would get a low rating. Two of the four options may be correct. It appears that options *d* and *a* are both possible. We could consider both *excluding* and *taking* as correct. Given that both the content and statistical analyses suggest Item 25 is problematic, we should probably not include it in the scoring of this test administration and revise it or remove it for future ones.

We will discuss Item 2 from Vocabulary Test 1 to see how IF can help with an item analysis. The B-Index is .00, meaning that students who showed mastery on the test did not do better or worse on the item than people who did not show mastery on the test. When we look at the item's IF, we discover the reason. All fifty-four test takers answered the item correctly. When all (or almost all) test takers respond correctly (or incorrectly) to an item, there will be no (or little) difference in the IF between masters and non-masters. In such cases, however, we do not immediately determine that the item is poor. Instead, we consider the item content, emphasizing the appropriateness of its difficulty for the context. A content analysis of Item 2 suggests that it is excellent for all five rating criteria. Importantly, the content and difficulty of the item aligns with the course criteria. The judge felt that the word "tone" was a very important word for the students to know, and that the item effectively measured knowledge of this word. As a result, even though the item does not help separate non-masters from masters, we may decide to include it on the test.

Time to Think 9.6

How would you explain what a B-index is to a university teacher who is trying to learn about evaluating CRTs?

Dependability

Dependability refers to how consistent mastery classifications are for CRTs, and is similar to the concept of reliability for NRTs. A dependable CRT consistently identifies the same test takers as masters and other test takers as non-masters of the targeted criterion. Dependability values can range from a low of .00, which means the test is not consistent at all in classifying masters and non-masters, to a high of 1.00, which indicates that the test perfectly classifies masters and non-masters. An appropriate dependability depends on the assessment context. In high-stakes contexts, the dependability values should be near .90 or higher. In low-stakes contexts, like formative classroom assessments, we might be satisfied with values near .70 or higher.

The most common method for calculating dependability for MC (or other dichotomously scored) items in language learning classroom contexts is **test-retest coefficient agreement** (Yan & Fan, 2022). This approach requires the same group of test takers to take the test twice (test-retest: see Chapter 5). We then compare which test takers did and did not show mastery in the two test administrations. When most test takers showing mastery on the first test administration also show mastery on the second, and most who do not show mastery on the first also do not show mastery on the second, the test scores are highly dependable. Since we administered Vocabulary Test 1 to the group of fifty-four test takers only once, we cannot use coefficient agreement to estimate its dependability. However, we will use the results from the first administration, and some hypothetical results from a hypothetical second administration, to demonstrate how we could use the test-retest coefficient agreement approach to calculate dependability for Vocabulary Test 1.

Let's assume that 25 of the 29 test takers who showed mastery on the first administration of Vocabulary Test 1 also showed mastery on the second. Let's also assume that 19 of the 25 who did not show mastery on the first administration of Vocabulary Test 1 also did not show mastery on the second. We can see this hypothetical data in a **contingency table** in Table 9.4. We use a contingency table to examine data that we can group and count across two or more variables. Our contingency table has two variables: mastery and administration number.

TABLE 9.4

Contingency table for mastery and test administration of Vocabulary Test 1.

		First administration of Vocabulary Test 1	
		Mastery	Non-mastery
Second administration of Vocabulary Test 1	Mastery	25	6
	Non-mastery	4	19

To calculate dependability, we add the decisions that were the same for both test administrations: 25 (mastery on both administrations, as shown in the upper left-hand box of the table) + 19 (non-mastery on both administrations, as shown in the lower right-hand box of the table) = 44. Then, we divide this value (44) by the total number of test takers (54) to get a dependability of .81. We should note that 10 of the 54 decisions did not agree. Four test takers showed mastery on the first administration but not the second, as shown in the bottom left-hand box of the table. Six test takers showed mastery on the second administration but not the first, as shown in the upper right-hand box of the table. We can interpret the value of .81 to indicate that we have 81 percent consistency in classification between masters and non-masters across the two test administrations. As this value is above our target of .70 for classroom contexts, we would be happy with this level of dependability.

Conclusion

In this chapter, we explored CRTs. We use CRTs to determine whether or not test takers have mastered language proficiency criteria or knowledge. We often use CRTs in classroom contexts to help us determine whether or not students have mastered course objectives and the materials that teachers present in a course. We discussed content and statistical analysis and how we can use these techniques to evaluate and/or increase the effectiveness of CRTs. We examined two approaches to standard setting: the Angoff method and the contrasting groups method. We concluded by discussing the concept of dependability for CRTs.

This chapter began with a story about an instructor who used an NRT approach to judge an assessment when a CRT approach would have been more appropriate. Unfortunately, this instructor's efforts were not very useful, because it is critical that we use appropriate techniques for judging the effectiveness of an assessment. People with language assessment literacy (LAL), like readers of this book, can be confident that they will not make similar mistakes.

Questions for Discussion

9.1 Imagine that you (and others) are responsible for evaluating a listening CRT for a tenth grade (15–16-year-olds) English as a foreign language (EFL) program. There are five sections of the class, and each has about thirty students. You have to decide on a standard setting method.
    9.1.1 Compare and contrast the Angoff method and the contrasting groups method for standard setting.
    9.1.2 Which of the methods would you use? Provide justification for your decision.

9.2 Why is content analysis more important in CRTs than in NRTs?

9.3 Compare the concepts of dependability and reliability. What are some similarities and differences?

Exercises

9.1 Analyze items 1 and 24 of Vocabulary Test 1. The items are in Example 9.1.
    9.1.1 Use the rating scale for judging a CRT item (Guidelines 9.2) and the statistical information provided in Table 9.3. Although you are not familiar with the curriculum, do your best to judge the content based on the description in the section on Vocabulary Test 1.
    9.1.2 Make a recommendation to keep as is, revise (if so, how), or exclude one or both of the items for future test administrations. Provide justification for your choices.

9.2 Create items for a criterion that is important for your own language learning context. For instance, you might use the objectives of a language course that you have taken or taught.
    9.2.1 Identify the construct that you want to measure.
    9.2.2 Write three items that would measure this ability by following the rating guidelines in Guidelines 9.1 and 9.2.
    9.2.3 Provide a justification of the items and how they measure the targeted criteria.

9.3 Evaluate the effectiveness of Vocabulary Test 2 (online materials: ISLA.VT2.9 and ISLA. Ex.9.3). The context is the same as the one we discussed in the section on Vocabulary Test 1. The cut score on Vocabulary Test 2 is 26 (79 percent).
    9.3.1 Calculate the median and mastery rate for the test scores.
    9.3.2 Calculate the IF and B-Index for each item.
    9.3.3 Use the IF, the B-Index, and the rating scale for judging a selected response item (Guidelines 9.1), and the rating scale for judging a CRT's item content (Guidelines 9.2) to identify the three best items and the three worst items.
    9.3.4 Justify your selection of the six items.

9.3.5 Let's assume that 31 of the 36 test takers who showed mastery on the first administration of Vocabulary Test 2 also showed mastery on a second administration of the same test. Let's also assume that 12 of the 17 who did not show mastery on the first test administration did not show mastery on the second.
  9.3.5.1 Create a contingency table for the data.
  9.3.5.2 What is the dependability of the scores, based on the test-retest coefficient agreement index?
  9.3.5.3 Interpret the meaning of the dependability value.
  9.3.5.4 Is the dependability of the scores sufficient for this context? Why or why not?

Additional Resources

Brown, J. D., & Hudson, T. (2002). *Criterion-Referenced Language Testing.* Cambridge University Press.
This book provides detailed explanations for how to create and analyze CRTs. The authors make the concepts clear by providing detailed examples. They explain statistics in a manner accessible to readers who have little math or statistics backgrounds. Chapter 3 may be of particular interest to language teachers who desire to create CRTs for their students.

Reckase, M. D. (2023). *The Psychometrics of Standard Setting: Connecting Policy and Test Scores.* CRC Press.
This book provides comprehensive coverage of the theory and practice of standard setting. It introduces various standard setting approaches and the relevant information that practitioners need to consider when selecting an appropriate one. It also details how to conduct standard setting in various contexts. This book is appropriate for readers who desire a much deeper understanding of standard setting.

Sawaki, Y. (2016). Norm-referenced vs. criterion-referenced approach to assessment. In D. Tsagari & J. Banerjee (Eds), *Handbook of Second Language Assessment* (pp. 45–60). De Gruyter Mouton.
This book chapter provides an excellent comparison between norm-referenced and criterion-referenced assessment theory and analysis. This chapter would be of particular interest to readers with backgrounds in norm-referenced assessment who want to expand their knowledge of criterion-referenced assessment.

16.3 Criterion Referenced Assessment https://youtu.be/7wm74U6kFtA
In this video, the speaker provides examples to explain how CRTs and NRTs are different. Because it is easily accessible to individuals with limited knowledge of CRTs, it might be a good approach to watch it before reading the chapter.

Appendix 9A Calculating the Median and Mastery Rate in Excel

This appendix will take us through the steps for calculating the median and mastery rate in Excel. We will use the Vocabulary Test 1 data (online materials: ISLA.Ap.9) to complete the activity. The online materials include a video that accompanies these instructions.

1. Open the ISLA.Ap.9 data file.
2. Complete the following steps to calculate the median. Select cell AB62 and type:
   =MEDIAN(AB2:AB55)

9 EVALUATING CRITERION-REFERENCED ASSESSMENTS

Press Enter. The median of 16.5 for the data set should appear. This command tells Excel to calculate the median for rows 2 to 55 (test takers 1 to 54) for column AB, which is the total score column.

3. Do the following to calculate the mastery rate. Note that we will use a cut score of 16.

   a. Select cell AB63 and type:

   =COUNTIFS(AB2:AB55,">=16")

   Press Enter. This tells Excel to count the cells from AB2 to AB55 (the total scores for each test taker) that have values that are greater than or equal to 16. The value of 29 should appear in the cell, indicating that 29 of the test takers got scores of 16 or higher.

   b. Select cell AB64 and type:

   =AB63/54*100

   Press Enter. This command tells Excel to divide the number of masters as shown in cell AB63 (29) by the total number of test takers (54). We multiply the value by 100 to convert it from a proportion to a percentage. You should see the mastery rate of 53.70 in cell AB64. This means that 53.70 percent of test takers showed mastery on the test.

Appendix 9B Calculating the B-Index in Excel

This appendix will take us through the steps for calculating the B-Index in Excel. We will use the Vocabulary Test 1 data (online materials: ISLA.Ap.9) to complete the activity.

1. Open the ISLA.Ap.9 data file.
2. Use the Excel sort function to sort the test takers by their total scores, from highest to lowest.

   a. Do the following to highlight the data that you want to sort:
      Select cell A1. Then place the cursor in the middle of this cell. The cursor should be a white cross. Press the mouse button. While holding the mouse button down drag to the right across the row until the column with the total score (AB) is highlighted. Continue to hold the mouse button down while dragging to the bottom row of the data, which is row 55 in this data set. Rows 1 to 55 for columns A to AB should be highlighted.

   b. Do the following to sort the data:
      While the data is highlighted from a. above, select the Data tab from the ribbon at the top of the screen and then select the Sort icon. A dialog box will appear. Select the "My data has headers" check box by clicking on it, so it shows a checkmark. Open the drop-down menu for the "Sort by" option to the far left of the dialog box and highlight Total Score (Column AB). You may need to scroll down to find Total Score. Open the drop-down menu at the far right of the dialog box and sort from largest to smallest score by selecting "Largest to Smallest". Select OK in the dialog box. You should now see the test takers sorted from highest to lowest on Total Score.

3. Do this to calculate the IFs.

   a. Select Cell C57 and type:

   =AVERAGE(C2:C55)

This command asks for the mean of the scores from C2 to C55. Press Enter. The IF of .44 for the first item should appear in the cell.

b. Select cell C57. Then put the mouse over the bottom right corner of the cell until the cursor becomes a small black cross. Click and hold down while dragging the mouse to the right until you have selected all the cells in this row up to and including cell AA57, which is the column for the last item. Release the mouse button. The IFs for the other twenty-four items should appear.

4. Calculate the IFs for the masters with the Excel Average command.

Because we set our cut score at 16 for this data set, we will identify masters as test takers who have scores of 16 or higher.

a. Calculate the IFs of the masters for the first item:

Select cell C58 and type:

=AVERAGE(C2:C30)

Press Enter. This will give the average of the masters for Item 1, which is .48 for this data set.

b. Calculate the IFs of the masters for items 2 to 24:

Select cell C58. Then put the mouse over the bottom right corner of the cell until the cursor becomes a small black cross. Click and hold down while dragging the mouse to the right until you have selected all the cells in the row up to cell AA58. Release the mouse button. All 25 cells in this row should be active and the IFs for the masters for the other 24 items should appear.

5. Calculate the IFs for the non-masters with the Excel Average command:

Non-masters are test takers with scores of 15 or lower.

a. Calculate the IF of the non-masters for the first item:

Select cell C59 and type:

=AVERAGE(C31:C55)

Press Enter. This will give the average of the non-masters for Item 1, which is .40 for this data set.

b. Calculate the IFs for the non-masters for items 2 to 24:

Select cell C59 and do the same as in step 4b to obtain the IFs for the other 24 items for the non-masters.

6. Subtract the IF of the non-masters from the IF of the masters to get the B-Index:

a. Obtain the IF for Item 1 by subtracting the IF of the non-masters from the IF of the masters for this item:

Select cell C60 and type:

=C58-C59

Press Enter. The command tells Excel to subtract the value in cell C59 from the value in cell C58. The B-Index for the first item, which is .08, should appear.

b. Obtain the B-index for items 2 to 24 by subtracting the IF of the non-masters from the IF of the masters for each item.

Select cell C60 and do the same as in step 4b to get the B-Index for the other 24 items.

PART IV
Judging Test Taker Performances

CHAPTER 10

Being Creative: Types and Delivery of Performance Assessments

FIGURE 10.1 University students having a discussion in the target language use situation.
Source: Hispanolistic/E+/Getty Images.

At one university where I worked, the faculty wanted to change the curriculum from teaching each of the four language skills of listening, speaking, reading, and writing separately to integrating them, as students often use them in the target language use (TLU) university context. They also needed to change the assessments to align with this new curriculum. The teachers had many questions about what kinds of assessments they could use to assess these new constructs. For example,

How do we assess students' abilities to effectively discuss a topic in small groups or give an oral presentation as they do in their university content courses?

How do we assess students' abilities to write essays based on information from written materials as they would for a research paper assignment?

How should we deliver these assessments? Should students talk to a teacher, classmate, or a computerized system when they take the test? If they talk to a teacher or classmate should it be face to face or online?

> **Time to Think 10.1**
> Select two of the teachers' questions and provide an answer and rationale for the answer.

Introduction

In this chapter, we will explore **performance assessments** which are test activities that require test takers to use language similarly to how they would in a TLU situation. Performance assessments require test takers to produce language rather than select an answer from a set of options. Because performance assessments aim to provide TLU opportunities for test takers to show their abilities, researchers have also used the labels "direct test" and "authentic test" to describe them. We use the term **test task,** or just **task**, to refer to the activity that we expect the test takers to complete, and **test prompt,** or just **prompt**, to indicate the test materials we use to get the test takers to produce particular targeted language. We will see several examples of tasks and prompts later in the chapter.

We usually use performance assessments to assess the productive language skills of speaking and writing independently and to assess a combination of two or more skills together, such as listening and speaking. Performance assessments are often appropriate because when the test and TLU tasks align, there is potential for providing an effective indication of test takers' language abilities or achievement and for promoting effective language learning practice. In other words, when test tasks are similar to ones test takers need to do in the real world, we can be more confident that the test scores will provide an appropriate indication of how effectively they can use the language for real purposes. Moreover, washback should be positive, since the test tasks align with the TLU tasks.

We will begin this chapter by discussing some important task features that we need to consider when we use performance assessments. After that, we will examine some common tasks for assessing speaking and writing. Next, we will discuss some tasks for assessing two or more language skills, such as reading and writing. Finally, we will explore some ways for delivering these tasks. In Chapter 11, we will discuss how to score performance assessments, and in Chapter 12, we will explore how to analyze them.

Independent, Integrated, and Interactive Tasks

Independent Tasks
Dividing language into the four skills of listening, reading, speaking, and writing is common in language learning and assessment contexts. For this reason, we often desire to assess each of the four language skills separately.

We explored some item types for assessing listening and reading in Chapters 6 and 7 and we will discuss some tasks for assessing speaking and writing in this chapter. When we think of language as four different skills, our assessments should use **independent tasks** or independent item types: language assessment activities that aim to assess only one of the four language skills. In fact, when we use independent tasks or items, we consider any difference in the scores resulting from other language skills to be construct-irrelevant variance. For instance, let's assume we want to assess speaking ability, and we use an assessment format that requires test takers to answer some questions that we ask orally. If the test takers' spoken responses are poor because their listening abilities limit their understanding of the questions, we would consider listening ability to be a source of construct-irrelevant variance. This would mean that we could not be confident that our scores provide an effective indication of test takers' speaking abilities.

Integrated Tasks

In other learning and assessment contexts, we do not divide language into the four skills of listening, reading, speaking, and writing. Instead, we think about language in terms of how we use it to complete a TLU task. For instance, if our TLU is a playground where children are playing (see Chapter 4), we may think of language as oral communication – language use that requires both listening and speaking. When we desire to assess language in these types of TLU situations, we use **integrated tasks**, which are assessment activities that require test takers to use two or more language skills.

We commonly use **listen-speak tasks**, which are assessment activities where test takers use both listening and speaking skills (like children on a playground might) and **read-write tasks**, which are assessment activities where test takers use both reading and writing skills (like university students might when writing a research paper). Integrated test tasks may require speaking or writing and any one or more of the other skills, depending on the language ability that we want to measure.

Interactive Tasks

Another important factor in performance assessment tasks is how interactive they are. **Interactive tasks** are assessment activities that require test takers to negotiate meaning about a topic with one or more other language users in real time. Talking or texting with other language users are examples of interactive tasks.

How interactive a task is can be particularly important for assessing oral communication, because we can use listen-speak tasks that are integrated and interactive to assess interactional competence, an important ability for orally communicating with other language users. Galaczi and Taylor (2018, p. 226) define interactional competence as the ability to "co-construct interaction in a purposeful and meaningful way, taking into account sociocultural and pragmatic dimensions of the speech situation and event." When we want to measure test takers' abilities to immediately and directly communicate with other language users, we need to consider how well a task can assess interactional competence. While interactional competence is mostly associated with oral communication, we will consider it in relation to both oral and written communication in this book.

Independent Test Tasks for Assessing Speaking and Writing

When we assess speaking or writing, we use performance assessment tasks that require test takers to produce language, oral for speaking and written for writing. We can then evaluate test takers' speaking or writing abilities by judging the quality and effectiveness of the language that they produce. In the next sections, we will explore some tasks that we can use for this purpose.

Prepared Oral Presentation Tasks

Prepared oral presentation tasks are assessment activities where test takers prepare and orally share information on a particular topic. We usually consider a prepared oral presentation as an independent, non-interactive task that assesses speaking ability. Test takers may use visual aids, such as electronic slide decks, to increase clarity of information. However, prepared oral presentations may also be integrated and/or interactive, depending on their format. For instance, they can be integrated if we require test takers to read some information and we then evaluate their oral presentations based, in part, on their understanding of the reading material that we gave them. Prepared oral presentations may also be interactive if someone asks test takers questions after test takers have delivered their presentations. Oral presentations are common in language learning classroom contexts. Students often present in pairs or small groups after having worked together to prepare their presentations.

We can see an example of a prepared oral presentation task in Example 10.1. The example includes the three parts of a performance assessment task: purpose, instructions, and scoring. We want our test takers to know why they are taking the test, what to do, and what factors we will use to score the test. Importantly, we want the task to be as clear as possible, and this may mean using simple language or explaining what to do in the test takers' first language.

Example 10.1 A prepared oral presentation task.

Purpose: This assessment measures your ability to work with two other students to orally present prepared information about a process (for example, making a cake).

Instructions: In a group of three, give a 7- to 8-minute presentation on a process. Groups will have two 50-minute classes to select, plan, and prepare a presentation on a process, such as how to make a cake. Presentations should include five slide decks, and each should have at least one image and no more than fifteen words. You may not use notes during the presentation.

Scoring: Scores depend on content (clarity of the process you describe), language accuracy (appropriateness of grammar and vocabulary), organization of ideas, delivery skills (verbal and non-verbal), and effectiveness of visual information.

Being able to give an effective oral presentation is a valuable skill that can help test takers in real-world contexts, including education and business. As a result, using them on assessments can have positive washback on language education practices. On the other hand, oral presentations can take a great amount of class time and may not be appropriate when classes are large. It may also be challenging to assess certain language features, such as fluency, when test takers can take as much time as they want to prepare. Moreover, test takers may get help from other when preparing the presentations, meaning we cannot effectively judge language features such as appropriateness of grammar and vocabulary.

Picture Tasks

Picture tasks are assessment activities where test administrators use visual input to help prompt test takers' responses. They are often independent and non-interactive, and we can use them to assess either speaking or writing. When we use picture tasks, test takers see one or more pictures and describe what they see, create a story from them, or use them to complete a specific task. For example, we might ask them to look at a city map and talk or write about how to get from the post office to the school. We will see an example of the use of pictures for assessing beginning-level test takers in Chapter 11. Pictures can be simple or detailed, depending on the level of the test takers and the construct that the developers aim to assess. We can see an example of a picture speaking task in Example 10.2.

> **Example 10.2** A picture task.
>
> **Purpose:** This test assesses your ability to orally describe a picture.
> **Instructions:** You have one minute to describe the picture in as much detail as you can.
>
>
>
> **Scoring:** scores depend on clarity of description, accuracy and appropriateness of vocabulary, grammar, pronunciation, and fluency.
> Source: Hagens World Photography/Moment/Getty Images.

We can use pictures to assess a range of language abilities. For instance, in the task in Example 10.2, beginners might only be able to say, "I see cows and one horse," while more advanced speakers might talk about the contrast between the snowcapped mountains in the background and the green pasture in the foreground. Single pictures are particularly effective at assessing test takers' ability to describe something, and a set of pictures can be effective for assessing their ability to tell a story. Another advantage of picture tasks in high-stakes contexts is that there is an unlimited number of pictures we can show test takers, making it difficult for them to try to use prepared answers when they respond.

On the other hand, when we use pictures, it can be challenging to provide appropriate scores for language ability, because test takers do not always interpret the picture(s) in the way that test developers and administrators expect. For example, test takers may create stories that do not seem logical to particular examiners. These examiners may incorrectly assume the test takers have lower levels of language proficiency than they actually have.

> **Time to Think 10.2**
>
> Have you ever taken, as a student, or given, as a teacher, a picture speaking task? If so, did you think it was effective for its purpose? If you have not yet used such a test, would you like to try to use one for your context? Why or why not?

Knowledge-Based Tasks

Knowledge-based tasks are assessment activities that require test takers to use only their personal experiences, knowledge, and/or opinions to produce the content of a response. These tasks are independent and non-interactive and do not include pictures, readings, or other external sources of information to help test takers complete the task. Writing a tweet, a blog, or an Instagram story are examples of knowledge-based tasks. We can see an example of a knowledge-based task for a university placement exam in Example 10.3.

> **Example 10.3** An independent writing task for a university placement exam.
>
> **Purpose:** This test assesses your ability to share your opinion about a topic effectively.
> **Instructions:** Write a blog which discusses whether or not university students should have part-time jobs. Type your answer and use the computer's word count function to ensure it is between 250 and 300 words.
> **Scoring:** Scores depend on effectiveness of organization, grammar, vocabulary, and persuasiveness.

When using knowledge-based writing tasks, test takers do not need to consider textual or graphical input, such as reading passages and graphs or diagrams. As a result, they can provide appropriate indications of writing without interference from a lack of other skills, such as reading or listening. On the other hand, knowledge-based tests have some limitations. In high-stakes contexts, even though they do not know what the prompt will be, test takers may prepare and memorize generic answers before they take the test. These prepared answers do not provide effective indications of test takers' language abilities. In addition, some test takers may find it difficult to think of an interest or experience that they can use to respond to a particular prompt.

Tasks for Assessing Integrated Language Skills

Retell and Summary Tasks

Retell tasks and **summary tasks** are assessment activities where test takers either read or hear some information and then write or retell its content. These tasks are integrated but not interactive and can be either oral or written. The difference between the two is that we allow test takers to use notes for summary tasks but not for retell tasks. When we use retell tasks, we should use short inputs that do not include specific details, because assessing test takers' memories is not a purpose of second language assessment. When we use summary tasks, because we allow note taking, inputs may be longer and include specific details.

Importantly, for summary or retell tasks, we do not expect test takers to write or say the exact words from the input. The aim is to determine how effectively test takers can comprehend and share the content of a message. We can see an example of an oral retell task in Example 10.4. The purpose of the test is to help determine how much support students of English as a Second Language (ESL) might need while studying at an English-medium university.

> **Example 10.4** An oral retell task for a university placement context.
>
> **Purpose:** This test assesses your ability to retell information about an academic topic.
>
> **Instructions:** Listen to a 40-second recording of a speaker talk about a university situation. You will then have 60 seconds to retell the speaker's view, and reasons for this view, in your own words. You may not take notes while listening.
>
> **Scoring:** Scores depend on comprehension of information and effectiveness of spoken vocabulary, grammar, pronunciation, and fluency.
>
> **Audio input:** I think everyone should take an exercise class in university, because they can help students perform better. After students spend time stretching out their bodies in the gym, they will have more energy to go to class, where they sit and passively listen to professors. After taking an exercise class last year, I know that it helped improve my performance on academic subjects. After the class, I felt energized and ready to study. So, I think it is a very good idea to spend time attending an exercise class even though students are busy with academic subjects.

Hearing or reading about a topic and then retelling the information is a common task in many TLU situations, and for this reason, retell or summary tasks are often appropriate. In addition, test takers do not need to use their background knowledge to complete these tasks, and this can be an advantage. When we want to assess general language proficiency, we do not want test takers to be able to prepare what they will say or write before they take the test. By using tasks that require test takers to respond to specific input, we reduce the chances that they can memorize generic content for responding to a particular prompt. On the other hand, although we do not expect test takers to memorize the information in retell or summary tasks, memory may have an effect and therefore may inappropriately affect scores.

Synthesis Tasks

Synthesis tasks are assessment activities that require test takers to either read or listen to information about a topic and then provide a written or oral response to it. For instance, test takers may read and/or hear two or more short passages about a topic, often with opposing opinions, and then compare the views of the authors, either with written or oral text. Synthesis tasks are integrated but not interactive and can be either oral or written. We can see a synthesis task for a university placement test in Example 10.5.

Synthesis tasks are common in school settings, especially for more advanced university students. They are therefore appropriate for educational TLU situations. We can use synthesis tasks to assess both comprehension of information and language production. They also have the advantage of requiring test takers to use specific input in their responses, making them appropriate for high-stakes proficiency tests.

Roleplay Tasks

Roleplay tasks are assessment activities that require test takers to imagine that they are in a particular TLU situation and then perform the part of one of the participants in this context. Roleplay tasks are both integrated and interactive. We commonly use them to assess oral communication skills (listening and speaking) for specific purposes. We can see an example of a roleplay task for young learners in Figure 10.2.

Example 10.5 A synthesis read-write task for a university placement context.

Purpose: This test assesses your ability to understand written information and to compare a person's or AI's viewpoint with your own in written form.

Instructions: Read the opinion about humans and their relationships with horses. Then compare your opinion about humans and their relationships with horses to the author's opinion on this topic. You have 30 minutes and should write between 300 and 350 words.

Scoring: Scores depend on effectiveness of organization, vocabulary, grammar, and comparison between writer's and author's opinions (should not use any of author's words).

Written input: Many people love horses. They can be fun to ride and good friends to people. However, I don't think we should have horses for leisure activities. First, horses require a great amount of resources. For instance, to produce enough hay for a horse to eat requires at least 8,000 square meters of excellent farmland. Horses also require a lot of space to live, since they need daily exercise and a comfortable place to sleep. Second, I don't think horses want people to control them. Humans should not try to take away horses' freedom.

FIGURE 10.2 Students taking the role of a prince and a princess in a classroom roleplay test task.
Source: blue jean images/Getty Images.

Roleplay tasks are especially effective when we want to assess **pragmatics**: an important part of interactional competence that relates to the way we connect linguistic forms and how we use them to achieve communication goals in specific social contexts (Taguchi & Roever, 2017). We can assess this ability with roleplays by requiring test takers to perform specific speech acts, such as complaining, suggesting, and requesting (Kasper & Youn, 2017). As a result, we often think of roleplays as the integration of the three language skills of reading, listening, and speaking. We can see an example of a roleplay task for a university setting in Example 10.6.

The task in Example 10.6 requires test takers to respond to a very specific situation that university students must be able to manage. By having test takers perform in specific situations, we have evidence of how well they can manage certain TLU tasks. However, this specificity also makes it challenging to infer how well they could perform in other language use situations. For this reason, roleplays can be effective for specific TLU contexts, but may not be

Example 10.6 A roleplay task for a university placement context.

Purpose: This test assesses your ability to use language to solve problems in a university setting.

Instructions: Imagine that you are a university student who used some ideas from an internet source for a writing assignment and forgot to give credit to the authors. The teacher was familiar with the source of the ideas and you got a failing grade on the assignment. The test administrator will play the role of the professor. You have three minutes and should address each of the points below.

1. Apologize for what you did and provide reasons for your mistake.
2. Try to convince the professor to let you resubmit the paper.
3. Thank the professor and end the conversation.

Scoring: Scores depend on how effectively you solve the problem by using polite language (pragmatic appropriateness), accuracy of vocabulary and grammar, pronunciation, and fluency.

effective for assessing more general language ability. In addition, not all test takers have the same level of comfort with roleplays. Some may enjoy acting and might be good at it, while others may not. Moreover, it can be difficult to separate language proficiency from acting ability when we use roleplays. As a result, test takers who are good actors may receive higher scores than are appropriate. Another challenge of roleplay tasks, especially for beginning-level test takers, is making it clear what we expect them to do without making it possible for them to read their role from a card. For example, in the task in Example 10.6, it would be possible to say, "Could I resubmit the paper?" The test taker could use *resubmit the paper* from the note card guidelines, and we may not be able to judge how much the test taker actually understood or could say.

> **Time to Think 10.3**
>
> Do you like to participate in roleplays? Do you think they are appropriate for assessing oral communication? Why or why not?

Interview Tasks

Interview tasks are assessment activities that require test takers to respond to questions in a one-on-one situation. Interviews can be either oral or written, but we will focus on oral interviews because they are the most common. They are integrated, since test takers need to both listen and speak, but we usually consider them non-interactive because test takers do not negotiate meaning with the interviewer. They simply respond to questions.

Oral interviews usually begin with questions that are easy and then continue with more challenging ones until the test taker can no longer respond effectively. The rationale underlying the oral interview is that by asking increasingly difficult questions, we can effectively identify test takers' language proficiency levels. Interviewers usually end with an easy question to help test takers finish the assessment on a positive note.

We often distinguish between interviews that are structured or semi-structured. In **structured interviews**, all of the questions are decided before the interview. The interviewer asks a question and waits for a response. This process continues until the interviewer has asked all of the questions or believes the test taker cannot answer sufficiently well to continue. In a **semi-structured interview**, after a test taker answers a preplanned question, the interviewer may ask follow-up questions based on the test taker's response. The interviewer may select these follow-up questions from a predetermined list or create them in real time. When interviewers create follow-up questions in real time, we might consider interviews somewhat interactive. We can see an example of a structured oral interview for beginning-level young learners in Example 10.7.

Example 10.7 An oral interview task for beginning-level young learners.

Purpose: To determine how well test takers can understand and respond to questions about themselves.

Instructions for interviewers

Ask the following questions one by one. Speak at a normal speed and with careful enunciation. If test takers do not respond after about 10 seconds, repeat the question. If they do not respond after you have repeated the question, ask the next question.

>Hi, how are you?
>What is your name?
>What kind of food do you like?
>What do you do in your free time?
>What is your favorite color?
>Okay. That's all the questions.
>Thank you.

Scoring: Scores depend on comprehension of the question, fluency, vocabulary, grammar, and pronunciation.

Interviews are flexible. We can create appropriate questions for almost any language assessment context. We can use them when we have test takers at very different levels of ability, because we can continue to ask increasingly difficult questions until the test taker can no longer effectively respond.

However, interviews are not without limitations. Of particular concern is the relationship between interviewers and test takers. Interviewers are often teachers or others who make decisions about whether or not test takers pass the test. As a result, many test takers feel high levels of anxiety when completing an oral interview. For this reason, and because responding to a list of questions is not a common activity in most target language use (TLU) domains, language experts have criticized oral interviews. Van Lier (1989) argued that when we assess oral communication, we should use tasks that are similar to ones that we would commonly use in TLU contexts. Van Leir suggests the use of conversations with peers to avoid the uneven power relationship in an interview, and because conversations are much more common language use situations.

Paired and Group Oral Discussion Tasks

In part due to the criticisms that Van Lier (1989) and others directed at the oral interview, paired and group oral discussions (sometimes just paired or group oral) emerged as tasks for assessing oral communication. A **paired oral** is an assessment activity that requires a test taker to discuss a topic and negotiate meaning with a test taker partner, while a **group oral** is a similar assessment activity with three or more test takers. This task type is both integrated and interactive, since test takers need to listen to others and speak and negotiate meaning with others in real time. In the most common format, test takers discuss an assigned topic without any support or interference from a test administrator. As a result, only the prompt and how test takers choose to respond to it control what test takers can say (see Figure 10.3).

FIGURE 10.3 Three test takers completing a group oral discussion task.
Source: miniseries/E+/Getty Images.

We can see an example of guidelines for a paired oral in Example 10.8. The purpose of the assessment is to determine whether or not students in an English-medium university need an English support course in their first year of university study.

Example 10.8 A paired oral task for a university placement context.

Purpose: This test assesses your ability to discuss an academic topic in a university setting.

Instructions: Some people think we should use standardized test scores for helping make university admissions decisions. Other people disagree. What do you think? Share your opinions and try to convince your partner that your view is correct. You will have four minutes for the discussion.

Scoring: Scores depend on effectiveness of interactional competence (communicates effectively with partner), appropriateness of fluency, accuracy of grammar and vocabulary, and effectiveness of pronunciation.

Paired orals have advantages over oral interviews. In most TLU contexts, we discuss topics with a partner as an equal, instead of answering questions as we do in an interview. Because of this potential for alignment between the test task and TLU situation, paired and group assessments may be more appropriate than oral interviews in many assessment contexts. To participate in a discussion effectively, we need to be able to interact with other language users. Paired and group discussions make it possible to assess interactional competence, an important part of communication.

On the other hand, because test takers and their partners have a lot of control over what they say in a paired or group assessment, it can be difficult to determine if test takers have certain language abilities. For example, some research suggests that test takers may fake understanding or change the topic when they cannot understand their partners. For instance, they may say, "Oh, I see," or "That's a good point," when in fact they do not understand. In such cases, it may be challenging to determine whether or not test takers understand each other (Ockey & Chukharev-Hudilainen, 2021). Other research suggests that the personal characteristics of the test takers' partners may affect group oral test scores. For example, partners' personalities (Berry, 2004; Ockey, 2009) and how familiar they are with each other (O'Sullivan, 2002) may affect a test taker's score. Finally, it may be difficult to separate the language abilities of test takers from the language abilities of their partners, because they co-construct language together (May, 2011).

Time to Think 10.4

Think of a situation where you believe a paired or group oral would be more appropriate than an oral interview. Provide support for your response.

Think of another situation where you think an oral interview would be more appropriate than a paired oral. Provide support for your response.

Elicited Imitation and Indirect Tasks for Assessing Speaking and Writing

We can find many other types of tasks that people use to assess speaking and writing, either independently or together with one or more other skills. Some people use **indirect tasks** for this purpose. These are assessment activities that do not require test takers to use language as they would in the real world. Instead, "an inference is made from performance on more artificial tasks" (Davies et al., 1999, p. 81). Because there is disagreement about the appropriate use of these task types, we can see a number of references in this section that interested readers may find useful.

One type of indirect task that people sometimes use to assess speaking or writing is **elicited imitation**. Elicited imitation is an assessment activity that requires test takers to listen to a sentence or phrase and then repeat what they hear. These tasks may be appropriate for assessing the ability to recognize and pronounce targeted sounds, and we commonly see pronunciation experts recommend their use for this purpose (Derwing & Munro, 2009, Levis, 2020). However, while some researchers argue that these task types are appropriate for assessing speaking more generally (Van Moere, 2012), others disagree. They argue that they are not appropriate because they may not require test takers to understand the meaning of the language that they hear and repeat. Test takers may be able to imitate what they hear without knowing the words or the meaning of the sentences or phrases (Chun, 2006; Ockey, 2024; O'Sullivan, 2013).

Some people use other indirect tasks to assess speaking or writing ability, such as selected response or short-answer items that we use to assess receptive abilities. For instance, to assess speaking, they may ask test takers to complete a written dialogue by selecting an appropriate option. With these tasks, we may be able to assess some aspects of speaking, such as grammatical proficiency or vocabulary knowledge. However, we may not be able to use them to assess interactional competence, pronunciation, fluency, or general speaking effectively. Moreover, such tasks may have poor washback. They may encourage test takers to practice imitating, which may result in limited development of speaking ability (Wagner, 2020; Wagner & Kunnan, 2015).

Time to Think 10.5

Think of a context familiar to you. What do you think about the use of an elicited imitation or indirect speaking or writing test for assessing speaking or writing in this context?

Delivery of Performance Assessment Tasks

When we use performance assessment tasks, we need to consider how we will deliver them. Delivery systems can use either a human or artificial intelligence (AI) partner and, if the partner is human, can be either face to face or virtual.

Face-to-Face Delivery

In a **face-to-face delivery model**, test takers complete tasks in the same place as one or more human test administrators or partners. We can use this model to deliver any of the performance assessments that we have discussed in this chapter. For instance, a trained human can deliver a semi-structured oral interview (see Figure 10.4). In this case the interviewer would judge the suitability of a particular question, create a follow-up question, and decide when to end the interview for a particular test taker.

FIGURE 10.4 A face-to-face oral interview task.
Source: Morsa Images/DigitalVision/Getty Images.

This delivery model is particularly effective at delivering roleplay or other task types that require social interactions. Trained humans, especially when they are physically with a person, can provide and react to almost any communication situation. For instance, they can effectively play the role of an angry professor in a roleplay task in which test takers try to convince an angry professor to forgive them for plagiarizing a class writing assignment. On the other hand, this human flexibility can limit the uniformity of test delivery, since different test moderators or partners will deliver assessments somewhat differently.

Virtual Delivery

In **virtual delivery** models, test takers complete assessment tasks with a human through an electronic delivery system. Test takers can orally converse with an assessment administrator in tasks such as an oral interview or roleplay, or with other test takers in tasks such as a paired oral. They can also use chat functions in these or other software programs to complete integrated-interactive read-write or read-speak tasks.

Video-Mediated Communication

One variation of a virtual delivery model is **video-mediated**. This technology makes it possible for test takers to see test administrators or other test takers while orally interacting. Some software applications that testers use for this purpose include Skype, Teams, WebEx, and Zoom. We can see an example of a virtual model delivery system in Figure 10.5.

FIGURE 10.5 Virtual delivery model: An interviewer is giving an oral interview to a test taker.
Source: SDI Productions/E+/Getty Images.

Virtual Environments

Another variation of a virtual with a human delivery model is the use of **virtual environment (VE)** software programs, such as Second Life (https://secondlife.com) or video-conferencing technology which has an avatar option, such as Zoom (www.zoom.us). In this model, individuals orally (or through writing) communicate in real time while seeing avatars that represent themselves and the other participants, such as an interviewer or other test takers. VEs use virtual characters that represent human users in virtual environments that we can design for particular TLU situations. In Figure 10.6 we can see an example of a VE that we might use if our TLU context is a business environment. The test taker may see a businessperson avatar and the

FIGURE 10.6 Virtual environment of a roleplay with an interviewer and a businessperson.
Source: luza studios/E+/Getty Images.

interviewer, and the interviewer may see a different avatar of a businessperson, representing the test taker.

VEs may have advantages when compared to face-to-face or video-mediated delivery models. When test takers complete VE assessments, they may feel less anxious than when they can see others, and this may mean we can obtain more appropriate oral performances. The game-like environment of VE assessments may motivate some test takers to perform at their highest level, particularly young learners. Moreover, their use may limit racial or other types of biases based on physical appearance.

Computerized Delivery

In a **computerized delivery model**, test takers complete assessment tasks with an electronic system. Humans may monitor the assessment, but they do not serve as a partner for a task. Computers can deliver both written and oral assessment tasks, and these can be independent or integrated and interactive or non-interactive. For instance, computers can deliver both structured and semi-structured interviews, and more complex tasks, such as a paired discussion.

Spoken Dialog Systems

One type of computerized system for delivering oral assessments is a **spoken dialog system (SDS)**, an electronic system that can orally "interact" with humans. SDSs can serve as a partner in an oral interview, a paired oral, or most other performance assessments. These systems have three main components: automated speech recognition, language processing, and text-to-speech. Depending on the language-processing component they use, SDSs can have a wide range of complexity. The simplest SDSs function by detecting key words or phrases in test taker speech and matching it with precomposed responses based on a homemade corpus that test developers create to respond to potential speech for a particular test prompt.

Ockey et al. (2023) used the key word approach to create an SDS that could deliver an integrated-interactive oral communication assessment that targeted the assessment of spoken interactional competence. After listening to two opposing points of view about a topic, such as the value of group work in a university setting, the test taker and SDS took different positions and defended them. The SDS responded to key words and phrases from the test takers' speech to engage the test taker in a discussion about the topic. When we use SDSs, the discourse that the test takers and SDS produce are not completely natural, but talking with an SDS can provide sufficient opportunities for test takers to demonstrate their oral language abilities.

Complex Language-Processing Models

To obtain a more natural exchange, we can also use more complex language-processing models. Examples of this technology include Google's BERT (https://arxiv.org/abs/1810.04805) and Open AI's GPT (https://openai.com/research/gpt-4). We briefly discussed this technology in Chapter 5 and used it to create MC assessments in Chapter 7. As we discussed previously, an example of one of these more complex models, ChatGPT, uses a large corpus (much of the language on the Internet) to create what it will say or write. The system builds a response based on probabilities of the next word a person might say, according to what people have said or written on the Internet. This makes it possible for ChatGPT to continue a discussion with another test taker. Because it uses a much larger corpus than an SDS, it can better manage unexpected speech from test takers. Another advantage of using large language models such as ChatGPT is their power to consider a wider context when responding to a test taker's turn. These models can consider all the words and phrases from several previous turns to create an appropriate response.

See Appendix 10 for example of how to use ChatGPT to create a performance assessment task.

Computerized delivery models have some advantages over face-to-face and virtual models. For instance, they can deliver oral assessments more uniformly than trained humans. Moreover, conversing with an electronic system is a common task in many TLU contexts. For these reasons, computerized delivery models may be suitable for some assessment contexts. On the other hand, communication is a social function, and responding to or interacting with a computerized system is different from the social interaction humans have with each other. For this reason, we may not be able to infer test takers' abilities to communicate with humans effectively when we use computerized delivery models. Another potential disadvantage of computerized delivery models is that it may be easier for test takers to cheat when humans are not present.

Time to Think 10.6

If you had to take a high-stakes oral communication language assessment, would you prefer to talk with a human or a computer? Why?

Conclusion

In this chapter, we discussed performance assessments: test activities that require test takers to use language similarly to how they would in a TLU situation. We discussed how to use performance assessments to assess speaking and writing independently and integrated with other skills, such as listening and reading. We considered various types of performance assessment tasks and discussed their appropriateness for particular contexts. To help make these tasks clear, we used a simple framework, which includes purpose, instructions, and scoring guidelines. Our final topic was about performance assessment delivery models, namely face-to-face, virtual, and computerized.

We will conclude this chapter by returning to the language assessment experience that we read about at the beginning of the chapter. The teachers conducted a language needs analysis to answer their questions. Based on their language needs analysis, they created two listen-speak tasks (an oral interview and a paired discussion) to assess oral communication, and two read-write tasks (summary and synthesis) to assess literacy. By following language assessment principles, they were able to answer their questions and develop a successful language assessment for their desired purpose.

Questions for Discussion

10.1 Discuss the pros and cons of a four-skills approach vs. an integrated skills approach for teaching and assessing.
10.2 Imagine you are teaching a group of fifteen-year-old intermediate English learners in the place where you are living now. An important goal of the course is for students to be able to orally communicate with other students in the class in English in a pragmatically appropriate manner. Compare the appropriateness of oral presentations, interviews, roleplays, and group discussions for this purpose. Which would you use? Provide justification for your choice.
10.3 Discuss the advantages and disadvantages of face-to-face, virtual, and computerized delivery models for your current language teaching or learning context. Assume that you have access to all of these systems at no cost.
10.4 In what situations do you think an integrated, interactive assessment would be better than an independent, non-interactive assessment?
10.5 In what situations do you think independent, non-interactive assessments might be better than integrated, interactive assessments?

Exercises

10.1 Create and try out a roleplay task. Assume the test takers are ten-year-old language learners in a foreign language context (for example Spanish learners studying Chinese in Spain). The students have studied the language for three years and have lower-intermediate levels of ability.
    10.1.1 Write the assessment prompt, including purpose, instructions, and scoring guidelines.
    10.1.2 Pilot your task by having friends, family members, or classmates complete the task with you.
    10.1.3 Discuss the effectiveness of your assessment based on the pilot.
10.2 Use an AI system to create an assessment prompt for a knowledge-based writing task. If you do not have access to an AI system, you can create one by hand. Assume the test takers are fourth-year university students who are majoring in English in Indonesia.
    10.2.1 Use an AI to create the assessment, including purpose, instructions, and scoring guidelines.

10.2.2 Try out your task by having friends, family members, or classmates complete it.

10.2.3 Discuss the effectiveness of your task.

10.3 Find a language performance assessment (possibly on the Internet, or another student's response to 10.1 or 10.2) and describe and discuss it.

10.3.1 What type of task is it (roleplay, oral interview, knowledge-based, etc.)?

10.3.2 Are the purpose, instructions, and scoring guidelines clear?

10.3.3 Is it independent, integrated, and/or interactive?

10.3.4 Discuss your experience with completing the task.

Additional Resources

Fulcher, G. (2003). *Testing Second Language Speaking.* Pearson-Longman.

This book provides details about defining speaking and then how to create speaking test tasks and rating scales. It includes many examples of types of speaking assessments that may be appropriate for a particular context.

Ockey, G. J., & Li, Z. (2015). New and not so new methods for assessing oral communication. *Language Value, 7*(1) 1–21. https://doi.org/10.6035/LanguageV.2015.7.2

This journal article provides a description of the challenges associated with assessing oral communication. It also evaluates various oral communication assessment tasks, with an emphasis on their strengths and weaknesses for particular contexts.

Ockey, G. J. & Neiriz, R. (2021). Evaluating technology-mediated second language oral communication assessment delivery models. *Assessment in Education: Principles, Policy & Practice, 28* (4), 350–368. https://doi.org/10.1080/0969594X.2021.1976106

This journal article introduces various types of oral communication delivery models, including spoken dialog systems, video-mediated models, and VEs.

Weigle, S. C. (2002). *Assessing Writing.* Cambridge University Press.

This book includes details about creating writing constructs, test tasks, and rating scales. It is accessible to readers with limited knowledge of assessment.

Appendix 10 Using ChatGPT to Create a Prompt for a Synthesis Task

In Chapter 7, we used ChatGPT to create a reading passage and its corresponding multiple-choice (MC) items. Now, we will use ChatGPT to help create a reading input for a read-write synthesis task. We will assume the test takers are fourth-year university students who are majoring in English in Indonesia. We can see our task below. We want to use ChatGPT to create (another) prompt for it.

1. Open https://chat.openai.com/
2. To ask ChatGPT to create the reading input, use the following prompt: "Create a 300-word text with three to four paragraphs on how to best learn a foreign language. There should be no bullet points."
3. As we learned in Appendix 7A, we may need to ask ChatGPT to modify the input or change it by hand if it is not appropriate.

Synthesis Read-Write Task

Purpose: This test assesses your ability to understand written information and compare a viewpoint with your own in writing.

Instructions: Read the following opinion piece about how to best learn a foreign language. Then, compare your opinion about how to best learn a foreign language to the author's opinion on this topic. You have 30 minutes and should write between 300 and 350 words.

Reading input:

Scoring: Comprehension of author's opinion, appropriateness of crediting author, organization, coherence, accuracy and appropriateness of grammar and vocabulary.

CHAPTER 11

Scoring Performance Assessments: Rating, Rating Scales, and Raters

FIGURE 11.1 A 10-point rating scale.
Source: AnthiaCumming/E+/Getty Images.

When one of my children was about ten years old, we were living in a country where English was not the first language of most people. My child spoke the local language quite well, but was a little below other students in reading and writing skills. As a result, my child took special language support classes to help improve these skills. In these support classes, there were students with very different language abilities. Some had abilities near the level of children who did not need the support classes, while others were at a very beginning level of writing.

To determine the language support needs of the students, the teachers had the students write sentence-length answers to questions, such as, "Tell me about your sports class." Some students left the page blank, while others – like my child – could respond with generally clear and effective answers that had minor errors. The teachers used dichotomous scoring, giving 1 point if the student answered the question and had no errors and 0 points if the student did not answer the question or made any language errors. For instance, a student who wrote, "My sports class is one of my **favrite** classes because the teacher makes a lot of funny jokes," and a student who wrote nothing would get the same number of points – zero. This dichotomous scoring led to students with very different language abilities getting the same level of instruction.

Time to Think 11.1

Do you think the scoring that the teachers used in the story you have just read was appropriate? Why or why not? If not, what type of scoring would you recommend? Why?

Introduction

Performance assessments are often appropriate for assessing the productive skills of speaking and writing, and integrated skills such as oral communication (listening and speaking) and literacy (reading and writing). This is because an important part of validity is appropriate alignment between test tasks and the target language use (TLU) situation. In Chapter 10, we examined some features of test tasks and discovered that there are many factors to consider when selecting, creating, or using performance assessment tasks for particular contexts. In this chapter, we will discuss scoring of performance assessments and some factors that affect them. We will consider an integrated listen-write assessment in this chapter and an oral communication (listen-speak) assessment in Chapter 12, where we discuss approaches to judging the effectiveness of performance assessments.

As we discussed in Chapter 6, we can use dichotomous scoring, where we score items as either right or wrong, or polytomous scoring, where we assign all possible points, no points, or some of the points for a response. When we use performance assessments, we usually use polytomous scoring, because it helps promote effective language learning practices and provides more accurate indications of the students' language abilities or achievement. We can distinguish among more proficient students by assigning higher scores, such as 3, 4, or 5, and among less proficient students with scores of 0, 1, or 2. Using a range of scores also makes it possible to provide students with levels of instruction more appropriate for their particular language needs. Moreover, by using a polytomous scoring approach, students, including ones that could not possibly write a perfect response, may be more motivated to prepare for the assessments. While more proficient test takers may aim for scores of 4 or 5, less proficient ones may target scores of 1 or 2.

In this chapter, we will learn about polytomous scoring by discussing how we could apply it to an assessment for eight- to ten-year-old learners of English. We will begin by discussing the context, purpose, and test task for this assessment. Next, we will examine some types of rating scales and some approaches to developing these rating scales. Finally, we will discuss how we can train both humans and machines to use rating scales to score performance assessment tasks.

A Listening and Writing Assessment for Young Saudi Learners of English

Context and Purpose

The assessment that we will discuss in this chapter – the Saudi Young Learner English Assessment – had the purpose of providing eight- to ten-year-old learners of English (and their parents) with information about their English proficiencies. The learners were all from Saudi Arabia and spoke English as a second language. They were studying in English-medium primary schools in the United States and received various levels of English support from their schools, families, and friends. A major aim of the assessment was to identify the children's strengths and weaknesses in English, so they (and their parents) could provide appropriate language support for school learning activities.

Constructs and Alignment

A common school activity that was challenging for these young learners was to listen to a teacher talk about a topic and then write about it. As a result, the test developers defined the construct that they wanted to assess as the ability to orally comprehend and write about age-appropriate academic topics in English.

Task

Based on the context, purpose, and construct, the test developers created an integrated listen-write assessment task that they felt would be age appropriate for assessing the ability to orally comprehend academic information and then report it in written form. They created a story about a child who looked for a lost dog and finally found it. The children listened to an adult that they knew well (usually a parent) read the story. While listening to the story, the children could see four pictures of the locations the child visited to find the dog. After the adult read the story once, the children could look at the pictures while they wrote the story in their own words. We can see the task in Example 11.1.

> **Example 11.1** The Saudi Young Learner English Assessment.
>
> **Purpose:** This assessment measures students' abilities to understand oral information and use their own words to retell the information in writing.
>
> **Instructions for test administrator**
> Print the two pages, the pictures for the story, and the piece of paper for writing, for each test taker. Be sure to print them on separate papers, not on opposite sides of the same paper.
> Give the test taker the pictures and the piece of paper on which to write the story.
> Say: "I am going to read a story. I will then ask you to write it. You can use the pictures to help you remember what happens in the story. I will only read the story once."
> Read the story at a natural pace. Be sure to use appropriate intonation to help make the story clear.
> "It was Saturday, and seven-year-old Li did not have to go to school today. After waking up, Li went to give the family's dog, Nip, its breakfast, but Nip was not in the backyard. Oh no! Where is Nip? Li thought. Then Li saw the backyard gate was open. Nip must have run away. Li began running down the sidewalk calling for Nip. Li and Nip loved to play at the school, so Li ran to the school. Nip was not at the school. Nip also liked to go to the park, so Li ran to the park. Nip was not at the park. Then Li remembered that the neighbors had a new puppy named Bam. Li ran to the neighbors' house. Li could hear dogs barking and ran to Bam's backyard. Yea! Nip was with Bam, and they were playing happily. Li ran to Nip and Bam and gave them both a big hug."
> Say: "Okay. Please use the picture to help you write the story about Li, Nip, and Bam. Try to fill the whole page with words."
> Once the test takers have finished writing, collect the responses. There is no time limit.
> **Scoring:** Scores depend on listening comprehension, writing coherence, grammar control, vocabulary effectiveness, writing conventions command, and handwriting neatness.

Printed with permission of Emiko Ockey

Please use the picture to help you write the story about Li, Nip, and Bam. Try to fill the whole page with words. [The assessment includes twenty blank lines where students write their responses.]

Time to Think 11.2

How effective do you think this task will be for assessing the young learners' abilities to orally comprehend information and then write about it?

Do you think the pictures help make the assessment more or less effective? Why?

Scoring Performance Assessments

Rating scales are ordered sets of descriptions of proficiency or achievement that we use to help us score performance assessments. We use them to connect test takers' language performances to the ability or achievement that we want to measure. We refer to the people or machines who use rating scales to judge test takers' abilities as raters (or judges). We can see an example of a 3-point rating scale in Table 11.1. The scale has three **proficiency bands** – Effective (3), Approaching Effective (2), and Developing (1) – and a score of 0 for no response. Language proficiency bands are descriptions of what test takers can do with a language. They distinguish among levels of test taker performance on an assessment. The test developers created this rating scale to help judge and describe the abilities of the young Saudi learners of English based on their performances on the Saudi Young Learner English Assessment.

Holistic Rating Scales

Language assessment researchers usually use either a holistic scale, like the one in Table 11.1, or an analytic scale, which we will discuss in the next section. We use a **holistic rating scale** to assign a score for test takers' overall ability on the construct we aim to measure. When we use holistic scales, our scores provide one number and a short generic description of a test taker's performance. For instance, if we use the holistic rating scale in Table 11.1, we would assign test

TABLE 11.1

Holistic rating scale for the Saudi Young Learner English Assessment.

Effective (3)

Students at an Effective Level demonstrate:

- ability to effectively comprehend and report all or almost all main elements of oral information
- ability to create coherent paragraphs that connect ideas effectively
- good control of grammatical structures, including using complete sentences with few errors that do not make meaning unclear
- ability to use vocabulary necessary for effectively sharing information
- command of writing conventions with few or no capitalization, punctuation, or spelling errors
- ability to handwrite clearly and neatly – handwriting does not require effort to read.

Approaching Effective (2)

Students at an Approaching Effective Level are able to demonstrate:

- ability to comprehend and report main elements of oral information with a few exceptions
- ability to create coherent paragraphs but connections among ideas are awkward
- fair control of grammatical structures, including using mostly complete sentences with some errors that do not make meaning unclear
- ability to use vocabulary that is mostly effective for sharing information; meaning is clear, but better word choice would be more appropriate
- general command of writing conventions, with most capitalization, punctuation, and spelling accurate
- ability to handwrite clearly but not neatly. Handwriting requires some effort to read, but lack of neatness does not lead to unclear meaning.

TABLE 11.1 (cont.)

Developing (1)

Students at a Developing Level demonstrate:

- limited ability to comprehend and report main elements of oral information
- limited ability to write coherent paragraphs; many ideas are not connected clearly
- limited control of grammatical structures, including using some incomplete sentences with numerous grammatical errors that sometimes make meaning unclear
- limited ability to use appropriate vocabulary for effectively sharing information; limited vocabulary sometimes leads to unclear meaning
- limited control of writing conventions, with many incorrect uses of capitalization and punctuation, and frequent spelling errors
- ability to handwrite, but not neatly. Lack of neatness sometimes makes the meaning unclear.

Note: Students who provide no response should receive a score of 0.

---

takers a score of 3 (Effective), 2 (Approaching Effective), 1 (Developing), or 0 (no response). The holistic rating scale in Table 11.1 has three proficiency bands (and a score option for no response). Each of these proficiency bands includes a description of six features, or subconstructs, of the ability to comprehend and report age-appropriate academic information.

> **Time to Think 11.3**
>
> Look at the holistic rating scales in Table 11.1. What are the six abilities that the test developers designed them to measure?

Analytic Rating Scales

Analytic rating scales present separate scores for different aspects of test takers' performances. We can see an example of an analytic rating scale for the Saudi Young Learner English Assessment in Table 11.2.

Instead of one rating scale at each proficiency band, like in a holistic rating scale, the analytical rating scale has six, which means that raters assign six different scores for each test taker's performance. By comparing the holistic (Table 11.1) and analytic (Table 11.2) scales, we can see that the language of the descriptors for the proficiency bands is almost the same. The difference is that the descriptor language is in one rating category in the holistic scale and separated into six rating categories in the analytic scale.

Comparison between Holistic and Analytic Rating Scales

The decision of whether to use holistic or analytic scales depends on the situation. An advantage of holistic scales is that they require less time and are therefore usually cheaper to use than analytic ones. On the other hand, analytic scales can provide more information about test takers' strengths and weaknesses. For example, test takers who get scores of Emerging (1) on one or more of the rating categories on the Saudi Young Learner English Assessment analytic rating scale may decide to spend more time working on their abilities on these language features than

TABLE 11.2

Analytic rating scale for the Saudi Young Learner English Assessment.

	Listening comprehension	Writing coherence	Grammar control	Vocabulary effectiveness	Writing conventions command	Handwriting neatness
Effective (3)	Ability to effectively comprehend and report all or almost all main elements of oral information.	Ability to create coherent paragraphs that connect ideas effectively.	Good control of grammatical structures, including using complete sentences with few errors that do not make meaning unclear.	Ability to use vocabulary necessary for effectively sharing information.	Command of writing conventions with few or no capitalization, punctuation, and spelling errors.	Ability to handwrite clearly and neatly; handwriting does not require effort to read.
Approaching Effective (2)	Ability to comprehend and report main elements of oral information with a few exceptions.	Ability to create coherent paragraphs but connections among ideas are awkward.	Fair control of grammatical structures, including using mostly complete sentences with some errors that do not make meaning unclear.	Ability to use vocabulary that is mostly effective for sharing information. Meaning is clear, but better word choice would be more appropriate.	General command of writing conventions with most capitalization, punctuation, and spelling accurate.	Ability to handwrite clearly but not neatly. Handwriting requires some effort to read, but lack of neatness does not lead to unclear meaning.

TABLE 11.2 (cont.)

	Listening comprehension	Writing coherence	Grammar control	Vocabulary effectiveness	Writing conventions command	Handwriting neatness
Emerging (1)	Limited ability to comprehend and report main elements of oral information.	Limited ability to write coherent paragraphs. Many ideas are not connected clearly.	Limited control of grammatical structures, including using some incomplete sentences with numerous grammatical errors that sometimes make meaning unclear.	Limited ability to use appropriate vocabulary for effectively sharing information, sometimes leading to unclear meaning.	Limited control of writing conventions, with many incorrect uses of capitalization and punctuation, and frequent spelling errors.	Ability to handwrite, but not neatly. Lack of neatness sometimes makes the meaning unclear.

on ones for which they get Approaching Effective (2) or Effective (3). They would not know which features are their strengths and weaknesses based on holistic rating scale scores.

It can also be easier for raters to assign scores on analytic scales to test takers who have uneven abilities across the rating categories. For instance, a test taker may have Effective (3) handwriting but Emerging (1) listening comprehension. Does this mean raters should assign a 3, because it is appropriate for the test taker's highest ability? Or should they assign a 1, because it is appropriate for the test taker's lowest ability? A 2 would not be in line with either of the abilities, but near both of them.

Both holistic and analytic scales can provide effective indications of test takers' language abilities and/or achievement. However, because they provide test takers with more specific feedback about their language strengths and weaknesses, analytic scales may be more appropriate than holistic scales in most contexts, particularly in classroom settings where promoting effective language learning practices may be the major assessment purpose.

Time to Think 11.4

Do you think it would be more appropriate to use the holistic (Table 11.1) or analytic (Table 11.2) scale to judge the abilities of the young Saudi learners of English to orally comprehend information and report it in writing? Why?

Considerations for Creating, Selecting, and Using Rating Scales

Many factors can affect scores and score meaning when we use rating scales. We need to consider these factors when we create, select, use, or interpret scores from rating scales for a particular context and purpose.

Strong and Weak Sense of Language Performance Assessment

We distinguish among rating scales based on whether they focus on task completion or language performance. In the **strong sense of language performance assessment**, raters judge performance based on how effectively test takers complete the assessment task. The focus is on successful task completion, and often both language and non-language factors (such as personality in a speaking task) contribute to test takers' success (McNamara, 1996). For the Saudi Young Learner English Assessment, if we use the strong sense of language performance assessment as our guide, we would focus on how well students tell the story about Li, Nip, and Bam. On the other hand, if we use the **weak sense of language performance assessment**, the focus would be on getting test takers to use language so that raters can judge their language proficiencies. Language use is the focus, not how effectively the test takers complete the task (McNamara, 1996). For the Saudi Young Learner English Assessment, the focus would be on the language features, including listening comprehension, coherence, grammatical accuracy, spelling, vocabulary usage, and neatness of handwriting.

Many rating scales, like the examples in Tables 11.1 and 11.2 for the Saudi Young Learner English Assessment, take into account both task completion and language usage. Raters consider how effectively test takers have completed the task and the quality and quantity of the language.

Test Takers' Characteristics

We also need to consider who the test takers are when we use rating scales. For instance, a writing performance that raters judge as "excellent" for the young Saudi learners of English would not be "excellent" for advanced university learners. We would need a different rating scale to effectively judge the advanced learners' abilities. Similarly, we rarely use rating scales that have either a perfect or a zero language ability proficiency band, because few language learners have either perfect or zero language ability.

Specificity

Another important consideration for using rating scales is their specificity. On one hand, we want them to be general, because this increases their **generalizability**. We use the term generalizability to indicate how effectively the scores on an assessment have meaning for various language use situations. For the young Saudi learners of English, it would be best if it were possible to generalize the score meanings to orally comprehending and reporting in writing all age-appropriate English. However, the task is for a narrative situation, and being able to comprehend and report a story does not mean the learners can also comprehend and report a class discussion or an expert's opinion about a science topic. For this reason, we might decide that the rating scales should be more specific and refer specifically to comprehension of age-appropriate stories and narrative writing.

Physical Layout

When we use rating scales, we also need to consider their physical layout and the numbers we use to indicate high and low scores. For instance, should the rating categories be horizontal and the proficiency bands vertical? Or should they be the opposite? If the proficiency bands are vertical, should the highest proficiency band be at the top or the bottom of the rating scale? The simple answer to these questions is to consider the context and use a rating layout that most raters prefer. However, when raters disagree with each other or do not have a strong view about the layout of rating scales, we might consider some of the research on this topic. Winke and Lim (2015) found that for a five-category vertically oriented analytic rating scale, raters in a US context spent the most time viewing the two descriptor bands furthest to the left and the least time viewing the two categories furthest to the right. This research suggests that when one or more rating categories is more important than the others, it is best to place the most important ones in the further left categories and the less important ones further to the right.

Weighting of Analytic Rating Scale Scores

When we use analytic rating scales, we need to consider how we will weight the scores for each of the categories. Should we consider all of the categories to be of equal importance? Or should we assign more weight to categories that we consider more important than the others? For the Saudi Young Learner English Assessment, the test developers decided to weight the listening comprehension rating scale more than the other categories, because they wanted comprehension to be an important part of the score. When calculating overall scores, they multiplied test takers' scores on this category by 3 and the other categories by 1. Let's assume a test taker got the following scores: listening comprehension, 2; writing coherence, 1; grammar control, 2; vocabulary effectiveness, 2; writing conventions command, 1; and handwriting neatness, 3. This test taker would get a total score of 15/24. The listening comprehension score of 2 would be multiplied by 3 to get 6, and the other scores would stay the same (6 + 1 + 2 + 2 + 1 + 3 = 15). Importantly, decisions about how to weight scores depends on the construct that the test developers and users consider most important.

Approaches to Creating Rating Scales for Performance Assessments

Knowing how test developers create rating scales is important for being able to use them effectively. When test developers create rating scales, they usually begin by considering the same factors they take into account when they create assessment tasks and items: the assessment purpose, including score use; and the assessment context (Knoch et al., 2021), for example test takers' ages, language abilities, motivations, and related social influences. Four approaches are common for creating rating scales: adaptation of existing rating scales, standards-based, theory-based, and performance-driven (Montee & Malone, 2014). In practice, we often use a combination of two or more of these approaches.

Adapting Existing Scales

A common (short-cut) approach to creating rating scales is to find existing ones that people use for similar purposes and contexts and adapt them to fit the new situation. A modification to this approach is to use generative AI, such as ChatGPT, to create a rating scale for our context that we can adapt for our specific purpose. When the test developers created the rating scales for the Saudi Young Learner English Assessment, they began by looking at rating scales that teachers use to evaluate young learners' English in school settings. They did not find a rating scale that they could adapt to their needs, but they did get some ideas about the types of scales that people use when assessing this population of test takers. Even when test developers do not plan to adapt existing scales, reviewing some is a good first step for creating them.

A Standards-Based Approach

We commonly use a **standards-based approach** for creating rating scales. For this approach, we create scales from an established set of standards or course objectives. We might consider this a short-cut approach, since we are relying on previous development of the constructs that we want to measure. This approach is common in school settings where teachers follow a set of course objectives. As we discussed in Chapter 4, course objectives should align with the ability or construct that we want to measure, making it appropriate to use them to guide rating scale development. Standards-based approaches often use category descriptors which compare performances to expected standards, such as Exceeds Standard, Meets Standard, Approaching Standard, and Emerging.

When the developers created the Saudi Young Learner English Assessment rating scales, they did not use a standards-based approach, since they did not aim to align the assessment with a particular curriculum. An example of creating rating scales with a standards-based approach would be to create a writing rating scale by making each of six writing course objectives into six rating scales. For instance, let's assume that one writing course objective is "To be able to write a five-paragraph essay with effective topic sentences." We might create a rating scale category for topic sentences that relates to the appropriateness of the topic sentences that the writer uses in the essay.

A Theory-Based Approach

When we use a **theory-based approach** to create rating scales, we begin by considering the ability that we want to measure for a particular group of test takers. Next, we carefully define the ability based on appropriate theory. Finally, we create rating scales that **operationalize** the ability that we want to measure. Rating scales operationalize abilities that we cannot observe, such as fluency, by connecting them to observable information, such as speech rate.

We used an example about assessing English as a lingua franca (ELF) to demonstrate the process of creating a construct from language theory in Chapter 4 (see Table 4.1). We will discuss how the developers of the Saudi Young Learner English Assessment used a theory-based approach, but first we will discuss a performance-driven approach.

A Performance-Driven Approach

Another approach to creating rating scales is to use the targeted language users' performances as guides. This **performance-driven approach**, or empirical approach, targets the specific assessment purpose and context (Fulcher, 2012). Step 1 is to collect language samples from the test takers or individuals with similar language abilities and backgrounds. In Step 2, test developers use these samples to help them identify language features that affect the quality of the performances. In Step 3, they use these features to create the rating criteria. In Step 4, they identify sample performances that represent distinct proficiency levels. In Step 5, they use the sample performances to describe the proficiency levels for each proficiency band.

The test developers of the rating scales for the Saudi Young Learner English Assessment used a combination of a theory-based and performance-driven approach to help guide their development of the rating scales (Tables 11.1 and 11.2). They began with a theory-based approach. They decided on the general construct that they wanted to measure: the ability to orally comprehend and report information in writing. Next, they identified four subconstructs that language learning theory indicates are important aspects of this ability: listening comprehension, written coherence, grammar, and vocabulary.

After using the theory-based approach to identify the subconstructs they wanted to measure, they used the performance-driven approach to determine 1) how well these four subconstructs were appropriate for measuring the ability to comprehend and report information, and 2) what proficiency levels would be appropriate for effectively distinguishing among the abilities of these learners. First, they asked some young Saudi learners of English who had similar ability levels and background characteristics as the test takers to complete the Saudi Young Learner English Assessment. After evaluating these samples, they believed they could distinguish among them with three proficiency levels. They selected the three samples in Figures 11.2a–c (Naila, Akeem, Farah; not their real names) for this purpose.

After considering the writing samples, the test developers decided to increase the number of subconstructs from four (listening comprehension, writing coherence, grammar control, and vocabulary effectiveness) to six. They added command of handwriting conventions (including punctuation and spelling) and handwriting neatness as subconstructs, because they were also important distinguishing features of the samples and contributed to the effectiveness of retelling the story. The developers used these six

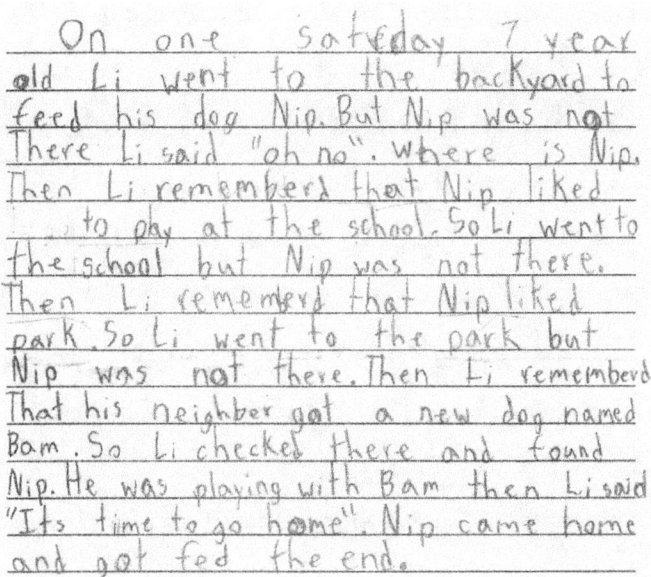

FIGURE 11.2a Effective-level writing sample for Saudi Young Learner English Assessment (Naila).

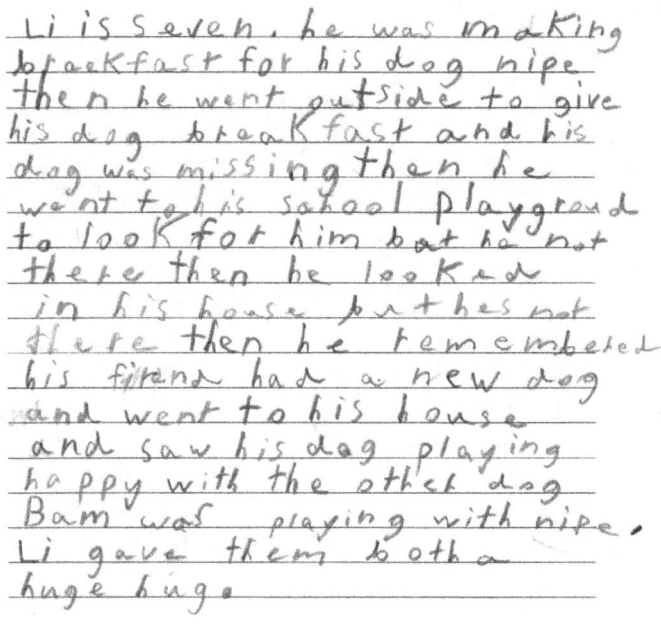

FIGURE 11.2b Approaching-Effective-level writing sample for Saudi Young Learner English Assessment (Akeem).

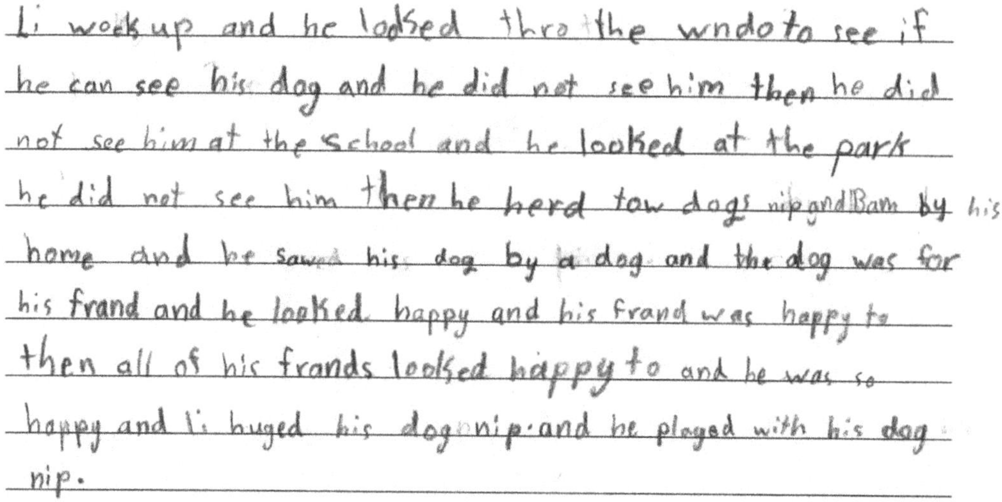

> Li wook up and he loAsed thro the wndo to see if he can see his dog and he did not see him then he did not see him at the school and he looked at the park he did not see him then he herd tow dogs nip and Bam by his home and he sawed his dog by a dog and the dog was for his frand and he looked happy and his frand was happy to then all of his frands looked happy to and he was so happy and li huged his dog nip·and he played with his dog nip.

FIGURE 11.2c Emerging-level writing sample for Saudi Young Learner English Assessment (Farah).

features to describe the holistic rating scale (see Table 11.1) and as the six categories of the analytic rating scale (see Table 11.2).

> **Time to Think 11.5**
> In addition to the six features of the performances that the test development team created, what features do you think might help distinguish among the performances?
> Which of the six features do you think is least important? Would you exclude this feature? Why or why not?

Finally, the test developers described the proficiency levels of each of the three samples and used these descriptions to create the three score bands for the holistic and analytic rating scales. The test developers judged that Sample a, Naila's, was strong across all six categories and used this sample to help define the features of Effective (level 3). Naila would get the total score possible of 24. In Sample b, Akeem does not accurately report important elements of the story, such as looking for Nip at the park. Moreover, the writing is not completely coherent, and grammar is only fairly well controlled. Moreover, Akeem only controls writing conventions to a fair degree. For instance, the writing has little punctuation. However, Akeem does demonstrate the ability to use vocabulary effectively, and handwriting neatness is effective. As a result, the test developers used Sample b to describe some of the features of Approaching Effective, including listening comprehension, writing coherence, grammar control, and writing conventions command. Akeem got scores of 6 (listening comprehension), 2 (writing coherence), 2 (grammar control), 3 (vocabulary effectiveness), 2 (writing conventions command), and 3 (handwriting neatness). The test developers used Farah's writing sample to help them describe the features of the Emerging category.

Time to Think 11.6

What analytic scores would you assign to Farah? Provide an explanation for your answer.

Preparing for Scoring Performance Assessments

In performance assessments, human raters or computer scoring are critical for connecting test takers' performances on test tasks to appropriate scores on rating scales. For this reason, we need to carefully prepare humans or computer software for this role.

Human Scoring

The goal of human rater preparation is to help raters identify the important features of test takers' performances and place appropriate value on these features when assigning scores (Davis, 2022). To ensure a fair scoring process, we want raters to be consistent with themselves (intra-rater reliability) and other raters (inter-rater reliability) when assigning scores. That said, we expect and usually desire a little variability in scoring. We consider each rater an independent expert, and we do not expect all experts to make exactly the same judgments when evaluating complex language abilities such as speaking or writing (Eckes, 2023). When high levels of rating accuracy are essential, we combine the scores of two or more raters to help ensure multiple expert perspectives on a performance and consistency in scoring. Helping raters understand the importance of the balance between being an independent expert and being acceptably consistent with the ratings of others is an important part of preparing raters. We discuss appropriate levels of reliability for particular contexts in Chapter 12.

When we prepare raters, we make an important distinction between **rater training** and **rater norming**. Training prepares raters to judge language performances based on an existing set of expectations. In norming procedures, all raters (experienced and new) work together to determine appropriate scoring expectations.

Rater Training

When we use a rater training approach to preparing raters, expert raters lead training sessions, and we expect new raters to align their rating with that of the experts. We often use rater training procedures in contexts where it is important to follow a set standard that should not change from one test administration to another.

While the exact procedures for rater training will depend on the particular context, we usually follow a fairly set process:

1. We introduce raters to the assessment purpose, context, and tasks. For the Saudi Young Learner English Assessment, this would mean talking about the backgrounds of the learners and showing and discussing the listen-write task.
2. We introduce raters to the rating scales, explaining the meaning of each rating category, the importance of each, and the test taker performance that we consider when we evaluate the features in a category. For the Saudi Young Learner English Assessment, we would introduce raters to the analytic rating scale (Table 11.2) and discuss the rating categories.
3. We provide raters with example responses that are representative of each of the proficiency bands. We include verbal or written explanations of the reasons for judging these examples as representing the associated proficiency level. For the Saudi Young Learner English

Assessment, we would share our examples of the three different proficiency levels (Figures 11.2a–c) and explain the scoring for each.
4. We provide the raters with further example performances and give them an opportunity to practice rating them. In most contexts, we do not ask them to share how they scored the examples. This approach allows new raters to conform to the rating standard without feeling a need to defend their scores. Instead, we provide them with the experts' scores for these examples and allow them to self-evaluate their ratings. Depending on the stakes of the assessment, we continue to have the new raters score additional test taker performances until they believe they are confident in their ability to rate effectively.

In high-stakes contexts, raters may need to pass a test after the training is complete. These certification tests, which are not part of the training process, usually require raters to judge a new set of examples with a certain level of accuracy.

Rater Norming

Rater norming and training procedures are similar, with one important exception. For rater norming, after more experienced raters have introduced the assessment's context, purpose, and rating scale, all the raters (experienced and new) discuss example performances and come to a shared understanding of their distinguishing features and the scoring for each. They continue to individually rate and then discuss until they sufficiently agree on their ratings. This process may be appropriate when maintaining a certain standard across different rating sessions is not important. An advantage of rater norming is that new raters may feel the more experienced team members value their expertise and views, which can lead to higher levels of cooperation.

Computer Scoring

The process of training computer systems to rate performance assessments is similar to the way we train humans. The Pearson PTE Academic, a writing assessment for intermediate to advanced English learners, uses computer scoring. According to Pearson, they design their computer scoring to align with the way expert humans rate an essay. They begin by having hundreds or even thousands of people respond to their writing tasks. Next, they have expert humans use analytic rating scales (usually three to four proficiency bands) to judge these responses. Then, they use these human expert ratings as sample data to determine what types of test taker responses align with particular proficiency bands on their rating scales. They can then use these test taker responses and expert human ratings to train automated scoring systems to assign test taker writing performances to the same proficiency bands as trained expert human raters assign them (Pearson/PTE, no date).

For the Saudi Young Learner English Assessment example, we could have asked hundreds of Saudi children to write the story, and then have twenty or thirty trained raters judge these written responses for listening comprehension, writing coherence, grammar control, vocabulary effectiveness, writing conventions command, and handwriting neatness. Then we would have used the Saudi children's writing samples and the trained raters' scores on these samples to train the computer to score the test. The computer would identify certain features of the writing samples that consistently aligned with certain scores on the tests and use these as criteria for assigning scores on unrated test taker writing performances. Importantly, when we use this approach to training computers to score performance assessments, they can be only as effective as the expert humans that we train them to follow.

Hybrid Scoring

Hybrid scoring is the process of combining scores from both humans and automated computer scoring systems. One approach to hybrid scoring is to use a computer score to confirm a human score. The Educational Testing Service has used hybrid scoring for the speaking and writing sections of the Test of English as a Foreign Language (TOEFL) iBT Test (www.ets.org/toefl.html), an academic test of English for university students. In this approach, when a computer score aligns with a human score, the test taker gets the score that the human assigned. When the computer score does not align with the human score, a second human rates the performance and the test taker gets an average of the two human scores. This approach gives more value to human scores than to computer scores. We could also give equal value to human and computer scoring by averaging the two scores, or we could weight either the human score or the computer score more than the other, depending on which we value more.

Another approach to hybrid scoring is to have humans judge some features of the quality of the language performance and computers judge others. Davis and Papageorgiou (2021) used this approach to have trained expert humans judge more global language features of oral communication and a computer system, SpeechRater^{SM}, judge more specific language features. This approach aims to take advantage of the strengths and weaknesses of both human and computer scoring approaches. Such an approach may be appropriate for the Saudi Young Learner English Assessment. Humans might judge the more global features of listening comprehension based on the content of the story and writing coherence, while computers might judge the more specific language features of grammar control, vocabulary effectiveness, and writing conventions command. Both might judge handwriting neatness.

Conclusion

In this chapter we discussed the use of rating scales to help provide polytomous scoring for performance assessments. We compared holistic and analytic rating scales. We use holistic rating scales to provide one general score for test taker performance on a task, and analytic rating scales to provide scores on multiple, specific language abilities. We explored four approaches to creating rating scales: adaptation of existing scales, including ones created by generative AI, standards-based, theory-based, and performance-driven. We concluded the chapter by discussing how we prepare humans and computers for scoring performance assessments.

We began this chapter with a story about the limitations of dichotomous scoring when we use performance assessments. The short-answer assessment scores that the teachers used did not effectively separate students into appropriate ability groups, and they did not provide the students with useful feedback. If the teachers had used rating scales to help them provide polytomous scoring, this may have led to more useful scores for placement and better feedback to the students. In Chapter 12, we will discuss how to analyze the effectiveness of the test content and scores when we use performance assessments.

Questions for Discussion

11.1   Compare the use of holistic and analytic rating scales for judging young learners' language proficiencies.

11 SCORING PERFORMANCE ASSESSMENTS

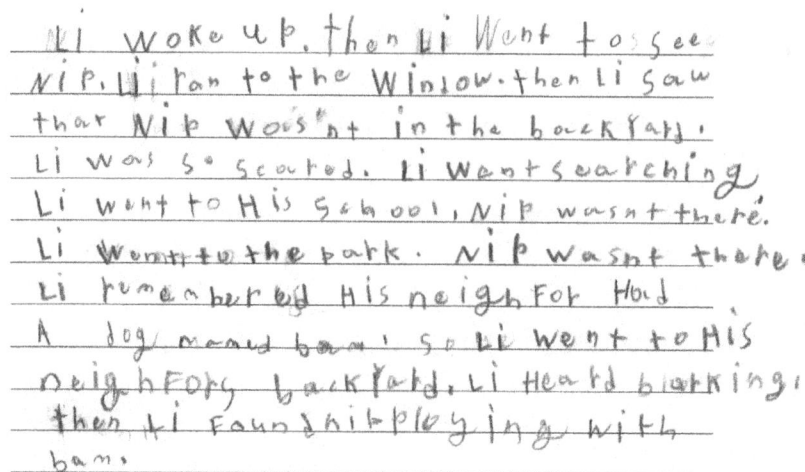

FIGURE 11.3 Writing sample for Saudi Young Learner English Assessment for Discussion Question 11.1.

11.1.1 Form a group. Let each person in the group, individually, use the holistic rating scale (Table 11.1) to rate the writing sample in Figure 11.3.

11.1.2 Discuss the ratings. Do your group members agree? Discuss how the scoring criteria may have led to any agreement or disagreement. How might you revise the scales to make them more effective for rating?

11.1.3 Have each person in your group, individually, use the analytic rating scale (Table 11.2) to judge the writing sample in Figure 11.3.

11.1.4 Discuss the ratings. Do your group members agree? Discuss how the scoring criteria may have led to any agreement or disagreement. How might you revise the scales to make them more effective for rating?

11.1.5 Add up each group member's scores. (Remember to multiply listening comprehension by 3, so scores will be between 8 and 24.) How similar or different is each group member's final score for the test taker? Do the scores appear to be reliable? (i.e., would the test taker get about the same score from all of the raters/group members?)

11.1.6 Compare the holistic and analytic ratings. Multiply the holistic scores by 8 (scores will be 8, 16, or 24) to make them comparable to the analytic scores.

11.1.7 Which scale do you think would be better for rating this group of test takers? Why?

11.2 Consider a context that is of interest to all members of your group.

11.2.1 Would human, computer, or hybrid scoring be more appropriate? Why?

11.2.2 What are some advantages of human scoring for this context? What advantages would computer scoring have for this context?

Exercises

11.1 Create and use a rating scale for the Saudi Young Learner English Assessment. Use one or more of the four approaches to rating scale development.

ADDITIONAL RESOURCES

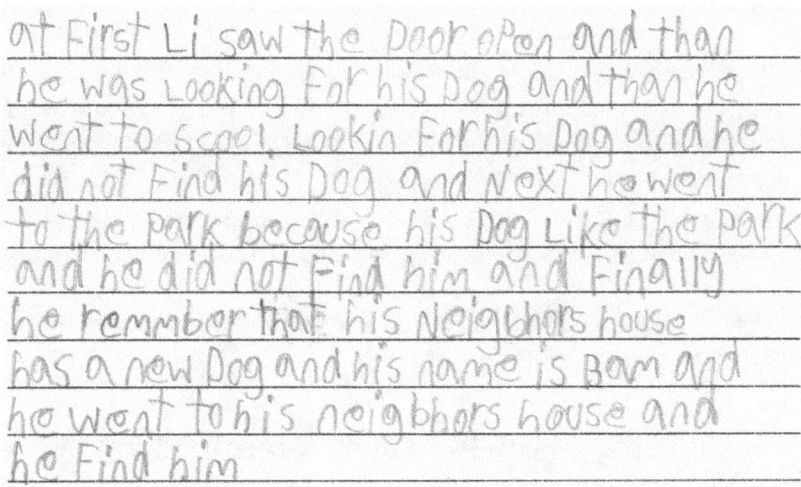

FIGURE 11.4 Saudi Young Learner English Assessment for Exercise 11.1.

11.1.1 Create a holistic rating scale for this purpose. Use an AI system to produce an existing rating scale (see Appendix 11) and then modify it by hand OR create and modify one by hand. Describe the process.

11.1.2 Create an analytic rating scale for this purpose. Use an AI system to produce an existing rating scale (see Appendix 11) and then modify it by hand OR create and modify one by hand. Describe the process.

11.1.3 Use your holistic scale to help you score the writing sample in Figure 11.4. Provide a few sentences to justify your scores.

11.1.4 Use your analytic scale to score the writing sample in Figure 11.4. Provide a few sentences to justify your scores.

11.1.5 Discuss how effectively you think your rating scales worked for rating the writing sample.

11.1.6 Discuss the advantages and disadvantages of holistic and analytic rating scales for rating in this context.

11.2 Compare and contrast the strengths and weaknesses of human and computer scoring systems for a context of interest to you.

Additional Resources

Galaczi, E., & Lim, G. S. (2022). Scoring performance tests. In G. Fulcher & L. Harding, (Eds), *The Routledge Handbook of Language Testing*, second edition (pp. 495–510). Routledge.

This book chapter provides an accessible introduction to developing and using rating scales. It also discusses both human and computer scoring and includes a useful list of references that interested readers can further pursue.

Knoch, U., Deygers, B., & Khamboonruang, A. (2021). Revisiting rating scale development for rater-mediated language performance assessments: Modelling construct and contextual choices made by scale developers. *Language Testing* 38(4), 602–626.

This journal article provides a discussion of the ways various contextual factors lead to different processes of creating a rating scale that is appropriate for a particular purpose.

Luoma, S. (2004). *Assessing Speaking*. Cambridge University Press.

Chapter 4 of this book provides a number of examples of types of rating scales for various purposes. It is a good place to begin when looking for ideas about what types of rating scales might be appropriate for particular contexts.

Montee, M., & Malone, M. (2014). Writing scoring criteria and score reports. In A. J. Kunnan (Ed.), *The Companion to Language Assessment*, Volume II, Part 7, Chapter 51 (pp. 1–13). John Wiley & Sons.

This book chapter provides a very accessible discussion of what rating scales are and the ways that test developers or others create and use them.

Appendix 11 Using ChatGPT to Help Create Rating Scales

This appendix provides guidance on how to use ChatGPT to help create a starting point for rating scales. We will use it to help us create some for the Saudi Young Learner English Assessment.

1. Open https://chat.openai.com/ and click on "Chat GPT." Then type in your commands in the "Send a Message" window.
2. Input the following: "Please create an analytic scoring rubric to evaluate young Saudi learners of English on a task where they listen to a story and then rewrite it. The learners are intermediate English learners and about ten years old. Include the following categories: listening comprehension, writing coherence, grammar control, vocabulary effectiveness, writing conventions command, and handwriting neatness. Use three score bands for each category. Put the rating scales in table form."
3. Continue to add commands to modify the scale until you think ChatGPT cannot help you further.

CHAPTER 12

Judging the Effectiveness of Performance Assessments: Validity, Reliability, and Dependability

FIGURE 12.1 Judges providing different ratings for the same performance.
Source: Noel Hendrickson/Photodisc/Getty Images.

As the director of a university English language oral communication placement assessment, I sometimes need to provide evidence of its effectiveness. While test takers, students in this case, generally trust multiple-choice (MC) or other selected response types of assessments, many question the results of human-rated performance assessments because of the potential subjectivity of humans. The most common questions I get are:

How do you know that the assessment can measure my ability to orally communicate at the university?

How do you know that the different teachers who rate the speaking performances assign the same scores for the same performance?

Do some raters fail students who would pass if they had another rater?

Do you have evidence that your tasks and scoring are fair?

Being able to convince these students that their oral communication assessment results are fair is critical to the success of the program.

Time to Think 12.1
Think of a time that you wondered about the appropriateness of your scores on a language performance assessment. What kinds of evidence would convince you that the scores were appropriate?

Introduction

In Chapter 10, we discussed some performance assessment tasks and principles, and in Chapter 11, we considered some approaches to scoring performance assessments. In this chapter, we will explore some methods to evaluate the effectiveness of the scores they produce. Because we often rely on human judgment when we score performance assessments, we have to be particularly concerned about the effectiveness of the scoring system. The story at the beginning of the chapter about test takers questioning the legitimacy of their scores is common when we use performance assessments. In fact, some people do not use performance assessments because of this concern. However, because of their strong potential for providing effective indications of test takers' language ability or achievement and promoting positive language learning practices, performance assessments are appropriate in many contexts.

We will begin this chapter by discussing an oral communication assessment that was part of an English support course in an English-medium university context. We will use this example to explore the kinds of evidence we use to evaluate the effectiveness of performance assessment scores for a particular purpose. We will begin by examining validity evidence for performance assessment contexts and then explore some approaches to estimating their score dependability and reliability.

The Assessment of Academic Oral Communication

Assessment Context and Purpose

The major purpose of the Assessment of Academic Oral Communication was to motivate English as a Second Language (ESL) students in a United States university to improve their English oral communication skills. The assessment was part of an English support course that students took in the seventh week of a fifteen-week course. There were five sections of the course, all with a different teacher, and fifty-six students in total. The classes were held three times per week, and each was 50 minutes. The teachers also used the assessment to compare the oral communication proficiencies of the students across the classes and assign course grades. They counted scores as 10 percent of final grades.

Assessment Constructs and Alignment

The teachers designed the assessment to align with the course objectives. The course had five learning goals, and the teachers designed the assessment to address three of them. These three learning goals were that students would develop:

1. the pragmatic speaking skills necessary for communicating with professors, classmates, and university staff
2. discussion skills for academic and non-academic situations
3. strategies for listening and speaking in academic situations.

Time to Think 12.2
Based on the context, purpose, and construct, do you think the assessment should be a norm-referenced test (NRT), criterion-referenced test (CRT), neither, or both? Why?

Assessment Task
Based on the context, purpose, and construct, the teachers decided to use a paired oral as the task type. As we discussed in Chapter 10, paired orals require test takers to discuss a topic with a partner. The teachers created six different prompts to help ensure that students who took the test last would not have the possible advantage of knowing their test prompt before taking it. We can see the assessment task with one of the six prompts in Example 12.1.

Example 12.1 The Assessment of Academic Oral Communication.

Purpose: This assessment measures students' abilities to discuss an academic topic in English.
Instructions for test administrator: Say, "I will begin by asking each of you a few warm-up questions. Your responses will not count toward your scores."
Warm-up questions:
Ask test takers about their names, home countries, and major area of university studies.
Ask test takers one question about their favorite holiday, summer holiday plans, or a related question.
Say, "Please look at the paper." Give the type-written prompt to the test takers and then read it aloud.
Prompt:
"Many people look for ways to be successful, but people disagree about what success means and how to reach it.
Student A (refer to one of the students by name): You believe that success as a student means to achieve a high grade point average and advanced degrees (master's, doctoral). Defend your position to Student B and try to convince your partner of your views on the topic. Provide reasons and examples to back your claims. Even if you do not necessarily agree with this statement, support this view.
Student B (refer to the other student by name): You believe that success as a student means to have a rich social life and to be very involved in campus clubs and volunteering. Defend your position to Student A and try to convince your partner of your views on the topic. Provide reasons and examples to back your claims. Even if you do not necessarily agree with this statement, support this view."
Say, "Okay, now the test will begin. You have four minutes for your discussion. Either of you can begin."
After four minutes, say, "Thank you. This is the end of the test."
Give the students a few words of positive feedback and wish them a happy day.
Scoring: Depends on fluency, interactional competence, pronunciation, and grammar/vocabulary.

Test Administration and Scoring

The teachers used a combination of theory-based, performance-driven, and standards-based approaches to create the rating scales. The assessment procedures for each pair took about eight minutes. Two classmates took the test together, and two teachers from classes different from the students' administered and scored the assessment. The teachers used an analytic rating scale that they discussed with the students before the assessment. As we can see in Table 12.1, it included four rating categories (interactional competence, pronunciation, fluency, and grammar/vocabulary) and had four proficiency bands (1, 2, 3, 4, with 1 indicating the least and 4 the most proficient). The teachers designed the rating scale with the expectation that students should achieve scores of 12 (an average of 3 per rating category) to demonstrate mastery in the course. We will assume that the teachers weighted each rating category equally.

Before they administered the assessment, the teachers followed rater norming procedures. They began by discussing the assessment purpose and context, and how to administer the task. Next, they talked about the rating scales and came to an agreement on the meaning of each of the rating categories. Finally, they observed video recordings of test takers completing a similar paired discussion task and came to an agreement about the scoring for each.

> **Time to Think 12.3**
>
> The rating scale in Table 12.1 uses adverbs, such as "usually," "sometimes," and "often," to distinguish among proficiency bands. Do you think this would make using these rating scales challenging? How could we limit this challenge without changing the rating scales?

Validity of Performance Assessment Scores and Their Interpretations

In this section, we will examine evidence and theory that we can consider to help judge the validity (see Chapter 4) of performance assessment scores and their uses. When we use listening or reading input for an integrated performance assessment, we use the same guidelines for creating or evaluating the input that we used for MC and other selected response item types (see Chapter 7, Guidelines 7.1). However, we use somewhat different guidelines for creating or evaluating performance assessment tasks. In Guidelines 12.1, we can see guidelines, modified from Brown (2005), for creating or evaluating performance assessment tasks.

Tasks Elicit Language Appropriate for Measuring Targeted Ability

For a task to elicit language appropriate for measuring the targeted language ability, it is important that test takers understand the task and have something to say or write about it. The prompt for the Assessment of Academic Oral Communication (Example 12.1) is similar to regular class activities. As a result, students should be able to understand what they are supposed to do, and they should have something to say about this topic.

TABLE 12.1

Analytic rating scale for the Assessment of Academic Oral Communication.

Interactional competence	Pronunciation	Fluency	Grammar/vocabulary
• Appropriateness of response to a given situation	• Individual sounds/word levels • Stress, linking, rhythm, and intonation • Listener effort to understand	• Speaking rate • Repetition/self-correction and pauses • Ability to speak naturally (e.g., effective use of fillers and markers)	• Accuracy and range of grammatical structures • Accuracy and range of vocabulary
4 Response is almost always appropriate in any given situation, for example: • initiating and expanding on own ideas • connecting own ideas to a partner's ideas • expanding on a partner's ideas • making relevant comments • taking turns appropriately • asking appropriate questions • (dis)agreeing politely • answering questions in an appropriate amount of time.	• Speech is almost always clear with well-articulated individual sounds and accurately pronounced words. • Speech shows good control of stress and intonation; words in an utterance are almost always accurately and effectively blended. • Speech variety does not require focused listening and does not interfere with comprehension.	• Speech is almost always at an appropriate pace. • Speech has very rare repetitions, self-corrections, or unnatural pauses. • Speech is almost always natural (e.g., effective use of fillers and markers).	• Speech almost always shows a range of accurate grammatical structures. • Speech almost always shows a range of accurate use of academic vocabulary.

TABLE 12.1 (cont.)

	Interactional competence	Pronunciation	Fluency	Grammar/vocabulary
3	Response is usually appropriate in any given situation, for example: • initiating and expanding on own ideas • connecting own ideas to a partner's ideas, but may not fully expand on a partner's ideas • making relevant comments • taking turns appropriately • asking appropriate questions • (dis)agreeing politely • answering questions in a somewhat appropriate amount of time.	• Speech is usually clear with well-articulated individual sounds and with accurately pronounced words. • Stress and intonation patterns may not be completely accurate, but this does not interfere with communication; words in an utterance are accurately and effectively blended. • Speech variety may require focused listening, but is completely comprehensible.	• Speech is usually at an appropriate pace. • Speech may have a few repetitions, self-corrections, or unnatural pauses. • Speech is mostly natural (e.g., effective use of fillers and markers).	• Speech usually shows a range of accurate grammatical structures. • Speech usually shows a range of accurate use of academic vocabulary.
2	Response is generally appropriate in any given situation, for example: • initiating, but may not expand on it very well • speaking without completely connecting own ideas to a partner's ideas • making relevant comments • taking turns appropriately	• A little mispronunciation of individual sounds and words might be present and may slightly interfere with communication. • Stress and intonation patterns may be present and may slightly interfere with communication; words are accurately and effectively blended in an utterance to some extent.	• Speech is generally at an appropriate pace. • Speech may have some repetitions, self-corrections, or unnatural pauses. • Speech is generally natural (e.g., a little misuse of fillers and markers).	• Speech generally shows a range of grammatical structures, and accuracy may not be completely consistent. • Speech generally shows a range of academic vocabulary. Some errors in vocabulary may be present but rarely hinder communication.

TABLE 12.1 (cont.)

	Interactional competence	Pronunciation	Fluency	Grammar/vocabulary
	• may ask questions that are not completely appropriate • may not (dis)agree completely appropriately/politely • may not answer questions in a completely appropriate amount of time	• Speech variety requires focused listening and may result in slight lack of comprehensibility.		
1	• Response is often not appropriate in any given situation. For example: • the rater may assume a speaker cannot understand questions or what a partner says • the speaker may: • not initiate and develop topics • may not contribute much to the discussion • may respond minimally and irrelevantly to a partner • may not ask appropriate questions • may not (dis)agree politely • may not answer questions in an appropriate amount of time	• Mispronunciation of individual sounds and words may often interfere with comprehensibility. • Stress and intonation patterns may be missing and may often cause difficulty for comprehension; words may not be accurately and effectively blended in an utterance. • Speech variety requires focused listening and may substantially interfere with comprehensibility.	• Speech is often too fast or too slow. • Speech may have frequent repetitions, self-corrections, or unnatural pauses. • Speech may not be quite natural (e.g., some misuse of fillers and markers).	• Speech often presents a range of grammatical structures; grammatical errors usually present. • Speech often shows a range of academic vocabulary. Some errors in vocabulary may be present and hinder communication to some extent.

> **Guidelines 12.1** Creating or evaluating performance assessment tasks.
>
> 1. The tasks elicit language appropriate for measuring the targeted ability.
> 2. The tasks elicit sufficient language.
> 3. The instructions are clear, for both test takers and administrators.
> 4. The scoring criteria are appropriate for measuring the targeted construct.
> 5. The scoring criteria are clear.
> 6. The proficiency levels are appropriate for making inferences about the targeted language proficiencies.

As we discussed in Chapter 10, when we use performance assessments, our goal is usually to get test takers to use language similarly to the way people use it in the target language use (TLU) situation. We can then judge this language performance with the aim of determining how effectively test takers can use language in the target situation. To achieve this aim, we select or create tasks that share as many of the language features of the TLU situation as possible. When we use performance assessments, we are particularly interested in how integrated and interactive tasks are in the TLU situation, so we can try to create tasks with similar levels of these language features. For the Assessment of Academic Oral Communication context, students need to communicate orally with professors, classmates, and university staff with appropriate discussion skills and listening and speaking strategies. This means that integrated listening and speaking tasks that require interaction are appropriate. The paired oral format used for the Assessment of Academic Oral Communication requires students to interact and use listening and speaking in an integrated way. In a paired oral, a speaking partner provides the oral input that test takers need to comprehend in order to provide a spoken response.

Tasks Elicit Sufficient Language

Tasks need to elicit enough language for effective judgments of test takers' language proficiencies. For instance, we would not expect that we could judge test takers' abilities to participate actively in a small-group classroom discussion based on language from a sample that required them to provide a few words. For our Assessment of Academic Oral Communication, test takers had four minutes to discuss a topic with another test taker. Therefore, we might expect the task to elicit sufficient language to judge their abilities for this purpose. However, one test taker may dominate the discussion, meaning the other test taker does not provide enough language for raters to make an effective judgment about language ability. For this reason, we need to monitor each pair of students to be sure that all students have sufficient opportunities to demonstrate their abilities.

Instructions Are Clear for Test Takers and Administrators

We need to make sure that test takers and test administrators know what to do to complete an assessment successfully. As we discussed in Chapter 10, performance assessment prompts usually include the test purpose, instructions, and scoring criteria. Instructions should include a clear explanation of what to do, as well as an appropriate response length and the time test takers can take to complete the task. The instructions for the Assessment of Academic Oral Communication provided this information (see Example 12.1). In some cases, it may be appropriate to show test takers an example of how to complete the task. For instance, if test takers have never had a group discussion, they might watch a video of test takers having a group discussion. For the Assessment of Academic Oral Communication, students practiced the task with a different prompt before they took the test. Moreover, they had discussed many topics in small groups as part of their classroom activities.

Scoring Criteria Are Appropriate for Measuring the Targeted Construct

The scoring criteria for measuring the targeted construct should be appropriate. In Chapter 11, we discussed how to align scoring criteria with the assessment purpose and targeted construct. The Assessment of Academic Oral Communication rating scale targets fluency, interactional competence, pronunciation/comprehensibility, and grammar/vocabulary. These constructs, particularly interactional competence, are in alignment with the course objectives. The focus of both is on university-level communication.

Scoring Criteria Are Clear

For performance assessments, whether we use human or computer scoring, the scoring needs to be clear to raters, test takers, and other stakeholders, such as teachers who need to help prepare their students for the assessment. As we discussed in Chapter 11, we use careful training procedures to prepare both humans and computers to understand the scoring criteria. For the Assessment of Academic Oral Communication, all of the instructors attended rater norming sessions. Students were familiar with the rating scales, since the teachers introduced them to the students during the first week of classes and referred to them occasionally during the course.

Rating Scale Proficiency Levels Are Appropriate for Making Judgments about Targeted Language Abilities

Proficiency levels need to be appropriate for making inferences about targeted language proficiencies. NRT scales need to distinguish among the proficiencies of the test takers, while CRT scales need to effectively separate proficient and non-proficient test takers. We judge the rating scales based on an understanding of the assessment context and purpose. For the Assessment of Academic Oral Communication, the major concern is between levels 2 and 3, since this separates mastery from non-mastery. As we can see in Table 12.1, the major difference between a 2 and a 3 is the use of the words "usually" and "generally." Based on these adverbs, we cannot say that the scale is appropriate for effectively distinguishing among the levels. However, it may be that this distinction would be clear if we observed the videos used during rater training of students with scores of 2 or 3. Reliability and dependability estimates, which we will discuss in the next section, also provide some insight into the effectiveness of the rating scales for distinguishing among the proficiency levels.

Reliability and Dependability of Performance Assessments

Uniformity, reliability, and dependability are important features of performance assessments. As we discussed in Chapter 5, by making assessments uniform, we increase our chances of reliable or dependable scores. We should therefore consider uniformity along with reliability or dependability when we judge the consistency of an assessment. We learned in Chapter 5 that reliability relates to the consistency of test scores for NRTs, and dependability relates to the consistency of test scores for CRTs.

Up to this point in the book, we have discussed CRTs and NRTs separately, but we will now discuss how we can sometimes treat one test as both a CRT and an NRT. This is possible when we desire to compare test takers to each other and to a criterion, when we have normally distributed scores (see Chapter 7), and when the content of the items or tasks align with the targeted criterion. The Assessment of Academic Oral Communication meets each of these requirements, so we will analyze it as both a CRT and an NRT. Our discussion will focus on measures of internal reliability and dependability, since it is the approach that we most often use in language assessment. As we discussed in Chapter 5, internal reliability and dependability relate to how consistent scores are within the same assessment.

To estimate reliability and dependability for performance assessments, we use the same logic that we used for MC and other dichotomously scored items. For both types of assessments, we are interested in score consistency. The major difference between the two approaches is that the most concerning sources of inconsistency are often not the same. For instance, when we discussed sources of test score inconsistency for dichotomously scored items in Chapters 8 and 9, our focus was on how test takers responded to items. If the scores on items rank the test takers in a similar order for NRTs, we consider them to be reliable, and if they classify masters and non-masters similarly for CRTs, we consider them to be dependable.

When we use human-scored performance assessments, differences in human judgments are usually the biggest source of score inconsistency. For this reason, we usually judge the reliability and dependability of these types of assessments based on the consistency of the human ratings. Importantly, this does not mean we ignore other potential sources of inconsistencies in our assessment process. For instance, when we have more than one test task, like when we had multiple items in Chapters 8 and 9, we should also consider how these different tasks affect score reliability or dependability.

Before we discuss the reliability and dependability of the Assessment of Academic Oral Communication, we need to distinguish among inter-rater, inter-rating, and intra-rater reliability and dependability. Inter-rater and inter-rating reliability and dependability are internal measures, while intra-rater reliability or dependability is a test-retest external measure. When we use **inter-rater reliability** or **inter-rater dependability**, we compare the consistency of the scores of two (or more) raters for each test taker performance. In contrast, when we use **inter-rating reliability** or **inter-rating dependability**, we compare the consistency of two (or more) ratings for each test taker, but the ratings do not come from the same two judges. This approach is common in assessment contexts where the same two raters are unable to rate all of the test taker performances. The five teachers used an inter-rating approach to score the students' performances on the Assessment of Academic Oral Communication, with two of the five teachers rating each student's performance.

We need to avoid confusing these two approaches with each other and with **intra-rater reliability** or **intra-rater dependability**, where the same rater judges the same test takers' performances at two different time periods (similar to test-retest reliability, which we discussed in Chapter 5). We use intra-rater reliability or intra-rater dependability when we want to determine how consistent raters are over time.

We will use the scores from the Assessment of Academic Oral Communication to help make our discussion of dependability and reliability of performance assessments clear. We can see data for the fifty-six students who took the assessment in Table 12.2.

TABLE 12.2

Scores from two raters for each of the four rating categories on the Assessment of Academic Oral Communication.

SID	Rating1	IC1	Pro1	Flu1	GV1	Tot1	Rating2	IC2	Pro2	Flu2	GV2	Tot2
1	1	3	3	4	3	13	2	3	4	3	4	14
2	1	4	3	4	3	14	2	4	3	3	3	13
3	1	3	3	4	4	14	2	4	4	3	4	15
4	1	3	3	3	3	12	2	2	4	3	4	13
5	1	4	4	4	3	15	2	4	4	4	4	16
6	1	4	4	4	3	15	2	3	3	4	4	14
7	1	2	3	3	2	10	2	3	4	3	3	13
8	1	3	3	3	4	13	2	4	4	3	4	15
9	1	4	3	3	2	12	2	4	3	4	3	14
10	1	4	3	4	3	14	2	3	3	3	4	13
11	2	4	4	4	4	16	4	3	3	3	3	12
12	2	3	3	3	3	12	4	3	3	3	3	12
13	2	3	4	4	4	15	4	3	3	3	3	12
14	2	3	3	3	4	13	4	3	2	3	3	11
15	2	4	4	4	4	16	4	3	3	3	3	12
16	2	2	3	3	3	11	4	3	3	3	3	12
17	2	3	3	2	4	12	4	3	3	2	3	11
18	2	4	4	4	4	16	4	3	4	4	3	14
19	2	3	4	3	4	14	4	3	3	3	3	12
20	2	4	3	4	4	15	4	3	3	3	3	12
21	2	3	4	4	4	15	4	3	3	4	3	13
22	2	3	3	2	4	12	4	3	3	3	3	12
23	2	2	4	3	3	12	4	2	4	4	4	14
24	2	2	3	3	3	11	4	2	3	3	3	11
25	3	2	2	2	3	9	5	2	2	2	3	9
26	3	4	4	4	4	16	5	4	4	4	4	16
27	3	3	4	3	4	14	5	3	4	3	3	13
28	3	3	3	3	3	12	5	3	3	2	3	11
29	3	4	3	4	4	15	5	3	4	4	4	15
30	3	2	2	2	2	8	5	2	3	2	2	9
31	3	2	2	2	3	9	5	2	3	2	2	9

TABLE 12.2 (cont.)

SID	Rating1	IC1	Pro1	Flu1	GV1	Tot1	Rating2	IC2	Pro2	Flu2	GV2	Tot2
32	3	4	3	3	3	13	5	3	3	3	4	13
33	3	2	2	2	2	8	5	2	2	2	2	8
34	3	4	4	4	4	16	5	3	4	4	4	15
35	3	4	4	3	3	14	5	4	3	4	4	15
36	1	3	3	3	4	13	4	3	3	4	4	14
37	1	4	3	4	4	15	4	3	3	4	4	14
38	1	4	3	4	4	15	4	3	4	4	4	15
39	1	3	4	3	4	14	4	3	4	4	4	15
40	1	4	3	4	4	15	4	3	4	4	3	14
41	1	3	3	3	3	12	4	3	3	4	3	13
42	1	2	3	3	4	12	4	2	3	4	3	12
43	1	3	2	3	3	11	4	3	2	3	3	11
44	1	3	3	3	3	12	3	3	2	2	2	9
45	1	3	2	3	3	11	3	4	3	3	4	14
46	1	4	3	4	4	15	3	4	3	3	4	14
47	1	4	2	3	4	13	3	3	2	2	3	10
48	1	3	2	2	3	10	3	4	2	3	4	13
49	1	3	4	4	4	15	5	4	3	3	4	14
50	1	4	3	4	3	14	5	3	3	4	3	13
51	1	3	2	3	3	11	5	2	2	3	2	9
52	1	4	3	3	4	14	5	3	3	3	3	12
53	1	3	3	3	3	12	5	2	3	2	2	9
54	1	3	4	4	4	15	5	3	3	3	3	12
55	1	3	2	3	2	10	5	2	3	2	2	9
56	1	3	4	3	4	14	5	4	4	3	3	14

Notes: SID = student identification number; IC = interactional competence; Pro = pronunciation; Flu = fluency; GV = grammar/vocabulary; Tot = total score; Rating1 = first rating; Rating2 = second rating

The furthest left column shows the student identification number (SID), and the column second to the left is the identification number for the teacher who assigned the first rating (Rating 1). For each test taker performance, two of the five raters (classroom teachers) assigned a score for each of the four rating categories. The scores from the first rating are in columns three (interactional competence: IC1), four (pronunciation/comprehensibility: Pro1), five (fluency: Flu1) and six (grammar/vocabulary: GV1) from the left. The next column to the right (Tot1) is the total of columns three, four, five, and six, with equal weighting. As we move to the right, columns eight (Rating 2: identification numbers of raters for the second round of rating), nine (IC2), ten (Pro2), eleven (Flu2), twelve (GV2), and thirteen (Tot2: total of second round of rating) show scores for the second rating.

> **Time to Think 12.4**
>
> Look at the data in Table 12.1. What patterns do you see? (Hint: consider the highlighted cells in the table.)
>
> Based on these patterns, do you think these scores are reliable and/or dependable? Why or why not?

By looking at the two ratings for each student's performance, we can see that the scores are generally reliable and dependable. Students who got low scores (test non-mastery) from one rater usually got low scores from the other, and students who got high scores (test mastery) from one rater usually got high scores from the other.

In the next section, we will discuss some approaches to estimate the reliability and dependability of these scores more systematically. We will consider the assessment as both a CRT and an NRT, since the teachers used it as a CRT to make decisions about course mastery and as an NRT to compare the oral communication proficiencies of the students across the class sections.

Dependability

We will begin by using a coefficient agreement approach to evaluate the dependability of the Assessment of Academic Oral Communication. As we discussed in Chapter 9, this is the most common approach to estimating the dependability of CRTs. Our concern is the dependability of the total scores in determining course mastery. In Table 12.2, we can see three differently shaded boxes for the total scores for ratings 1 and 2: unshaded, lightly shaded, and heavily shaded. Unshaded boxes indicate that both raters assigned a mastery score of 12 total points (the test has a cut score of 12) or higher to the student. Lightly shaded boxes indicate that both raters assigned non-mastery scores of 11 total points or lower, and heavily shaded boxes with scores in bold indicate that one rater assigned a mastery score and the other assigned a non-mastery score. We can see this information divided into four categories in the contingency table in Table 12.3.

TABLE 12.3

Contingency table for mastery and non-mastery of the Assessment of Academic Oral Communication.

		Rating 2	
		Mastery	Non-mastery
Rating 1	Mastery	38	6
	Non-mastery	4	8

The raters agreed about mastery for 46 of the 56 students. As we can see in the unshaded boxes in Table 12.2 and the upper left-hand box in Table 12.3, two raters assigned mastery scores to 38 students. We can see in the lightly shaded boxes in Table 12.2 and the lower right-hand column of Table 12.3 that two raters assigned non-mastery scores to 8 students (SIDs 24, 25, 30, 31, 33, 43, 51, 55). The raters only disagreed about mastery for 10 students. As we can see from the heavily shaded boxes and scores in bold in Table 12.2 and the lower left-hand box in Table 12.3, the first rater assigned non-mastery to 4 students (SIDs 7, 16, 45, and 48) to whom the second rater assigned mastery. We can see from the heavily shaded boxes and scores in bold in Table 12.2 and the upper right-hand box of Table 12.3 that the second rater assigned non-mastery to 6 students (SIDs 14, 17, 28, 44, 47, and 53) to whom the first rater assigned mastery.

With the information in Table 12.3, we can calculate the level of dependability. We add the decisions that were the same for both raters. We have 38 (mastery) + 8 (non-mastery) for a total of 46 (ratings that agree on the decision for a test taker). Then we divide this value by the total number of students, which is 56. (Ten of the ratings were not in agreement.). So, we divide 46 by 56 to get a dependability of .82. We can interpret this value to indicate that the raters classified students into masters and non-masters with 82 percent consistency. As we noted in Chapter 9, we typically target a dependability of .70 or higher for most classroom contexts. The value of .82 is an indication that the Assessment of Academic Oral Communication is sufficiently dependable for its purpose.

> **Time to Think 12.5**
>
> What factors might have resulted in 10 of the 56 decisions about mastery and non-mastery being different for the two ratings?

Reliability

Because the teachers also use the Assessment of Academic Oral Communication to provide feedback to students on their oral communication proficiency compared to other students in the classes, the teachers should also have an indication of the reliability of the scores. Our concern with the reliability of NRTs relates to how consistently the raters rank order the test takers. We will use Cronbach's Alpha for this purpose. As we discussed in Chapter 8, we can use Cronbach's Alpha to estimate the internal reliability of an assessment.

Now that we have a better understanding of reliability, we will look more closely at how we calculate Cronbach's Alpha. We can see the Cronbach's Alpha formula in Equation 12.1.

$$\alpha = \frac{(k)(\overline{Cov})}{Var + (k-1)(\overline{Cov})} \qquad (12.1)$$

When we use human-rated performance assessments, average **covariance** ($\overline{Cov}$) relates to how consistently the raters rank order the test takers based on proficiency. Covariance is the unstandardized form of correlation (see Chapters 7 and 8). If both teachers' ratings rank order test takers in the same way, covariance will be positive and large in the same way that correlation is positive and large. Variance (Var) relates to how much the scores vary from the mean (see Chapter 7), and the number of scores (k) is the number of ratings for each test taker. We include the number of ratings in the formula, since more ratings for each test taker would mean we could be more confident in that person's score. Higher values for covariance indicate that raters are consistently rank ordering the test takers. As we discussed in Chapter 8, Cronbach's Alpha can have a value between .00 and 1.00, and a value of .70 or higher is generally acceptable for a classroom assessment.

We can use Equation 12.1 to calculate Cronbach's Alpha reliability for the Assessment of Academic Oral Communication scores. We have two ratings (k = 2). Since we only have two

RELIABILITY AND DEPENDABILITY OF PERFORMANCE ASSESSMENTS

ratings, we only have one covariance (see Chapter 8 for a discussion about correlation and how scores can relate with each other), which means the average covariance is the covariance between the two ratings. The value is 2.74. We can calculate the average variance by summing the variance of Rating 1 and Rating 2. The variance for Rating 1 is 4.34 and 4.00 for Rating 2.

 See Appendix 12 for how to use Excel to calculate the average covariance and the average variance for the Assessment of Academic Oral Communication.

We can insert the values that we got from completing Appendix 12 into our formula for Cronbach's Alpha and complete the calculations. We can see these calculations in Table 12.4.

TABLE 12.4

Calculation of Cronbach's Alpha for the Assessment of Academic Oral Communication.

This is the formula for Cronbach's Alpha:	$\alpha = \dfrac{(k)(\overline{Cov})}{\overline{Var} + (k-1)(\overline{Cov})}$
• Insert values for each of the variables. k is the number of ratings (2). The average covariance between the two ratings is 2.74. • The variance for the first rating is 4.34 and for the second it is 4.00.	$\alpha = \dfrac{(2)(\overline{2.74})}{\overline{4.34} + \overline{4.00} + (2-1)(\overline{2.74})}$
• Sum $\overline{4.34}$ and $\overline{4.00}$ to get $\overline{8.34}$. • Subtract 1 from 2 to get 1. • Multiply $\overline{2.74}$ by 2 to get $\overline{5.48}$. Since there are only two raters (we only have one covariance), average covariance equals covariance, so $\overline{5.48} = 5.48$.	$\alpha = \dfrac{(2)(\overline{2.74})}{\overline{8.34} + (1)(\overline{2.74})}$
• Find the average of 8.34 for two ratings by dividing 8.34 by 2 (each of the 2 ratings has variance in scoring). This removes the average sign above 8.34 and gives a value of 4.17. • Multiply 2.74 by 1 to get 2.74.	$\alpha = \dfrac{5.48}{4.17 + 2.74}$
• Sum 4.17 and 2.74 to get 6.91. • Divide 5.48 by 6.91 to get .79.	$\alpha = \dfrac{5.48}{6.91}$ $\alpha = .79$

Our resulting value is .79, which means that 79 percent of the differences in the scores is consistent. If we assume that our assessment measures oral communication, we can be confident that 79 percent of the differences in scores is due to oral communication proficiency. This estimate of reliability is above the .70 value we expect for classroom contexts, indicating that the scores are appropriately reliable for their purpose.

Time to Think 12.6

If we calculate Cronbach's Alpha for each of the four subconstructs separately, would you expect the reliability estimates to be higher or lower than for the total scores? Why?

Conclusion

In this chapter, we explored approaches to evaluating performance assessments. We considered types of validity evidence and approaches to estimating score dependability and reliability. We learned that these types of evidence are similar to the ones we discussed for selected response or short-answer items. We also discovered that we have to pay particular attention to scoring, since there is no right or wrong answer for performance assessments. We evaluated a paired oral discussion test. We found that the validity evidence suggested it was appropriate for its purpose and that the scoring was acceptably consistent for making decisions about course mastery and comparing the proficiencies of the students across the classes.

At the beginning of the chapter, we discussed a story about test takers questioning their scores on an oral communication placement assessment. After discussing the assessment and their scores, not all test takers agreed that their scores were effective indicators of their abilities to perform in an English-medium university. However, when presented with the types of evidence we discussed in this chapter, they generally accepted the decisions. Being able to provide evidence for decisions about test takers' language abilities or achievement is an important part of being a successful language teacher or other language expert.

Questions for Discussion

12.1 Evaluate the Saudi Young Learner English Assessment in Chapter 11 (Example 11.1). Use Guidelines 12.1.

12.2 Work together to estimate the dependability of the scores for interactional competence on the Assessment of Academic Oral Communication (Table 12.2). Assume the cut score is 3.
 12.2.1 How many students showed mastery for interactional competence?
 12.2.2 How many students demonstrated non-mastery for interactional competence?
 12.2.3 What was the dependability of the decisions?
 12.2.4 Discuss and interpret the dependability of the subconstruct of interactional competence. Is it appropriate for its purpose? Why or why not?

12.3 Discuss how you would explain the difference between dependability and reliability to a group of high school teachers who have no formal assessment knowledge.

Exercises

12.1 Create and evaluate a performance assessment task. Two twelfth grade teachers have sixty students (17 to 18 years old) who are studying a foreign language. They need to divide the students into two equal sections. Their course aims to prepare students for university reading and writing.
 12.1.1 What type of task would you use? (Hint: See Chapter 10.) Why?
 12.1.2 Create a task for this purpose.
 12.1.3 Evaluate the task based on the principles in Guidelines 12.1.
 12.1.4 What type of scoring (human or computer, analytic or holistic scale) would you use? (Hint: See Chapter 11.) Why?

12.1.5 Assume the two teachers judge the performances and then use inter-rater reliability procedures to evaluate the score consistency. Cronbach's Alpha is .45. Should the teachers be satisfied with this result? If so, why? If not, what should they do to make the situation better?

12.2 A different group of students took the Assessment of Academic Oral Communication. Evaluate the scores (online materials: ISLA.Ex.12.2). Assume the same cut score of 12.

12.2.1 Calculate dependability based on coefficient agreement and interpret the result.
12.2.2 Calculate Cronbach's Alpha and interpret the result.

Additional Resources

Ockey, G. J. (2022). Item response theory and Many-Facet Rasch Measurement. In G. Fulcher & L. Harding (Eds.).*The Routledge Handbook of Language Testing*, second edition (pp. 462–476). Routledge.
This chapter is for readers who are deeply interested in statistics for performance assessments and want to read about more advanced approaches that we do not cover in this book. The chapter introduces Many-Facet Rasch Measurement, emphasizing the value of understanding rater behavior in more detail than we can with the statistics that we discuss in this book.

Yan, X., & Fan, J. (2022). Reliability and dependability. In G. Fulcher & L. Harding (Eds.).*The Routledge Handbook of Language Testing*, second edition (pp. 477–494). Routledge.
This chapter is accessible to readers who want to know more about reliability and dependability. The authors provide clear examples to help them explain these two concepts for both selected and constructed response item types.

Appendix 12 Using Excel to Calculate Average Covariance and Average Variance for Performance Assessment Scores

This appendix will take us through the steps for calculating the average covariance and average variance in Excel for the Assessment of Academic Oral Communication 1. We need these two values for the formula for Cronbach's Alpha (Equation 12.1 and Table 12.4):

$$\alpha = \frac{(k)(\overline{Cov})}{\overline{Var} + (k-1)(\overline{Cov})}$$

Note that k is the number of ratings (2 for this data). We will use the online materials: ISLA. Ap.12 data to complete the activity. The online materials include a video that accompanies these instructions.

1. Open the data file ISLA.Ap.12.
2. Complete this step to calculate the average total rating variance:

    a. Calculate the variance for the first rating:
    Select cell G59 and type:
    =VAR.P(G2:G57)

Press Enter. This command tells Excel to calculate the variance of the scores in cells G2 to G57. The variance of 4.34 for the first rating's variance should appear.

b. Calculate the variance for the second rating:
Select cell M59 and type:

=VAR.P(M2:M57)

Press Enter. The variance of 4.00 for the second rating's variance should appear.

c. Calculate the average variance of the ratings:
Select cell G60 and type:

=AVERAGE(G59,M59)

Press Enter. The average variance of 4.17 for the variance of the two ratings should appear in cell G60.

3. Complete this step to calculate the total score covariance:

Select cell G61 and type:

=COVARIANCE.P(G2:G57,M2:M57)

Press Enter. The covariance of 2.74 for the two total ratings should appear. Since there is only one covariance for two ratings, this is also the average covariance for the two ratings. Use Table 12.4 to complete the calculations of Cronbach's Alpha for the scores.

PART V

Reflecting and Self-Assessment

CHAPTER 13

Evaluating Our Language Assessment Literacy

FIGURE 13.1 Reflecting on what we have learned
Source: SDI Productions/E+/Getty Images.

Introduction

Throughout this book, we have emphasized that language assessment literacy (LAL) is much more than memorizing some assessment vocabulary and assessment frameworks. Being able to effectively select or create appropriate assessments for a particular purpose and context and then administering, scoring, and evaluating them are at the heart of LAL. We have discussed and applied various language assessment principles to specific assessment contexts to help achieve the aim of gaining sufficient LAL.

In this final chapter, we will assess our LAL. We will begin by reflecting on how language assessment literate we thought we were prior to reading this book, how well we have met our LAL goals, and what we plan to learn about language assessment in the future. Then we will evaluate two language assessments based on what we have discussed in the previous chapters. These evaluations will further help us gain an understanding of our LAL and what areas we need to develop further.

Judging Our Language Assessment Literacy

In Chapter 1, we discussed LAL. We considered Kremmel and Harding's (2020) nine aspects of LAL to help us determine the areas and degrees of LAL that we need in order to be effective language experts in our particular fields of practice. We can see these nine aspects in Guidelines 1.2 of Chapter 1. As we discussed in Chapter 1, Kremmel and Harding also found that language teachers, developers, and researchers needed different levels of expertise in each of the nine areas (see Figure 1.4). Comparing our LAL with what we knew when we began to read the book, our goals at that time, and what we know now can help us in determining if we need to gain more LAL and, if so, what kind and how much.

To achieve this aim, we will begin by completing the self-assessment in Table 13.1. For each of the nine areas of LAL, we can assign ourselves a value between 1 (0–19 percent) and 5 (80–100 percent).

TABLE 13.1
Scale for self-assessment of LAL.

	1 0–19%	2 20–39%	3 40–59%	4 60–79%	5 80–100%
1. Developing and administering language assessments	1	2	3	4	5
2. Assessment in language pedagogy	1	2	3	4	5
3. Assessment policy and local practices	1	2	3	4	5
4. Personal beliefs and attitudes	1	2	3	4	5
5. Statistical and research methods	1	2	3	4	5
6. Assessment principles and interpretations	1	2	3	4	5
7. Language structure use and development	1	2	3	4	5
8. Washback and preparation	1	2	3	4	5
9. Scoring and rating	1	2	3	4	5

After completing the LAL self-assessment scale, the next step is to refer back to how we evaluated ourselves when we completed this same scale at the beginning of the book (Table 1.1). We can use the following steps to help us determine how much we have learned from reading the book, whether we think we need to gain more LAL, and, if so, in what areas and how much:

1. Complete Table 13.2. The values for column 2 (your level of LAL before reading this book) and column 3 (the level of LAL you believed you needed before reading this book) should

TABLE 13.2

Levels of LAL before and after reading this book.

Column 1	Column 2	Column 3	Column 4	Column 5	Column 6
	Level believed to have before reading book	Level believed to need before reading book	Level believed to have after reading book	Column 4 minus column 2	Column 4 minus column 3
1. Developing and administering language assessments					
2. Assessment in language pedagogy					
3. Assessment policy and local practices					
4. Personal beliefs and attitudes					
5. Statistical and research methods					
6. Assessment principles and interpretations					
7. Language structure use and development					
8. Washback and preparation					
9. Scoring and rating					
Total					

come from Table 1.1. We should base the values for column 4 on our self-evaluation of our current level of LAL (Table 13.1).
2. After filling in columns 2–4, we can compare the level of LAL we had before reading this book to the level we now have, by subtracting column 2 from column 4 in each of the nine areas. We can put this value in column 5.
3. Next we can compare the level of LAL we believed we needed before reading this book to the level we now have in each of the nine areas. We do this by subtracting column 3 from column 4. We can write this value in column 6.

Now, we can add up ratings across the nine aspects for columns 2 to 6 and write the total score for each of these columns at the bottom of the table. The differences between the total scores and the scores in each of the nine areas for the five columns should give us the information we desire. Now, we can consider the self-evaluated change in LAL and the desired level of LAL.

The final step is to determine how much more LAL we desire (if any) and in which areas. Readers may find that after completing the book they discover that they overestimated their LAL after reading Chapter 1. This is an indication that they were not aware of many language assessment concepts that they now know.

The Language Assessment Literacy Test

In the next sections, we will have an opportunity to evaluate our LAL by completing the Language Assessment Literacy Test. Each part of the test includes a language assessment context, an example of a particular type of assessment, and questions to guide our evaluation of the assessment. The Language Assessment Literacy Test includes two MC reading assessments and an oral communication performance assessment.

Evaluating a Multiple-Choice Reading Assessment

Two Indonesian English teachers decide to create a reading test for their second to fourth grade students (ages 7 to 10) as part of the end-of-year exam. They will use it to help determine who is ready for the next reading class level. The main reading objectives they have for their English as a Foreign Language (EFL) class are 1) reading for global comprehension, 2) reading for detailed information, and 3) reading for making inferences about unstated information. Because one teacher, Ajij, has a class in the morning and the other, Mega, has a class in the afternoon, half of the students must take the exam in the morning and the other half in the afternoon. The teachers are worried that the students taking the test in the morning may share the test content with the afternoon students. Ajij and Mega agree to create two reading tests, one for the morning group (Test 1) and the other for the afternoon group (Test 2). Two topics that the teachers discuss in the class are zoo animals and school subjects, so the teachers decide to make the tests about these two topics. Ajij decided to create a reading assessment about animals and Mega one about school subjects.

Reading Test 1: Visiting the Zoo with My Family

Ajij decided to make a computer-delivered assessment that the students would take in the computer room. Ajij wrote a short story (about a family that went to the zoo), created four multiple-choice (MC) questions, and put the information into a computer app that would deliver the test. The app delivered the assessment as follows:

13 EVALUATING OUR LANGUAGE ASSESSMENT LITERACY

1. Computer screen 1: A screen with the test instructions: "On the next screen, you will see a story. You will have five minutes to read and prepare to answer four questions about it. You cannot take any notes about the story. After you read the story, you will see and answer the four questions on a different screen. When you are ready, you can push the continue button." The instructions were in both English and Indonesian.
2. Computer screen 2: The second screen showed the story. Students could see the story and a countdown timer. After the timer counted down five minutes, the story disappeared.
3. Computer screen 3: The students could see the four MC questions about the story. They had five minutes to type the letter of their preferred answer in the blank space for each question. After five minutes, the computer would record the responses to a score sheet.

We can see the information on computer screens 2 and 3 of Reading Test 1: Visting the Zoo with My Family in Example 13.1.

Example 13.1 Reading Test 1: Visiting the Zoo with My Family.

Input for Reading Test 1 (computer screen 2)

Visiting the Zoo with My Family

My family and I took a long car ride to visit the zoo last Saturday. We got there at 9:00 AM, even though the zoo is about a two-and-a-half hour drive from our home. After we got there, we began by visiting the monkeys. My sister was very excited to see them. My sister also saw the zookeepers feed them and some gorillas. At lunchtime, we were hungry. My parents bought food. We ate it under some trees. Next, we visited the big cats. My parents liked the lions. We watched them for a long time. Before we left the zoo, we visited the crocodiles. They looked scary. After that, we were very tired. My sister and I slept on the way home. It was a fun weekend.

Questions for Reading Test 1 (computer screen 3)

Type the letter for the correct answer in the space. You will receive 1 point for each correct answer.

1. The family went to the zoo on _____

   a. Friday   b. Monday   c. Saturday   d. Thursday

2. The family probably woke up at about _____.

   a. 6:00 AM   b. 7:00 AM   c. 8:00 AM   d. 9:00 AM

3. At lunchtime, my parents bought some food because we were _____.

   a. hungry   b. scary   c. thirsty   d. tired

4. The _____ fed the monkeys.

   a. parents   b. sister   c. writer   d. zookeeper

Reading Test 2: Seemi's Math and Art Classes

Mega created a paper-and-pencil test that the students would take in their regular classroom. Mega wrote a short story about a student's opinions of art and math classes, created four MC comprehension questions about the story, and printed both the story and questions on one side of a sheet of paper. Mega delivered the test as follows:

1. Mega spoke Indonesian to tell the students that after they got the test, they had ten minutes to read the story and answer the four questions by circling the correct answer.
2. Mega gave the students the story and questions.
3. Mega spoke Indonesian to ask the students if they had any questions about how to complete the test. If any students asked a question about the testing procedures, Mega answered it, but did not answer any questions about the content of the story or the questions.
4. After ten minutes, Mega collected the tests from the students.

We can see Reading Test 2: Seemi's Math and Art Classes in Example 13.2.

Example 13.2 Reading Test 2: Seemi's Math and Art Classes.

Input for Reading Test 2: Story and questions (printed out)
Seemi's Math and Art Classes
I like my art class more than my math class. Actually, I hate math. I cannot remember multiplication tables. My math teacher does not let us use calculators in class. The teacher thinks we should memorize a lot. On the other hand, I love my art class because I can be creative. I enjoy the drawing and painting assignments because I can use my imagination instead of my memory! My art teacher put one of my paintings in a local art contest, and I won first place.

Circle the letter of the correct answer. You will receive one point for each correct answer.

1. Seemi dislikes math class because it _____.

   a. difficult   b. requires memory   c. boring   d. does not allow calculators

2. Seemi likes art class because it _____.

   a. after lunch   b. has no homework   c. requires creativity   d. easy

3. Seemi was happy to _____.

   a. pass art class   b. win a math award   c. pass math class   d. win an art award

4. Seemi _____.

   a. likes drawing   b. likes talking   c. likes painting   d. likes math problems

1. Evaluate the effectiveness of Test 1's reading passage. Consider the following:
   a. Genre for assessing targeted construct
   b. Topic accessibility
   c. Delivery
   d. Length
   e. Grammatical complexity and vocabulary difficulty
   f. Non-language input

2. Evaluate the effectiveness of Test 1's items. Consider the following:
   a. How well they assess the targeted construct
   b. Whether or not information in one item affects responses to others
   c. How straightforward they are
   d. How similar and concise the options are
   e. How appropriate the order of the options is
   f. How effectively they require comprehension of the reading passage to answer correctly
3. Evaluate the effectiveness of Test 2's reading passage. Consider the following:
   a. Genre for assessing targeted construct
   b. Topic accessibility
   c. Delivery
   d. Length
   e. Grammatical complexity and vocabulary difficulty
   f. Non-language input
4. Evaluate the effectiveness of Test 2's items. Consider the following:
   a. How well they assess the targeted construct
   b. Whether or not information in one item affects responses to others
   c. How straightforward they are
   d. How similar and concise the options are
   e. How appropriate the order of the options is
   f. How well they require comprehension of the reading passage to answer correctly
5. How parallel are Reading Test 1 and Reading Test 2? Consider their uniformity for the following:
   a. Context
      i. Physical environment
      ii. Equipment
      iii. Administrative procedures
   b. Materials
      i. Input
      ii. Expected response
      iii. Scoring
   c. Do you consider the two tests parallel? Why or why not? If you do not consider the tests parallel, what would you do to make them parallel?

Evaluating an Oral Communication Performance Assessment

A hotel hired a testing team to create an assessment to evaluate hotel receptionists' ability to communicate effectively with English-speaking guests in Seoul, Korea. All test takers are adults and have studied English for at least six years. The testing team first conducted a language needs analysis. They decided to collect information about the target language use (TLU) situation by observing effective hotel receptionists interacting with English-speaking guests. Based on the needs analysis, the testing team defined the test construct as "the ability to check in guests, address complaints in a polite manner, and answer guests' questions about the tourism sites in the city." They then developed an oral communication roleplay test task where test takers respond to a guest complaint. We can see the test in Example 13.3.

Example 13.3 Roleplay task for assessing hotel receptionists' abilities to interact with hotel guests.

Roleplay task: Responding to a guest complaint

Purpose: The test assesses test takers' ability to interact effectively with hotel guests.

Instructions: The test administrator will play the role of an unhappy customer, and the test taker will play the role of a hotel receptionist. Use the notecards to guide the roleplay.

Scoring: Scores depend on how effectively the test taker (hotel receptionist) responds to the test administrator (hotel guest), including the use of polite language (pragmatic appropriateness), accuracy of vocabulary and grammar, pronunciation, and fluency.

Test administrator (Unhappy customer) notecard:

Say: "My room is terrible. It's a non-smoking room, but the smell of smoke is so strong that I started coughing as soon as I entered."
Listen to response and then provide one follow-up demand based on it.
Possible follow-up demands:
"Can you at least get a fan in there and open the windows?"
"Why can't you put someone else in that room and move me to another one?"
"Are all the rooms smoky?"
Say: "Also, I could not find a place to park my car. I had to park on the sidewalk, and I am sure I will get a parking ticket. The hotel needs to pay for it!"
Listen to response and then provide one follow-up demand based on it.
Possible follow-up demands:
"Can someone move my car to a legal location?"
"Can someone show me where I can park my car?"
Say: "I appreciate your efforts in trying to solve these problems."

Test taker (Hotel receptionist) notecard:

Situation: The hotel has no vacant rooms, all hotel staff are busy, and you cannot offer any money or refund.
Use the above information when responding to the unhappy customer's complaints. Your goal is to try to calm the person and solve the problems, but you must not agree to anything that goes against the guidelines in the Situation.

Rating Scale for Roleplay Task: Responding to a Guest Complaint

4	Test taker understood each complaint and used appropriately polite language to solve the problems and calm the customer. Language was appropriately accurate, clear, and fluent.

(cont.)

3	Test taker understood each complaint. Language addressed the problems, but it was not sufficiently polite and effective at calming the customer. Language was completely understandable, but it required careful listening and was not completely fluent.
2	Test taker understood most of the complaints but did not effectively use polite language to solve the problems or calm the customer. Even with careful listening, a little of what the test taker said was not understandable. The test taker sometimes struggled to think of appropriate words to say, making the response slow and strained.
1	The test taker was unable to understand much of what the test administrator said. The responses did not effectively address the problems. Even with careful listening, much of the language was not understandable. The language was very slow and strained.

1. What is the test purpose?
2. What is the construct that the team wants to assess?
3. How well do you think the test developer conducted a language needs analysis? Defend your view.
4. Evaluate the content of the assessment by considering:
   a. how well the task elicits language appropriate for measuring the targeted ability.
   b. to what degree tasks elicit sufficient language.
   c. how clear the instructions are for the test takers and administrators.
   d. how appropriate the scoring criteria are for measuring the targeted construct. As part of your answer, indicate whether it would be better to use an analytic rating scale or a holistic rating scale.
   e. how clear the scoring criteria are.
   f. how appropriate the rating scale proficiency levels are for making judgments about the targeted language abilities. What level (1, 2, 3, or 4) would be acceptable for hiring decisions? Defend your answer.
5. What is the possible washback (positive and/or negative) that the test would have on learning and teaching practices?
6. Discuss how you would improve the test.

Evaluating Our Own Performance on the Language Assessment Literacy Test

Time to Think

Were you more confident in your ability to evaluate the MC or the performance assessment? Why?

What do you think you did well on the Language Assessment Literacy Test? Why?

> What do you think you did less well on the Language Assessment Literacy Test? Why?
>
> Based on your performance on the Language Assessment Literacy Test, modify your goals for areas of LAL that you would like to further develop.

Conclusion

In this chapter, we reflected on what we have learned from the book and evaluated our own LAL. We compared our knowledge about language assessment prior to and after reading the book and considered areas that we want to develop further. We also completed some language assessment activities to help us get a better understanding of our LAL strengths and weaknesses. We can use this experience to help determine what areas of language assessment we might further explore.

I began this book with a story about a major reason I decided to write it. A language teacher who had very good intentions forced me (and my classmates) to take an assessment that did not provide an accurate indication of my language ability or achievement. The task of writing a story on a chalkboard with limited time, knowing that my teacher would criticize me while my peers observed, made it impossible for me to demonstrate my actual language ability. I believe that if my teacher had followed the principles in this book, my score on that test would have been a better indication of my language ability. Moreover, I believe that I would have become more motivated to study and learn the language. I hope that learning the language assessment principles in this book leads to language assessment practices that provide effective indications of language ability or achievement and promote effective language learning and teaching practices throughout the world.

Glossary

Accommodations	Procedures or aids, such as large font or hearing aids, that help students demonstrate their language abilities despite their disabilities, without giving them any unfair advantage over students who do not have the disability.
Alignment	How well test content and test takers' response processes match the test construct's content and response processes.
Analytic rating scale	An instrument we can use to assign separate scores for different aspects of test takers' performances.
Angoff method	A test-centered approach to standard setting which requires content judges to estimate the odds of a minimally competent test taker passing each item. We can use these estimates to set cut scores.
Artificial intelligence (AI)	A technological system that can approximate human intelligence.
Assessment	Any way of collecting evidence about a test taker or group of test takers for the purpose of estimating their knowledge of and ability to use a language. It includes both formal and informal measurements.
Assessment resources	Materials test developers and users need in order to create or select and carry out assessments.
At-home assessments	Computer-delivered tests that test takers complete online at their homes or other internet-connected locations.
Authentic input	A type of listening input where test developers find and use real-world spoken texts. For example, they might record some students discussing a topic in class to use for the input.
Authenticated input	A type of listening input where test developers create semi-scripted oral texts. They create the general outline of a speaking situation, and then actors use the semi-scripted texts to help them construct discourse in real time based on the situation.
B-Index	The difference in scores between test takers who pass and ones who fail. To get the B-Index, the item facility of the ones who fail is subtracted from the item facility of those who pass.
Cognitive validity	How well the processes that test takers use to complete an assessment align with those they use to complete real-world tasks.
Computerized delivery model	An approach where test takers complete assessment tasks with an electronic system.
Consequential validity	The appropriateness of the interpretations or decisions that result from assessment scores. The impacts of the assessment, including washback on learning, are important indicators of consequential validity.
Construct	An ability that we cannot observe directly, such as listening.

GLOSSARY

Construct-irrelevant content	Something that we do not want our test to measure, such as reading ability or test taking strategies when we desire to assess listening.
Construct-relevant content	What we desire to measure with our assessment. For example, when we assess listening, information that is relevant to listening is construct-relevant content.
Construct underrepresented content	The part of the ability we want to assess that the assessment does not measure.
Content judges	Experts who evaluate the quality of test items for a criterion-referenced test.
Context validity	The relevance and representativeness of the assessment content, including language input, questions, and timing.
Contingency table	A way to group data across two or more variables that makes it possible to identify the consistency of test scores.
Contrasting groups method	A test-taker-centered approach to setting cut scores where experts divide test takers into two groups: those they think will be able to pass the test and those they think will not. They then use the test score that best distinguishes these groups as the cut score.
Corpus (plural: corpora)	An organized electronic storage of language, usually written or spoken, that we can use for linguistic analysis (Barker, 2014). Corpora make it possible for test developers to determine the characteristics of language for particular spoken and written contexts.
Correlate	To compare students' scores for two tests to see how similarly their patterns match.
Correlation	A statistical technique that we use to determine the degree of a relationship between two variables. It can be a value between −1.00 and 1.00.
Covariance	The unstandardized correlation among a set of scores.
Criterion-referenced tests (CRTs)	Assessments that compare a person's knowledge or skills against a predetermined standard, learning goal, performance level, or other criterion.
Criterion-related validity	How well an assessment's scores correlate with scores on other assessments with the same construct.
Cronbach's Alpha	A measure of the internal consistency of a set of test scores for norm-referenced tests.
Culture	"The values, beliefs, systems of language, communication, and practices that people share in common and that can be used to define them as a collective" (Cole, 2020).
Cut score	The score that determines whether or not a test taker passes or fails a criterion-referenced test.
Dependability	How consistent mastery classifications are for criterion-referenced tests.
Diagnostic test	An assessment that aims to identify the strengths and weaknesses of a test taker with the purpose of guiding teaching and learning.

Dichotomous scoring	An approach where we mark an item either correct or incorrect. We do not assign test takers any credit for partially correct answers.
Distractor	A wrong answer option in a multiple-choice or other type of selected response item type.
Dynamic assessment (DA)	An assessment approach that emphasizes the relationship between learning and assessment. Learning and assessment are fundamentally connected, and learning should always drive assessment. The approach relates closely to the Zone of Proximal Development.
Elicited imitation	An item type that requires test takers to listen to a sentence or phrase and then repeat or write what they hear.
English as a Lingua Franca (ELF)	The use of English for communication among a community of people in which at least one is not a first language English speaker.
English as a Second Language (ESL)	The learning of English in a context where English is the first language of the majority of the language users.
Face-to-face delivery model	An approach where test takers complete tasks in the same place as one or more human test administrators or partners. The participants can see each other.
Formative assessment	Assessment which aims to determine the learning a student achieves in a course and provide an indication of how future learning should progress.
Generalizability	How effectively the scores on an assessment have meaning for various language use situations. We generally desire scores that are highly generalizable.
Group oral (discussion task)	A performance assessment where two or more test takers discuss a topic with each other. The test takers control the discussion while a test administrator monitors (and rates) them.
Histogram	A chart that we use to represent how many test takers get a particular number of items correct.
Holistic rating scale	An instrument we can use to assign a score for test takers' overall ability on the construct we desire to measure.
Hybrid scoring	The process of combining scores from both humans and automated computer scoring systems to arrive at a final score for a test taker.
Independent task	A language assessment activity that aims to assess only one of the four language skills of listening, reading, speaking, and writing.
Indirect task	An assessment activity that does not require test takers to use language as they would in the real world. Instead, "an inference is made from performance on more artificial tasks" (Davies et al., 1999, p. 81).
Integrated task	An assessment activity that requires test takers to use two or more language skills. Note that this is not the same as an integrative task (see Ockey, 2024).
Intelligibility	How well we can understand a speaker.
Interactional competence	The ability to "co-construct interaction in a purposeful and meaningful way, taking into account sociocultural and pragmatic

	dimensions of the speech situation and event" (Galaczi & Taylor, 2018, p. 226).
Interactive task	An assessment activity that requires test takers to negotiate meaning about a topic with one or more other language users in real time.
Internal reliability	An approach that provides an indication of how consistent scores are within one test administration.
Inter-rater dependability	How consistent the same two or more judges' mastery classifications are when we use criterion-referenced tests. Mastery classifications are from the same two or more judges for the same test administration.
Inter-rater reliability	The consistency of the scores of two (or more) raters for test takers' performances. Ratings are for the same test administration.
Inter-rating dependability	How consistent two or more judgments about test takers' mastery classifications are when we use criterion-referenced tests. Mastery classifications come from a pool of raters for the same test administration. The same two raters do not judge the performances of all test takers.
Inter-rating reliability	The consistency of two (or more) ratings for test takers' performances. Ratings for a test taker do not come from the same two raters. They come from a pool of raters.
Interview task	An assessment activity (usually oral) that requires test takers to respond to questions in a one-on-one situation.
Intra-rater dependability	How consistent a judge's mastery classifications of test takers are when we use criterion-referenced tests. The same judge(s) determines the mastery classification for each test taker at two different time periods.
Intra-rater reliability	The consistency of two or more ratings of test takers' performances. The same rater judges the same test takers' performances at two different time periods.
Item discrimination	The effectiveness of an item to distinguish among high- and low-scoring test takers.
Item facility (IF)	How easy an item is for a group of test takers. IFs are between 0.00 (no test takers got the item correct) and 1.00 (all test takers got the item correct).
Item preview	Presenting test takers with the question stems, answer options, both, or neither before they read or listen to the input that we use to assess their language comprehension.
Item type	The kind of assessment activities that test takers must complete to demonstrate their language abilities.
Key	The response option on a multiple-choice or other selected response item type that we consider correct.
Knowledge-based task	An assessment activity that requires test takers to use only their personal experiences, knowledge, and/or opinions to produce the content of a response.

Kurtosis	A measure of how peaked a score distribution is. Kurtosis can be positive (distribution is peaked) or negative (distribution is flat).
Language assessment literacy (LAL)	What language teachers and other language experts need to know about language assessment to be effective in their work.
Language corpus	An organized electronic storage of written or spoken language that we can use for linguistic analysis.
Language needs analysis	A collection of information about a language use situation and the language we need to function effectively in it.
Learning-oriented assessment (LOA)	An assessment approach that emphasizes the learning aspect of assessment by using teachers' judgments of student classroom performance to promote learning.
Listen-speak task	An assessment activity which requires test takers to use both listening and speaking skills.
Mastery rate	The percentage of test takers who pass a criterion-referenced test.
Maximum (max)	The highest score that any test taker got on a test.
Mean	The average score for an assessment. We calculate the mean by adding up each test taker's score and dividing by the number of test takers.
Median	The score at the midpoint of a set of test scores that we have ordered from highest to lowest.
Minimum (min)	The lowest score that any test taker got on a test.
Multimodal input	A type of listening input that includes both verbal and visual stimuli.
Multiple-choice (MC)	Selected response item types that require test takers to respond to a statement or question by selecting from a list of options.
Negative point-biserial	A quality when the scores on an item negatively correlate with the total test scores. Scores on these items disagree with the overall test scores, so these items decrease the reliability of the scores.
Normal distribution	A spread of scores where test takers' abilities range from high to low, with many test takers getting scores near the average and few test takers getting very high or very low scores. The shape of the curve is like a bell, so we sometimes call it the bell curve.
Norm-referenced tests (NRTs)	Measures that rank order test takers from most to least proficient, making it possible to identify the test takers who have the highest level of ability among a certain group of test takers.
Objective assessments	Measures that we score according to a predetermined answer, for example tests which require students to select whether a statement about the content of a reading passage is true or false.
Operationalize	The process of making unobservable abilities measurable by connecting them to observable information. We commonly have test takers demonstrate their language ability, and then we use rating scales and raters to judge the test takers' abilities.
Option	An answer choice that a test taker can choose from to respond to a selected response item.
Oral communication	Language use that requires both listening and speaking.

GLOSSARY

Paired oral (discussion)	An assessment activity that requires a test taker to discuss a topic and negotiate meaning with a test taker partner.
Parallel forms reliability	An estimate of how well two versions of an assessment provide consistent indications of test takers' abilities.
Performance assessment	Test activities which require test takers to use language similarly to how they would in a target language use (TLU) situation. We then judge their abilities based on these performances.
Performance-driven approach	An approach to developing rating scales where we use the targeted language users' performances on an assessment task to help us distinguish among their abilities. We then select performances to identify ability levels.
Picture task	Assessment activities where test administrators use visual input to help prompt test takers' responses.
Pilot	Trying out an assessment to see if it works acceptably well before using it.
Point-biserial (PB)	The correlation between the score on an item and the total test scores. When they are high and positive, it means the item is functioning to rank order the test takers in a similar way as the total test scores.
Polytomous scoring	An approach where we can assign partial credit, such as 3 points on a 5-point scale.
Portfolio assessment	A collection of examples of learners' language-related work that we can judge to measure their language abilities.
Positive point-biserial	A quality of an item when it positively correlates with the total test scores. Items with positive point-biserials rank order the test takers in a similar way that the total scores rank them, thus increasing the reliability of the scores.
Power test	An assessment where the focus is on ability level without considering time to complete the activity. We give test takers enough time to complete the assessment.
Pragmatics	An important part of interactional competence that relates to the way we connect linguistic forms and how we use them to achieve communication goals in specific social contexts.
Prepared oral presentation task	An assessment activity where test takers prepare and orally share information on a particular topic.
Productive skill	The skills we use to produce language, namely speaking and writing.
Proficiency band	Description of what test takers can do. They distinguish among levels of test taker performance on an assessment.
Proficiency test	An assessment that provides a general indication of a test taker's ability.
Range	A measure of the difference between the minimum and maximum.
Rater norming	An approach to preparing raters to judge test takers' performances based on the expertise of all raters. Raters work together to come to a shared interpretation of the rating scales.

Rater training	An approach to preparing raters to judge test takers' performances based on an existing set of expectations. Expert raters lead training sessions and new raters align their ratings with those of the experts.
Raters	People or machines who use rating scales to judge test takers' abilities.
Rating scales	Ordered sets of descriptions of proficiency or achievement that we use to help us score performance assessments.
Read-write task	An assessment activity where test takers use both reading and writing skills.
Receptive skills	The skills we use to comprehend language, namely listening and reading.
Reliability	How consistent and stable test scores are for a particular group of test takers and context.
Response processes	The techniques and procedures (including mental processes) test takers use when completing an assessment.
Retell task	An assessment activity where test takers either read or hear some information and then write or retell its content. Test takers cannot take notes while listening or reading.
Roleplay task	An assessment activity that requires test takers to imagine that they are in a particular TLU situation and then perform the part of one of the participants in this context.
Scatter plot	A graphic where we plot the values of two variables to see their relationship with each other.
Scoring validity	The consistency and generalizability of test scores.
Scripted input	A type of listening input where test developers write the input based on their ideas or a corpus of what people often say in a particular situation. The test developers then have actors read or memorize these scripts, so they say exactly what the test developer has written.
Selected response items	Items where test takers choose a best answer from two or more options.
Self-assessment	A process where individuals think about and assess the quality of their own work and ability.
Semi-structured interview	An oral interview task where, after a test taker answers a pre-planned question, the interviewer asks follow-up questions based on the test taker's responses.
Setting	An assessment's physical environment, equipment, and administrative procedures.
Short-answer item	An item type where test takers produce a short answer, usually one word or a short phrase.
Skewness	How centered the scores are compared to the mean. When most scores are to the left of the mean, the score distribution is positively skewed, and when most scores are to its right, they are negatively skewed.
Speech variety	The pronunciation patterns of a particular group of people who speak a language.

GLOSSARY

Speeded test	An assessment which includes how fast test takers can complete an activity. Strict time constraints are important.
Split-half reliability	An approach where we divide test questions into two equal parts, for example a first half and a second half or odd and even, and then compare the consistency of test takers' scores on the two halves.
Spoken dialog system (SDS)	An electronic system that can orally "interact" with humans. Humans train the program with a corpus of potential responses to what a human might say.
Stakeholder	Anyone who has an interest in an assessment or its results.
Stakes	The seriousness of the impact an assessment will have on test takers and others, such as teachers, families, and institutions. Results based on high-stakes assessments have important consequences that we cannot easily reverse, while it is easier to reverse the consequences of low-stakes assessments.
Standard deviation (SD)	The average number of points the scores are from the mean.
Standardized test	An assessment that requires all test takers to respond to equivalent questions, and for test administrators to score them in a highly consistent manner. We use them to provide an indication of test takers' language achievement or proficiency.
Standards-based approach	An approach to developing rating scales where we create scales from an established set of standards or course objectives.
Standard setting	The process of setting cut scores for a criterion-referenced test.
Stem	A word, phrase, sentence, or question that presents a multiple-choice item.
Strong sense of language performance assessment	An approach where raters judge test takers' performances based on how effectively they complete the assessment task. The focus is on task completion rather than the language test takers use to complete the task.
Structured interview	An oral interview task where the test developer decides all of the questions before the interview. The interviewer does not ask follow-up questions.
Subjective assessment	An assessment that does not have a clearly defined right or wrong answer.
Summary task	An assessment activity where test takers either read or hear some information, take notes, and then write or retell its content.
Summative test	An assessment that provides an indication of a student's mastery of course criteria or objectives in school settings.
Synthesis task	An assessment activity that requires test takers to either read or listen to information about a topic and then provide a written or oral response to it.
Target language use (TLU) situation	A real-world situation in which test takers complete language use tasks. An example is children using language to play together in a park.

GLOSSARY

Test	A formal way of collecting evidence about a test taker or group of test takers for the purpose of estimating their knowledge of and ability to use a language.
Test-centered approach	An approach to standard setting where a panel of experts judge the difficulty of the test input and items. The experts' aim is to determine which items a minimally competent test taker could answer correctly. They then set the cut score accordingly.
Test content	Instructions, items, and language and non-language input for an assessment.
Test prompt (or just prompt)	The test materials we use to get test takers to produce targeted language in a performance assessment.
Test-retest coefficient agreement	A value that indicates how consistently test scores from two different criterion-referenced test administrations separate test takers into masters and non-masters.
Test-retest reliability	An approach that provides an indication of how well test takers' scores on the same assessment are consistent across different time periods.
Test-taker-centered approach	An approach to standard setting where a panel of expert judges, who are familiar with the test takers' ability levels, select test takers that they believe have sufficient language knowledge or ability to meet the targeted criteria, and test takers that they believe do not. They then create the cut score from the score that best separates these two groups of test takers.
Test task (or just task)	The activity that we expect test takers to complete in a performance assessment.
Theory-based approach	An approach to developing rating scales where we use language and assessment theory to guide our descriptions of language ability.
True–false item	A type of test question where test takers read or hear a statement and select true if they believe the statement is correct or false to indicate that they believe it is wrong.
Uniformity (uniform assessment)	The consistency of the assessment setting, content, and scoring procedures.
Validity	How confident we can be, considering theory and evidence, that the language test scores and their interpretations are effective indicators of test takers' abilities for the assessment's purpose.
Variable	A characteristic that we can measure. Language assessment variables are usually language ability indicators, such as item scores or test scores, or test taker characteristics, such as age and first language.
Variance	How much the scores vary from the mean.
Video-mediated (technology)	Technology that makes it possible for test takers to see test administrators or other test takers, remotely, while orally interacting.
Virtual delivery model	Test takers complete assessment tasks with a human through an electronic delivery system.
Virtual environment (VE)	Technology that makes it possible for individuals to orally (or through writing) interact in real time while seeing an avatar that

represents themselves and avatars representing the other test takers or test administrators.

Washback — An assessment's effect on teaching and learning practices. Assessments with positive washback lead to more effective learning and teaching practices.

Weak sense of language performance assessment — An approach where raters judge test takers' abilities based on the effectiveness of the language they used to complete a task. Language use is the focus, not how effectively test takers complete the task.

Zone of Proximal Development (ZPD) — The range of a person's (language) abilities that are in the process of developing and may be most responsive to instruction.

References

AERA (American Educational Research Association), APA (American Psychological Association), & NCME (National Council on Measurement in Education) (Eds). (2014). *Standards for Educational and Psychological Testing*. American Educational Research Association. Retrieved April 20, 2022, from https://www.testingstandards.net/uploads/7/6/6/4/76643089/standards_2014edition.pdf

Andrade, H., & Du, Y. (2007). Student responses to criteria referenced self-assessments. *Assessment & Evaluation in Higher Education, 32*(2), 159–181.

Angoff, W. H. (1971). Scales, norms and equivalent scores. In R. L. Thorndike (Ed.), *Educational measurement*, 2nd ed. (pp. 508–600). American Council on Education.

Bachman, L. F., & Dambock, B. (2017). *Language Assessment for Classroom Teachers*. Oxford University Press.

Bachman, L. F., & Palmer, A. S. (1996). *Language Testing in Practice*. Oxford University Press.

Bachman, L. F., & Palmer, A. S. (2010). *Language Assessment in Practice: Developing Language Assessments and Justifying Their Use in the Real World*. Oxford University Press.

Barker, F. (2014). Using corpora to design assessment. In A. J. Kunnan (Ed.), *The Companion to Language Assessment*, Volume 2, Part 8 (pp. 1–16). John Wiley & Sons. https://doi.org/10.1002/9781118411360.wbcla102

Berry, V. (2004). A study of the interaction between individual personality differences and oral performance test facets. Unpublished doctoral dissertation. King's College, University of London.

Biber, D., Conrad, S., Reppen, R., Byrd, P., Helt, M., Clark, V., Cortes, V., Csomay, E., & Urzua, A. (2004). *Representing Language Use in the University: Analysis of the TOEFL 2000 Spoken and Written Academic Language Corpus*. (ETS TOEFL Monograph Series, MS-25). Educational Testing Service.

Brown, J. D. (2005). *Testing in Language Programs: A Comprehensive Guide to English Language Assessment*. McGraw-Hill.

Brown, J. D. (2022). Classical test theory. In G. Fulcher & L. Harding (Eds), *The Routledge Handbook of Language Testing* (pp. 447–461). Routledge.

Brown, J. D., & Hudson, T. (2002). *Criterion-Referenced Language Testing*. Cambridge University Press.

Chapelle, C. (2021). *Argument-Based Validation in Testing and Assessment*. Sage.

Chapelle, C., Enright, M., & Jamieson, J. (2008). *Building a Validity Argument for the Test of English as a Foreign Language*. Routledge.

Chun, C. W. (2006). Commentary: An analysis of a language test for employment: The authenticity of the PhonePass test. *Language Assessment Quarterly, 3*(3), 295–306. https://doi.org/10.1207/s15434311laq0303_4

Cole, N. L. (2020, August 27). So what is culture, exactly? Retrieved February 12, 2024, from https://www.thoughtco.com/culture-definition-4135409

Cox, T. L., & Dewey, D. P. (2020). Measuring language development through self-assessment. In P. Winke & T. Brunfaut (Eds), *The Routledge Handbook of Second Language Acquisition and Language Testing* (pp. 382–390). Routledge.

Cummins, P., & Davesne, C. (2009). Using electronic portfolios for second language assessment. *Modern Language Journal* (Special Issue) *93*, 848–867.

Davies, A., Brown, A., Elder, C., Hill, K., Lumley, T., & McNamara, T. (1999). *Studies in Language Testing: Dictionary of Language Testing*. Cambridge University Press.

Davies, M. (2008–) The Corpus of Contemporary American English (COCA). Retrieved February 12, 204, from https://www.english-corpora.org/coca/

Davis, L. (2022). Rater and interlocutor training. In G. Fulcher & L. Harding (Eds), *The Routledge Handbook of Language Testing*, second edition (pp. 322–338). Routledge.

Davis, L., & Papageorgiou, S. (2021). Complementary strengths? Evaluation of a hybrid human-machine scoring approach for a test of oral academic English. *Assessment in Education: Principles, Policy, & Practice, 28*, 437–455.

Derwing, T. M., & Munro, M. J. (2009). Comprehensibility as a factor in listener interaction preferences: Implications for the workplace. *Canadian Modern Language Review, 66*(2), 181–202. https://doi.org/10.3138/cmlr.66.2.181

Earl, L. (2013). *Assessment as Learning: Using Classroom Assessment to Maximize Student Learning*. Corwin.

Eckes, T. (2023). *Introduction to Many-Facet Rasch Measurement: Analyzing and Evaluating Rater-Mediated Assessments*. Peter Lang.

Fernández, P. O. (2021). Derivation of ironical implicatures by English foreign language learners: Do language proficiency and culture play a role? Unpublished thesis. Universidad del Pais Vasco.

Fulcher, G. (2012). Scoring performance tests. In G. Fulcher & F. Davidson (Eds), *The Routledge Handbook of Language Testing* (pp. 378–392). Routledge.

Galaczi, E., & Taylor, L. (2018). Interactional competence: Conceptualizations, operationalizations, and outstanding questions. *Language Assessment Quarterly 15*(3), 219–236.

Giraldo, F. (2022). *Language Assessment Literacy and the Professional Development of Pre-service Foreign Language Teachers*. Editorial Universidad de Caldas.

Hall, E. (1976). *Beyond Culture*. Doubleday.

Hall, E., & Hall, M. (1990). *Understanding Cultural Differences: Germans, French, and Americans*. Intercultural Press.

Harding, L., & McNamara, T. F. (2018). Language assessment: The challenge of ELF. In J. Jenkins, M. J. Dewey, & W. Baker (Eds), *Routledge Handbook of English as a Lingua Franca* (pp. 570–582). Routledge.

Kane, M. T. (1992). An argument-based approach to validity. *Psychological Bulletin, 112*(3), 527–535.

Kasper, G., & Youn, S. J. (2017). Transforming instruction to activity: Roleplay in language assessment. *Applied Linguistics Review, 9*(4), 589–616.

Knoch, U., Deygers, B., & Khamboonruang, A. (2021). Revisiting rating scale development for rater-mediated language performance assessments: Modelling construct and contextual choices made by scale developers. *Language Testing, 38*(4), 602–626.

Koyama, D., Sun, A., & Ockey, G. J. (2016). The effects of item preview on video-based multiple-choice listening assessments. *Language Learning & Technology, 20*(1), 148–165.

Kremmel, B., & Harding, L. (2020). Towards a comprehensive, empirical model of language assessment literacy across stakeholder groups: Developing the language assessment literacy survey. *Language Assessment Quarterly, 17*(1), 100–120.

Larson-Hall, J. (2016). *A Guide to Doing Statistics in Second Language Research Using SPSS and R*, second edition. Routledge.

Levis, J. (2020). Revisiting the intelligibility and nativeness principles. *Journal of Second Language Pronunciation, 6*(3), 310–328. https://doi.org/10.1075/jslp.20050.lev

Livingston, S. A., & Zieky, M. J. (1982). *Passing Scores: A Manual for Setting Standards of Performance on Educational and Occupational Tests*. Educational Testing Service.

May, L. (2011). Interactional competence in a paired speaking test: Features salient to raters. *Language Assessment Quarterly, 8*(2), 127–145.

McNamara, T. (1996). *Second Language Performance Assessment*. Addison Wesley Longman.

McNamara, T. (2005). 21st century Shibboleth: Language tests, identity and intergroup conflict. *Language Policy, 4*, 351–370.

Montee, M., & Malone, M. (2014). Writing scoring criteria and score reports. In A. J. Kunnan (Ed.), *The Companion to Language Assessment*, Volume II, Part 7, Chapter 51 (pp. 1–13). John Wiley & Sons.

Nishimura, S., Tella, S., & Nevgi, A. (2008). Communication style and cultural features in high/low context communication cultures: A case study of Finland, Japan and India. Subject-Didactic Symposium, Helsinki, pp. 783–796.

Norton, B., & Stein, P. (1998). Why the "Monkeys Passage" bombed: Tests, genres, and teaching. In A. J. Kunnan (Ed), *Validation in Language Assessment* (pp. 231–249). Lawrence Erlbaum.

Ockey, G. J. (2009). The effects of a test taker's group members' personalities on the test taker's second language group oral discussion test scores. *Language Testing, 26*(2), 161–186.

Ockey, G. J. (2024). Assessing listening. In E. Wagner, E. Galaczi, & A. Batty (Eds), *Routledge Handbook of Second Language Acquisition and Listening* (pp. 230–240). Routledge.

Ockey, G. J., & Chukharev-Hudilainen, E. (2021). Human versus computer partner in the paired oral discussion test. *Applied Linguistics, 42*(5), 924–944. https://doi.org/10.1093/applin/amaa067

Ockey, G. J., Chukharev-Hudilainen, E., & Hirch, R. (2023). Assessing interactional competence: Interactional Competence Elicitor (ICE) vs a human partner. *Language Assessment Quarterly*, *20*(4–5), 377–398.

Ockey, G. J., & French, R. (2016). From one to multiple accents on a test of L2 listening comprehension. *Applied Linguistics*, *37*(5), 693–715.

Ockey, G. J., & Hirch, R. R. (2020). A step toward the assessment of English as a lingua franca. In G. J. Ockey & B. Green (Eds), *Another Generation of Fundamental Considerations in Language Testing* (pp. 9–28). Springer.

Ockey, G. J., & Wagner, E. (2018). An overview of the issue of using different speech varieties on L2 listening tests. In G. J. Ockey & E. Wagner (Eds), *Assessing L2 Listening: Moving towards Authenticity* (pp. 67–82). John Benjamins.

Onion, R. (2013). Take the impossible "Literacy" Test Louisiana gave black voters in the 1960s. Retrieved February 12, 2024 from https://slate.com/human-interest/2013/06/voting-rights-and-the-supreme-court-the-impossible-literacy-test-louisiana-used-to-give-black-voters.html

O'Sullivan, B. (2002). Learner acquaintanceship and oral proficiency test pair-task performance. *Language Testing*, *19*(3), 277–295.

O'Sullivan, B. (2013). Assessing speaking. In A. J. Kunnan (Ed.), *The Companion to Language Assessment* Volume 1, Part 2 (pp. 1–16). John Wiley & Sons.

Pearson/PTE (no date). Using automated scoring. Retrieved February 12, 2024 from https://www.pearsonpte.com/scoring/automated-scoring

Poehner, M., & Lantolf, P. (2023). Advancing L2 dynamic assessment: Innovations in Chinese contexts. *Language Assessment Quarterly* (Special Issue), *20*(1), 1–19.

Popham, W. J. (1981). *Modern Educational Measurement*. Prentice-Hall.

Purpura, J. E. (2004). *Assessing Grammar*. Cambridge University Press.

Qian, D. (2002). Investigating the relationship between vocabulary knowledge and academic reading performance: An assessment perspective. *Language Learning*, *52*(3), 513–536.

Sawaki, Y. (2016). Norm-referenced vs. criterion-reference approach to assessment. In D. Tsagari & J. Banerjee (Eds), *Handbook of Second Language Assessment* (pp. 45–60). De Gruyter Mouton.

Schedl, M., O'Reilly, T., Grabe, W., & Schoonen, R. (2021). Assessing academic reading. In X. Xi & J. M. Norris (Eds), *Assessing Academic English for Higher Education Admissions* (pp. 22–60). Routledge.

Shohamy, E. (2005). *Language Policy: Hidden Agendas and New Approaches*. Routledge.

Shulruf, B. (2018). Standard setting. In B. Frey (Ed.), *The SAGE Encyclopedia of Educational Research, Measurement, and Evaluation*. Sage. https://doi.org/10.4135/9781506326139

Taguchi, N., & Roever, C. (2017). *Second Language Pragmatics*. Oxford University Press.

Turner, C., & Purpura, J. (2016). Learning-oriented assessment in second language classrooms. In D. Tsagari & J. Banerjee (Eds), *Handbook of Second Language Assessment* (pp. 255–274).

Van Lier, L. (1989). Reeling, writhing, drawling, stretching, and fainting in coils: Oral proficiency interviews as conversation. *TESOL Quarterly*, *23*(3), 489–508.

Van Moere, A. (2012). A psycholinguistic approach to oral language assessment. *Language Testing*, *29*(3), 325–344. https://doi.org/10.1177/0265532211424478

Vygotsky, L.S. (1934/1978). *Mind in Society: The Development of Higher Psychological Processes*. Harvard University Press.

Wagner, E. (2020). Duolingo English Test, Revised Version July 2019. *Language Assessment Quarterly*, *17*(3), 300–315. https://doi.org/10.1080/15434303.2020.1771343

Wagner, E., & Kunnan, A. (2015). The Duolingo English Test. *Language Assessment Quarterly*, *12*(3), 320–331. https://doi.org/10.1080/15434303.2015.1061530

Wagner, E., & Ockey, G. J. (2018). An overview of the use of authentic, real-world spoken texts on L2 listening tests. In G. J. Ockey & E. Wagner (Eds), *Assessing L2 Listening: Moving towards Authenticity* (pp. 13–28). John Benjamins.

Weir, C. (2005). *Language Testing and Validation: An Evidence-Based Approach*. Palgrave MacMillan.

Winke, P. (2020). Foreword. In S-A. Abdolhamid & P. de Costa (Eds), *The Sociopolitics of English Language Testing* (pp. xvi–xxii). Bloomsbury Academic.

Winke, P., & Lim, H. (2015). ESL essay raters' cognitive processes in applying the Jacobs et al. Rubric: An eye-movement study. *Assessing Writing*, *25*, 38–54.

Wu, J. (2016). A socio-cognitive approach to assessing speaking and writing: The GEPT experience. *Japan Language Testing Association Journal*, *19*, 3–11.

Yan, X., & Fan, J. (2022). Reliability and dependability. In G. Fulcher & L. Harding (Eds), *The Routledge Handbook of Language Testing*, second edition (pp. 477–494). Routledge.

Yanagawa, K., & Green, A. (2008). To show or not to show: The effects of item stems and answer options on performance on a multiple-choice listening comprehension test, *System, 36*, 107–122.

Zwick, R. (2006). Higher education admissions testing. In R. Brennan (Ed.), *Educational Measurement* (pp. 647–679). American Council on Education and Prager.

Zwick, R. (2022). A century of testing controversies. In E. Clauser & M. Bunch (Eds), *The History of Educational Measurement: Key Advancements in Theory, Policy, and Practice* (pp. 136–154). Routledge.

Index

accommodation, 22, 67
achievement, 76, 139
alignment, 23, 58, 60, 86, 169, 178, 205
American Educational Research Association, 50, 58
Andrade, H., 24
Angoff method, 143, 144, 146
artificial intelligence, 72, 170
assessment
  dynamic, 22
  formal, 3, 10, 13, 23, 41
  formative, 24, 46, 91, 150
  objective, 18, 19, 57, 81
  performance, xx, 159, 160, 161, 170, 172, 178, 180, 191, 192, 198, 200, 204, 205, 206
  portfolio, 25
  subjective, 18
  summative, 26, 91, 137, 143
authentic, xvii, 87, 88, 89, 90, 98, 159

Bachman, L. F., 54, 61, 67
Barker, F., 56, 227
Berry, V., 169
BERT, 173
bias, 6, 26
Biber, D., 57
B-Index, 148
Brown, J. D., 50, 60, 99, 135, 142, 148, 200

Chapelle, C., 61, 62, 85
ChatGPT, 72, 97, 98, 99, 114, 173
Chukharev-Hudilainen, E., 169
Chun, C. W., 170
COCA, xvii, 56
Cole, N. L., 37, 227
communicative competence, 52
complexity, 70, 91
computer-automated, 19
computerized, 173
consequences, 18, 61
construct, 51, 52, 54, 55, 56, 57, 58, 59, 60, 83, 85, 87, 91, 92, 98, 100, 125, 131, 132, 139, 140, 142, 159, 162, 179, 187, 188, 199, 222
content analysis, 99, 100, 101, 102, 111, 126, 128, 129, 131, 138, 139, 142, 147, 150

contingency table, 209
contrasting groups method, 144
corpora, 52, 56, 57
covariance, 210, 211
Cox, T., 24
culture, 37
Cummins, P., 25

Dambock, B., 61
Davesne, C., 25
Davies, A., 143, 169
Davies, M., 56
Davis, L., 191, 193
dependability, 74, 150, 151, 205, 209, 210
Derwing, T. M., 169
Dewey, D. P., 24
distractor, 101
distribution, 21, 107, 108, 109, 110, 146, 148
Du, Y., 24

Earl, L., 4
Eckes, T., 191
elicited imitation, 169
English as a Lingua Franca, 52

Fan, J., 150
Fernández, P. O., 37
Fulcher, G., 188

Galaczi, E., 160
generalizability, 61, 186
Giraldo, F., 10
Grammar Tense Test, 102, 104, 106, 110, 120, 126, 127, 128, 129, 130, 131
Green, R., 86
group oral, xviii, 168, 169

Hall, E., 37, 38
Hall, M., 37
Hamilton, M., 31
Harding, L., 10, 11, 90, 217
high stakes, 18, 26, 27, 51, 57, 58, 62, 126, 131, 139, 143, 150, 162, 163, 164, 192
histogram, 107, 110
Hudson, T., 142, 148

IELTS, 16, 26, 92
intelligibility, 36

interactional competence, 55, 160, 165, 169, 172
item
  discrimination, 125
  facility, 147
  preview, 86, 92
  selected response, xx, 81, 82, 99, 101, 111, 140, 170, 200

Kane, M. T., 61
Kasper, G., 165
Knoch, U., 187
Koyama, D., 86
Kremmel, B., 10, 11, 217
Kunnan, A., 170
kurtosis, 107, 108, 109, 110

language assessment literacy, 10, 111, 216, 219
language needs analysis, 54, 55, 222
Lantolf, P., 23
Larson-Hall, J., 109, 110, 118
Levis, J., 36, 169
Lim, G. S., 195
Lim, H., 186
Livingston, S. A., 144

Malone, M., 187
mastery rate, 146
maximum, 104
May, L., 169
McNamara, T., 4, 5, 90, 185
mean, 104, 106, 107, 108, 146, 234
median, 146
minimum, 104
Montee, M., 187
multimodal, 91, 92
multiple-choice, 119, 219
Munro, M. J., 169

Nishimura, S., 37
Norton, B., 36

O'Sullivan, B., 169, 170
Ockey, G. J., 90, 169, 170, 172
Onion, R., 5
operationalize, 188
oral communication, 160, 164, 167, 168, 172
oral interview, 6, 166, 167, 170, 171, 172

INDEX

paired oral, 168, 171, 172, 199, 204
Palmer, A. S., 54, 67
Papageorgiou, S., 193
Pearson PTE, 192
performance-driven, 188
picture task, 161, 162
pilot, 36, 41, 126
Poehner, M., 23
point-biserial, 121, 148
Popham, W. J., 67
pragmatics, 165
prepared oral presentation, xxi, 161
proficiency band, 182, 186, 188, 191, 192, 200
Purpura, J., 23, 85

Qian, D., 91

rank order, 73, 74, 75, 106, 124, 129, 130, 132, 138, 142, 210
rater norming, 191, 192, 200, 205
rater training, 191
rating category, 182, 191, 200
rating scale
   analytic, 182, 185, 186, 190, 191, 192, 200
   holistic, 181, 182, 185, 190
read-write task, xxi, 160, 165
reliability
   coefficient agreement, 151
   Cronbach's Alpha, 129, 131, 137, 210, 211
   internal, 75, 129, 130, 206, 210
   inter-rater, 191, 206
   inter-rating, 206
   intra-rater, 191, 206
   parallel forms, 73, 74, 75, 130
   split-half, 75
   test-retest, 73, 130, 150, 206
response process, 59, 60, 86
retell task, 163
Roever, C., 165
roleplay, 164, 166, 171, 222

Saudi Young Learner English Assessment, 181, 182, 185, 186, 187, 188, 191, 192, 193
Sawaki, Y., 138
scatter plot, 121, 124
Schedl, M., 85
scoring
   computer, 40, 71, 191, 192, 193, 205, 219
   criteria, 65, 150, 188, 204, 205
   dichotomous, 71, 177, 178
   human, 71, 191, 193, 205, 206, 210
   hybrid, 193
   polytomous, 178
scripted input, 87, 89
self-assessment, 24, 25, 83, 217
Shohamy, E., 40
short-answer, 84, 85, 170
Shulruf, B., 143
skewness, 107, 109, 110
social influences, 187
Socio-cognitive Framework, 61
sociopolitical, 36, 40
speech variety, 36, 41, 90
spoken dialog system, 172, 233
stakeholder, 41, 43, 83, 205
standard deviation, 106
standard setting, 143
standards-based approach, 187
statistical analysis, 102, 111, 131
Stein, P., 36
summary task, 163, 164

Taguchi, N., 165
task
   direct, 159
   independent, 159, 161, 163, 172
   indirect, 170
   integrated, 160, 161, 163, 164, 166, 168, 171, 172, 179, 200, 204
   interactive, 160, 161, 164, 167, 168, 171, 172
   knowledge-based, 163
Taylor, L., 160

test
   at home, 46, 68
   criterion-referenced, 138
   diagnostic, 25
   norm-referenced, 21, 73, 96, 137
   power, 87
   proficiency, 26, 66, 73, 102, 164
   speeded, 87
   standardized, 16, 26, 27
test-centered approach, 143
test-taker-centered, 143, 144
theory-based approach, 188
TOEFL, 26, 57, 62, 193
Turner, C., 23

uniformity, 66, 67, 68, 69, 70, 71, 73, 171, 205

validation, xvii, 61, 62
validity, 50, 51, 52, 57, 58, 59, 85, 178
   argument-based, xvii, 61, 62
   criterion-related, 60, 61
Van Lier, L., 168
Van Moere, A., 169
variance, 210
video-mediated, 87, 171, 172
virtual environment, 171
Vocabulary Test 1, 138, 139, 140, 144, 146, 148, 150, 151
Vygotsky, L. S., 22

Wagner, E., 90, 170
washback, 11, 27, 43, 44, 61, 159, 161, 170
Weir, C., 61
Winke, P., 40, 186
Wu, J., 61, 62

Yan, X., 150
Yanagawa, K., 86
Youn, S. J., 165

Zieky, M. J., 144
Zone of Proximal Development, 22
Zwick, R., 36, 39

For EU product safety concerns, contact us at Calle de José Abascal, 56–1°, 28003 Madrid, Spain or eugpsr@cambridge.org.

www.ingramcontent.com/pod-product-compliance
Lightning Source LLC
LaVergne TN
LVHW081524060526
838200LV00044B/1988